MOUNTAIN SPIRIT

MOUNTAIN SPIRIT

The SHEEP EATER INDIANS
of YELLOWSTONE

Lawrence L. Loendorf & Nancy Medaris Stone

THE UNIVERSITY OF UTAH PRESS
Salt Lake City

The Defiance House Man colophon is a registered trademark of the University of Utah Press. It is based upon a four-foot-tall, Ancient Puebloan pictograph (late PIII) near Glen Canyon, Utah.

LIBRARY OF CONGRESS CATALOGING-IN-PUBLICATION DATA

Loendorf, Lawrence L.
  Mountain spirit : the Sheep Eater Indians of Yellowstone / Lawrence L. Loendorf and Nancy Medaris Stone ; illustrations by David Joaquin.
    p. cm.
  Includes bibliographical references and index.
  ISBN-13: 978-0-87480-868-1 (cloth : alk. paper)
  ISBN-13: 978-0-87480-867-4 (pbk. : alk. paper)
    1. Tukuarika Indians—Yellowstone National Park—History. 2. Tukuarika Indians—Yellowstone National Park—Social life and customs. 3. Shoshoni Indians—Yellowstone National Park—History. 4. Shoshoni Indians—Yellowstone National Park—Social life and customs. 5. Mountain sheep hunting—Yellowstone National Park. 6. Bighorn sheep hunting—Yellowstone National Park. 7. Yellowstone National Park—History. 8. Yellowstone National Park—Social life and customs. I. Stone, Nancy Medaris, 1939– II. Title.
  E99.T85L64 2006
  978.7'52004974574—DC22   2006002051

www.UofUpress.com

Printed by Sheridan Books, Inc., Ann Arbor, Michigan
Interior printed on recycled paper with 50% post-consumer content.

Contents

CONTENTS

Illustrations

(Following page 128)

Prologue

||||||||||||||||||||||||||

What's in a Name?

"What's in a name?" Juliet Capulet asked Romeo Montague from the balcony of her boudoir. *"That which we call a rose / By any other name would smell as sweet."* While Shakespeare's young heroine is correct in claiming that if a bouquet of long-stemmed flowers were called "turnips" instead of "roses" it would be just as pleasing to the recipient, she fails to realize that the names attached to human beings often have much greater significance. Romeo and Juliet belonged to feuding families, so even if Romeo had complied with Juliet's request—"Romeo, doff thy name"—their lineages, social milieu, and unhappy fate would have remained the same.

Names also matter a great deal to historians and ethnographers, who need to be able to distinguish among and classify groups of people prior to recording observations and developing generalizations about their behavior, past and present. The conventions for naming are different, however, among many of their human subjects, nowhere more so than in the large, linguistically affiliated group of western Indians whose generic tribal designation is *Shoshone*.[1]

For millennia, the Shoshone lived in small, interrelated groups scattered throughout the intermountain West, sharing similar lifeways and common food pursuits. When Euro-Americans first appeared in the region, Shoshone peoples occupied a territory extending from California to Montana and spoke one of many Uto-Aztecan languages. In Idaho and Wyoming, groups sometimes referred to as the Northern and Eastern Shoshone spoke a Central Numic language. The Colorado Ute, their neighbors to the south, spoke Southern Numic, while the Oregon Paiute were Western Numic speakers.

Within this community could be found groups of people whose names reflected their major source of protein, such as the *Tukudika*, which is the Shoshone name for several bands of hunters living in the mountainous region surrounding Yellowstone National Park.[2] *Tuku* means "meat," and *dika* is translated as "eaters of," and because of the preponderance of bighorn sheep in the Tukudika diet, they were also called Sheep Eaters. Several hundred miles to the north and west, in Idaho and Montana, another Shoshone subgroup, the *Agaidika*, or Salmon Eaters, acquired their name because of their dependence on specific aquatic resources.

Both of these *dika* groups were also commonly referred to as the Mountain Shoshone and, somewhat less frequently, as the Mountain Snakes. The latter designation has ambiguous roots, but an argument has been made for its being derived from the Shoshone word for grass, which is *sonip*. This would have been appropriate because these groups often lived in grass-covered houses, but the connection to reptiles is based on the following misunderstanding. In the nineteenth-century gesture language used by many North American Indian groups, the sign for "grass" was a waving hand and may have been misinterpreted as the similar sign for "snake." Before anyone accepts this etymology as gospel, however, reference must be made to another competing explanation derived from behaviors associated with fishing for and processing the Ling fish found in deep glacial lakes, such as Dinwoody and Torrey, in the Wind River Mountains. Once caught, these fish were skinned and then dried by hanging them in the surrounding trees. It has been said that the drying fish resembled snakes, and, perhaps as a joke, the reptile's name ended up sticking to the folk doing the fishing.

It may not be possible for historians to discern which of these explanations is correct, but, like Juliet, Shoshone people of that period would not have found this fact especially troubling. The names that Shoshone bands would be called—by themselves as well as others— were subject to change, depending on what endeavors were involved in their subsistence. If, for example, a band of Sheep Eaters traveled to the Portneuf River in Idaho, where there were abundant root vegetables to exploit, they would have been called the *Kuyedika*, or the Eaters of Tobacco Roots (*Valeriana obovata*). The Swedish anthropologist Sven Liljeblad has described how this linguistic convention worked:

> Nowhere among the Northern Shoshoni did these or other names relating to special foods denote clearly defined local groups or individual bands. Rather, they referred to regional resources utilized by people who might travel widely. An individual, a family, or an entire

band could be named differently at different times according to temporary whereabouts or to the seasons and the corresponding foods.[3]

It is difficult for persons in the twenty-first century to appreciate
the security that a mobile way of life conferred on hunter–gatherer
groups living in regions with diverse resources and at population levels that did not exhaust those resources. And for those of us dedicated
to researching our family genealogies in terms of patronymics that
have conveniently remained the same for many generations, it is even
more difficult to imagine that as households moved across large areas
of the landscape in the course of an annual round, they were referred
to by various names.

By the time Robert Lowie, an anthropologist at the University of
California, Berkeley, best known for his research with Crow Indians,
visited the Shoshone in 1906, both Agaidika and Tukudika groups had
been forced to give up their mobile lifeways and were living together
at the Lemhi Valley Agency in northern Idaho.[4] As part of his analytical effort, Lowie classified the two groups together in one taxon—
the Northern Shoshone—a practice that was followed by anthropologist Julian Steward when he collected information from Shoshone
bands in 1935 and 1936.[5] Shortly after Lowie's visit to the Lemhi
Agency, the Agaidika and Tukudika were moved to the Fort Hall
Agency, near Pocatello, Idaho, where they joined other groups of
Shoshone. By that time, their mobile way of life was a thing of the
past, but they kept the last iteration of their *dika* names, though the
foods they now ate were entirely different.

The task of sorting out just who is who becomes even harder
when the *Kukundika*, or Buffalo Eaters, are added to the mix. They
were the primary Shoshone group settled on the Wind River Reservation near Lander, Wyoming, and are sometimes called the Eastern
Shoshone or the Plains Shoshone. Groups of Sheep Eaters also moved
out of the mountains and settled on the Wind River Reservation, but
when Lowie's student Demitri Shimkin studied these Shoshone in
1937 and 1938, he did not differentiate among the various bands. In
fact, he placed more emphasis on buffalo hunting and barely mentioned bighorn sheep and their importance to Sheep Eaters.[6]

Some details of the moves and reservation settings of the Shoshone, emphasizing the whereabouts of the Mountain Shoshone in
the historic period, are discussed in a subsequent chapter, but it is not

possible to identify specific lineages or individual groups. The approach we take in this book is to distinguish between the Mountain Shoshone (Agaidika and Tukudika) and the Plains Shoshone (Kukundika) and then to focus on the Sheep Eater contingent of the Mountain Shoshone. To develop an adequate understanding of the Mountain Shoshone, we have also treated separately the period before the introduction of the horse and the era that came after that momentous technological, economic, and social innovation.

Our intent throughout this book is to present Sheep Eater life in the context of the landscapes in which it was lived, which includes what is now Yellowstone National Park. Our focus is not meant to suggest, however, that Tukudika were the only Indians to live in the greater Yellowstone region. Salish-speaking Flathead and Pend d'Oreille groups were ancient inhabitants of the park, as were Sahaptin-speaking Nez Perce bands and Tanoan-speaking Kiowa peoples. After AD 1500, groups of Siouan-speaking Crow and Bannock Indians made extensive use of the park's resources and interacted with Sheep Eaters both socially and economically.[7] Some of these encounters are discussed in subsequent chapters as we meet and come to know the group of people whose several names—Mountain Shoshone, Sheep Eaters, Tukudika—only begin to express the rich variety of the hunting and gathering life that they made for themselves.

MOUNTAIN SPIRIT

1

Objects of Pity

History—according to the first definition offered by the *Oxford English Dictionary*—is "a relation of incidents (in early use, either true or imaginary; later only of those professedly true)."[1] It is a misfortune that many of the incidents related about the Sheep Eater Indians of southern Montana and northwestern Wyoming are decidedly imaginary, eclipsing more "professedly true" accounts of their way of life. Sheep Eaters have been described as miserably poor, mentally retarded cowards, and that characterization is one of the *least* derogatory in the ethnohistoric record. For more than one hundred years, disparaging and inaccurate descriptions of these montane hunters have been repeated with such consistency that the Sheep Eater reputation has long demanded rehabilitation.

The primary goal of this book is to present the Sheep Eaters as they really were—intelligent, inventive, congenial tenants of a high-latitude landscape that they occupied without initiating conflict. In the process, we hope to expose the sources of and reasons behind the biased and substantially incorrect view of this intrepid group of people that has been accepted without critical evaluation by contemporary writers, archaeologists, and historians.[2]

It has often been acknowledged that, from their first appearance as a distinct entity within the larger geographic distribution of Shoshone peoples, the Sheep Eaters traversed and exploited a piece of real estate that in the late nineteenth century was designated as Yellowstone National Park. The imposition of lines on a map defining more than two million acres of mountains, valleys, lakes, and rivers as a new jurisdiction controlled by a distant federal bureaucracy—and subject to its rules—must have been unfathomable to the human groups that for generations had lived among and used the many resources the area offered. It is perhaps not surprising that many of the stereotypically degrading Sheep Eater images are found in reports and other publications associated with the park. For example, Hiram Chittenden, the first person to chronicle Yellowstone Park history, referred to the Sheep Eaters as follows:

> Utterly unfit for warlike contention, they seem to have sought immunity from their dangerous neighbors by dwelling in the fastnesses of the mountains. They were destitute of even savage comforts....Their rigorous existence left its mark on their physical nature. They were feeble in mind and diminutive in stature, and are described as a "timid, harmless race."[3]

Had they known of Chittenden's assessment of their character, the Sheep Eaters might have been forgiven any outrage over their portrayal as dull-witted and harmless, but compared to other slanderous depictions, Chittenden's account is actually quite mild. A case in point is the commentary offered by Charles Coutant, a distinguished Wyoming historian. In addition to labeling the Sheep Eaters as cowards, Coutant accuses them of incest: "Not cultivating the acts of war, they became a timid and inoffensive tribe, marrying among themselves and at last became dwarfed and were despised by war-like nations."[4]

Reading these descriptions, as hundreds of people have, it is easy to see why there are so many misconceptions about the Sheep Eaters. Unfortunately, Chittenden's and Coutant's characterizations have been repeated time and again, without any apparent effort to determine their correctness, with the result that fallacious stereotypes have morphed into historical verities. Some authors have displayed a screenwriter's originality, inventing preposterous reasons for imagined Sheep Eater behavior. In his acclaimed account about John Colter, widely credited as the first non-Indian to trek through Yellowstone Park, the Harvard-educated, Wyoming native Burton Harris notes that

> the only inhabitants of Yellowstone Park in the vicinity of the lake in Colter's time were the furtive Sheepeaters. The presumption is that this wretched, primitive tribe were outcasts from the various Shoshone bands, and that they lived in the region only because the other tribes shunned the geysers. The Sheepeaters possessed few weapons, and had been cowed so thoroughly by their enemies that their principal method of defending themselves was to cower near geysers they feared no less than their pursuers.[5]

The caricature of cringing Sheep Eaters huddled for protection within the folds of Mother Nature's misty skirts is disproved by the hundreds of archaeological sites in Yellowstone's geyser basins that contain extensive evidence of activities related to daily life. One has to wonder how these sites were generated in thermal areas if, as asserted, Indians feared the geysers. There are also dozens of ethnographic accounts of the use of Yellowstone Park by the Crow, Flathead, Pend d'Oreille, Blackfoot, Bannock, Kiowa, Shoshone, and other tribes. In the face of the archaeological and historical evidence that unequivocally tells us that Indians did not fear the geysers, we are left with the conclusion that many historians have been guided by that well-known methodological imperative: "Please, don't confuse me with the facts."[6]

One of the sources to which historians *could have turned* had they wanted to investigate allegations that Sheep Eaters were feebleminded, cowardly, defenseless dwarfs consists of the memoirs and journal of Osborne Russell, a capable mountain man and free trapper who lived in and near Sheep Eater territory between 1834 and 1841. Traveling in the Lamar Valley of Yellowstone National Park in 1835, Russell observed:

> Here we found a few Snake Indians...who were the only Inhabitants of this lonely and secluded spot. They were all neatly clothed in dressed deer and Sheep skins of the best quality and seemed to be perfectly contented and happy. They were rather surprised at our approach and retreated to the heights where they might have a view of us without apprehending any danger, but having persuaded them of our pacific intentions we then succeeded in getting them to encamp with us.[7]

We shall have reason to return throughout this book to other parts of Russell's description, but at this point it is important to underscore that he found the Sheep Eaters to be contented, happy, and neatly clothed. Although they retreated when Russell and his party first approached, after being assured that the trappers had come with peaceful intent, they soon descended to the party's camp and settled in to trade.

CAPTAIN BONNEVILLE'S JOURNEY

In nineteenth-century America, the eastern appetite for tales about the expeditions and adventures of travelers west of the Mississippi was enormous, and nowhere did this passionate curiosity burn with more intensity than in the heart of Captain Benjamin L. E. Bonneville (Figure 1.1). A graduate of West Point,

> he was stationed at various posts in the Far West. Here he was brought into frequent intercourse with Indian traders, mountain trappers, and other pioneers of the wilderness; and became so excited by their tales of wild scenes and wild adventures, and their accounts of vast and magnificent regions as yet unexplored, that an expedition to the Rocky Mountains became the ardent desire of his heart, and an enterprise to explore untrodden tracts, the leading object of his ambition.[8]

Once Captain Bonneville had successfully raised the large sum of money necessary to finance his expedition, in 1832 he disappeared into the western horizon. By the time he returned three years later, it was widely believed that he had died or gone AWOL. Washington Irving, author of *The Legend of Sleepy Hollow* and *Rip Van Winkle*, encountered Captain Bonneville shortly after his return from his journey of discovery. Irving was so captivated by the tale told in Bonneville's journal—described as a "mass of a manuscript"—that he subsequently acquired it, rewrote it in the third person, and published it to great acclaim under the title *The Adventures of Captain Bonneville*.

The Irving publication reports that during the time Bonneville was in the Wind River Mountains near present-day Lander, Wyoming, a scouting party spotted some Indians who fled when approached. After the scout reported the incident to Bonneville, the latter concluded (on the basis of what information or intuition is not known) that these Indians were part of a

> hermit race, scanty in number, that inhabit the highest and most inaccessible fastnesses. They speak the Shoshonie language, and probably are offsets from that tribe, though they have peculiarities of their own, which distinguish them from all other Indians. They are miserably poor; own no horses, and are destitute of every convenience to be derived from an intercourse with the whites. Their weapons are bows and stone-pointed arrows, with which they hunt the deer, the elk, and the mountain sheep. They are to be found scattered about the countries of the Shoshonie, Flathead, Crow, and Blackfeet tribes; but their residences are always in lonely places, and the clefts of the rocks.... These forlorn beings, forming a mere link between human

Figure 1.1. Captain Benjamin L. E. Bonneville, a western explorer whose contact
with Sheep Eater Indians is recorded in *The
Adventures of Captain Bonneville* by Washington Irving. Illustration by Davíd Joaquín,
based on a photograph by John Brandow
appearing on the National Park Service–
Yellowstone National Park Web site.

nature and the brute, have been looked down upon with pity and con-
tempt by the creole trappers, who have given them the appellation of
"les dignes de pitié," or "the objects of pity." They appear more worthy
to be called, the wild men of the mountains.[9]

There will always be some uncertainty about whether the terms in
which this encounter is recorded reflect Bonneville's own sentiments
or whether the original text might have been distorted or modified by
Irving during his editing and rewriting of the manuscript. It should be
emphasized, however, that regardless of any possible changes, there
was no actual face-to-face encounter between Bonneville or his men
and the Sheep Eaters until a month or so later, when Captain Bonneville came upon a group of "les dignes de pitié" while camped on the
Snake River. At this meeting, Bonneville discovered that the Sheep

Eaters were actually better off than he had originally imagined: "The captain had the good fortune to meet with a family of those wanderers of the mountains, emphatically called 'les dignes de pitie,' or Poordevil Indians. These, however, appear to have forfeited the title, for they had with them a fine lot of skins of beaver, elk, deer, and mountain sheep."[10]

OTHER CLOSE OBSERVERS

The preceding excerpt describing the meeting between Bonneville and the Sheep Eaters is seldom quoted, perhaps because it contradicts more popular misconceptions. It contains information, however, that would not have been overlooked by any mountain man who was anxious to trade: the Sheep Eaters were well endowed with furs and prepared to do business with the American traders. Another mountain man and trapper, Warren Ferris, recorded experiences similar to those of Osborne Russell, emphasizing that he found the "Snake Indians without horses" to be well clothed, some wearing beaver-skin moccasins and beaver-fur clothing.[11]

As early as 1854, the observations of a Middle Oregon Indian agent, R. R. Thompson, challenged another canard—the belief that Sheep Eaters lacked sufficient intelligence to cope in the modern world:

> The Mountain Snake Indians are a branch of the Root Diggers, (who, in the extreme south, are presumed to be the lowest order of the aboriginal race) and have a common language. They occupy the country on the north end east of Fort Hall, and to the south to include Bear River valley. These Indians gradually improve in their habits and intelligence as they approach the northern and eastern extremities of their country.[12]

Almost seventy years later, Episcopal churchwoman Sarah Olden described her encounter with Sheep Eater Indians during a visit with the Reverend John Roberts on the Wind River Reservation. Her assessment of Sheep Eater mental capacity corroborates the testimony of Agent Thompson, but she appears to interpret the presence of hunting paraphernalia as indicative of their readiness to engage in armed conflict: "This band was more intelligent, and very warlike. They wandered off into the mountains and took their dogs with them. They found mountain sheep in abundance; when the dogs saw the sheep on an eminence, they surrounded them and holding them at bay, waited until the Indians came forward to kill them."[13]

Several earlier accounts corroborate that Sheep Eaters were capable warriors, among them Humfreville's assertion that Sheep Eaters were a "fierce tribe that lived near the headwaters of the Salmon River" and Lander's description of them as "very fierce and wild, rarely visiting whites."[14]

THE EARLY PARK SERVICE VIEW

It is interesting that prior to the creation of Yellowstone National Park in 1872, none of the accounts of trappers, Indian agents, and missionaries described the Sheep Eaters as diminutive or commented on their lack of intelligence. Quite the opposite is true, which suggests that the Department of the Interior had a vested interest in applying considerable negative spin to earlier perceptions of Sheep Eater capabilities and attitudes as an excuse ultimately to ban their presence in the park. Government pressure to control the Indian use of Yellowstone intensified in 1877, following the capture of a party of tourists by a group of Nez Perce traveling through the park. A similar trek by Bannock Indians the next year resulted in considerable political pressure on the park's second superintendent, Philetus Norris, to take the steps necessary to make the park a safe and popular tourist attraction.

Even though Norris was a student of archaeology—and collected and shipped to the Smithsonian Institution some of the most important artifacts found in Yellowstone Park—he was also a practical administrator and recognized the need to diminish the status of "wild" Indians within his jurisdiction. As part of this effort, his reports to Congress identified the Sheep Eaters as a timid group of harmless, pygmy Indians. He also traveled to the Lemhi Agency in northern Idaho to inform the Shoshone (and any Sheep Eaters in their midst) that they had been given a reservation and should stay on it.[15] The message was clear: Indians were no longer welcome in Yellowstone National Park.

Park superintendents who succeeded Norris continued to enforce the policy declaring that the park should be an Indian-free zone. In 1887, Moses Harris, the first military officer to serve as superintendent, reported that eastern visitors "were not accustomed to seeing

Indians in their wild state" and were understandably uneasy. Tourism and the development of amenities to make the visitor experience enjoyable were the government's highest priorities, so there is a logic to the steps taken to transform policy into reality. By today's standards, however, the treatment of the Sheep Eaters represents one of the many injustices of the nineteenth-century pacification of the West. It is a cruel irony that indigenous and well-adapted tribal groups were evicted from their lands in order for urban tourists to enjoy the wondrous landscapes without running the risk of unanticipated encounters with the former occupants.

THE DEHUMANIZING FABRICATIONS CONTINUE

It is one thing to realize that events in the past unfolded in terms of the knowledge or ignorance, the strengths or weaknesses, of the participants. It is much more difficult to understand—in what has been characterized as the Information Age—how inaccurate stereotypes of the Sheep Eaters are allowed to persist. Contemporary histories continue to chronicle make-believe images of culturally impoverished Sheep Eaters. The recent memoirs of a chief ranger of Yellowstone National Park sound a depressingly familiar refrain:

> Known as the Tukudikas, or "Sheepeaters," they [are] the lowliest of the low in the Shoshone Indian tribes. Lacking either the will or the courage to compete in a world upset by the introduction of the horse and gun, they sought to eke out an existence in the then mostly undesired rugged country.... They stayed mostly to themselves, were timid, small in stature.... Dirty, destitute, primitive ... the Sheepeaters were anything but fodder for the Indian romancer.[16]

Not only are there many similar descriptions in the contemporary literature, but at least one artistic depiction of Sheep Eaters has been influenced by dehumanizing fictions. In one of his works, the accomplished sculptor Richard Greaves represents dull-looking Sheep Eaters hiding in trees, hanging from the branches in apelike poses (Figure 1.2).

In fairness to early historians like Hiram Chittenden, we must note that in the 1860s Sheep Eater lifeways had been severely disrupted by the discovery of gold in areas they frequented in Idaho and Montana. Hunters from the new mining communities exhausted the

Figure 1.2. Sketch of a portion of the Sheep Eater sculpture by Richard Greaves showing a woman crouching in a tree. Note that she is unclothed and holding onto the tree with a simian-like grasp. Illustration by Davíd Joaquín.

supply of game, polluted the streams, overfished the lakes, and cut down the forests. The simultaneous introduction of domestic sheep into the region had a devastating effect on the millions of northern Rocky Mountains bighorns, which had no immunity to domestic sheep diseases. William Baillie-Grohman, hunting bighorns in the Absaroka and Wind River mountains between 1879 and 1881, observed that within only a few years the bighorn herds had been reduced to a fraction of their original numbers.

With the loss of their primary food resource, Sheep Eaters were forced to rely more intensively on other subsistence strategies such as fishing, but their access to fish, too, had been altered by Euro-Americans. The newly built dams and weirs in the region's rivers significantly reduced the upstream migrations of many species, with the result that when Chittenden encountered Sheep Eater groups in and around Yellowstone Park in the 1880s, their condition may have justified his conclusion that they were miserably poor. But his assumption that hunger and a sense of futility had imposed mental feebleness and diminutive stature on the once-proud people whom Osborne Russell had met in 1834 is very far off the mark. It is the early Sheep Eater Indians—the highly capable mountaineers who developed remarkable strategies for survival in a rigorous environment and left behind a legacy worth reporting to others—whom we want to chronicle in this book.

2

IIII

"We Are All the Same People, All the Way Back": Looking for Sheep Eaters in the Historic and Archaeological Records

For an imaginary line, the Continental Divide of North America has great clout. In its 8,000-mile length, it runs along a nearly continuous series of elevated geological formations from the northwest coast of Alaska to Central America. Its course was determined over eons by the hundreds of episodes of upheaval, tilt, and erosion that created the features of the continent's surface as we know it and led to its role in a scenario of nature having immense consequences. The location of the Great Divide, as it is sometimes called, coupled with gravity, determines the direction of the flow of all surface water in North America. In this case, "all" refers to the water from the smallest creeks and streams to the largest rivers and watersheds, which, flowing west of this boundary, ultimately ends up in the Pacific Ocean and, flowing east, empties into the Atlantic Ocean.

Seen from above by a migratory bird setting out from the Chukchi Sea, the Great Divide runs almost due east through northern Alaska, passing through the Arctic National Wildlife Refuge before crossing into Canada's Yukon Province. There it drifts south across the Arctic Circle and then heads southeast into British Columbia, where it links up with the northern tip of the Rocky Mountains and forms the southern half of the provincial boundary between British Columbia and Alberta. Crossing into the Lower Forty-eight at Waterton Lakes, Montana, it wanders southeast through some magnificent national forests until it hangs a left south of Butte and travels about ninety miles to the Idaho border. Turning to the south again, it follows the interstate border through the Bitterroot Range to Beaverhead National Forest, makes a hairpin turn to the east in the Targhee

National Forest, and sets out for Wyoming and Yellowstone National Park. There it loops south around Old Faithful and Yellowstone Lake before veering southeast out of the park and running the entire length of the Wind River Range.

Continuing to head south, the Great Divide sticks with the Rockies until they peter out in southern New Mexico, and then, crossing an international boundary for the third time, it takes off into Mexico on an excursion along the ridges of the Sierra Madre Occidental. It almost dips into the Gulf of Tehuantepec as it traverses the coastal range in southern Chiapas Province, on its way through Mayan ruins to the cloud forests of Costa Rica's Puntarenas Province. The end of the line for the Great Divide occurs with a bump at the locks of the canal on the Isthmus of Panama.

First Encounters

On August 11, 1805, along a stretch of the Beaverhead Mountains where the Great Divide delineates what is now the Idaho–Montana border, the tired, hungry, and dispirited members of a contingent of Lewis and Clark's Corps of Discovery had a remarkable encounter with a group of Mountain Shoshone led by a headman named Cameahwait. In Lewis's journal entry describing the encounter (the original spelling is preserved in the following excerpt and all others that we quote), he observes that the group

> live in a wretched stait of poverty. yet nothwithstanding their extreem poverty they are not only cheerfull but even gay, fond of gaudy dress and amusements; like most other Indians they are great egotists and frequently boast of heroic acts which they never performed. they are also fond of games of wrisk. they are frank, communicative, fair in dealing, generous with the little they possess, extreemly honest, and by no means beggarly. each individual is his own sovereign master, and acts from the dictates of his own mind; the authority of the Cheif being nothing more than mere admonition supported by the influence which the prop[r]iety of his own examplary conduct may have acquired him in the minds of the individuals who compose the band.[1]

The Indians and the Easterners both had some pressing needs and some resources that the other group wanted. Meriwether Lewis had just discovered that there were no westward-flowing navigable waterways through the mountains of Idaho and was now trying to find local Indian groups with horses to trade so that the expedition could continue its trek to the Pacific Ocean. Cameahwait's group was gearing up for the fall buffalo hunt on the Plains to the east and needed weapons and various supplies.

Captain Clark, the Indian guide Sacajawea, and other members of a side party were off scouting the terrain, but when they rejoined Lewis near what has become the town of Dillon, Montana, Sacajawea discovered—as every American schoolchild knows—that Cameahwait was the brother from whom she had been forcibly separated many years earlier.[2] This fortuitous reunion played a major role in the success of the expedition, not only because Cameahwait's group of Shoshone—who would later be known as the Lemhi—had many horses but also because they provided the corps with essential information about the Indians and terrain the corps would soon encounter.

As Lewis noted in his journal, by means of a chain of translation proceeding from English, to French, to Hidatsa, to Shoshone, and back again,

> I soon obtained three very good horses. for which I gave an uniform coat, a pair of legings, a few handkerchiefs, three knives and some other small articles the whole of which did not cost more than about 20$ in the U' States. the Indians seemed quite as well pleased with their bargin as I was. the men also purchased one for an old checked shirt a pair of old legings and a knife.[3]

All told, Lewis successfully negotiated for twenty-nine horses, promising that on his return trip—a pledge apparently never kept— he would bring Cameahwait the requested guns his group needed for hunting and self-defense.

Horses had become available to the Mountain Shoshone around AD 1730 through an extensive trade network originating in the Spanish settlements of New Mexico. The replacement of human foot-powered transport, which was slow and geographically constraining, with "horse power" (in the original sense of the term) radically changed most western Indian societies. Possession of horses allowed the Mountain Shoshone to travel many miles eastward to the Plains, where increased mobility enabled them to scout, chase, and kill bison and then carry home large quantities of meat. The risks associated with these logistical hunting forays were best met by observance of the maxim "there's safety in numbers," so Shoshone groups aggregated into larger bands better able to contend with competition and aggression from other Plains tribes.

At the time of the Lewis and Clark transect through Sheep Eater territory, successful bands of horse-riding Shoshone were living throughout the greater Yellowstone region. In addition to the Lemhi, other equestrian bands were attracted by the excellent winter pastures along the Snake River near what became—a half-century later—Fort Hall, Idaho. As many thousands of Mountain and Basin Shoshone restructured their group size, mobility, and subsistence options, some bands moved into the good horse-grazing country near Black's Fork, Wyoming.[4] Led in the historic period by the renowned Chief Washakie, these groups are now referred to as the Eastern or Plains Shoshone. Other groups left Montana and Wyoming to position themselves closer to the sources of horses in New Mexico and in the process emerged with a new name—the Comanche—and a reputation throughout Texas and New Mexico for the audacity of their exploits.

It is important to remember, however, that prior to the arrival of horses, those groups coalescing as equestrian tribes were indistinguishable from the Sheep Eater, Salmon Eater, and other Mountain Shoshone groups that were *not* swept up into the new mobile way of life but, instead, continued to maintain their reliance on the pedestrian foraging adaptation that had sustained them for centuries.[5] Trying to identify these traditional Mountain Shoshone groups both in the historical era and in prehistory is a challenge, but fortunately there are some sources for the inquisitive researcher to consult. Once Euro-American trappers arrived in the Yellowstone region, textual references to Sheep Eaters began to occur, along with a set of historical maps originating with the Corps of Discovery but augmented by the experiences of other early adventurers in the region.

MAPPING THE SHOSHONE

Several years after returning from his four-year journey with Meriwether Lewis, William Clark prepared two maps. The first, known as "the Clark 1810 map," includes for its time a remarkably accurate depiction of the geographical features of the greater Yellowstone region. It lacks, however, any information about the Indians inhabiting the area. The second map, referred to as "the 1814 Clark map," is of interest because Indian names were provided by John Colter and George Drouillard, two well-known mountain men who had been trusted members of the Lewis and Clark team.

Both men had spent several years independently exploring the Yellowstone region in the early 1800s. Colter spent the winter of 1806–07 with two other trappers somewhere north of present-day Cody, Wyoming, and then joined up with Manuel Lisa's trading expedition, which had left Saint Louis that spring for points west. After constructing the Fort Raymond trading post at the point on the Yellowstone River where it is joined by the Bighorn, Colter and Drouillard were instructed by Lisa to spend the winter searching for streams with abundant beaver dens and to make trading contacts with the Indians.[6] To fulfill this assignment, both men made remarkable treks throughout the greater Yellowstone region and had much of interest to report on subsequent visits to Clark in Saint Louis.

Colter apparently did not present Clark with a map, but Drouillard made two maps, one of which was a pencil sketch that included no information about tribal locations. It is the second map and its accompanying notes that contain significant information about the Indians encountered on his 1807–08 trek across northern Wyoming.[7] Drouillard may have worked directly with Clark, the latter writing details on his own draft map during their discussions. Clark in turn transferred his version of the geographical data to Nicholas Biddle, who had served as the editor of the Lewis and Clark journals and had engaged Samuel Lewis, a map engraver, to produce the 1814 Clark map (Figure 2.1).

One group of Indians on the 1814 Clark map, located on the upper reaches of the Madison River to the northwest of Yellowstone National Park, is identified as "Ne-Moy" "600 souls" "Band of Snake Indians." Linguists have pointed out that, historically, the Shoshone would sometimes refer to themselves using an archaic construction—the "Ne'me," "Ne'we," or "Nü:wɜ," with stress on the first syllable.[8] These designations, and other variations, all mean the same thing: "a person speaking our native tongue."[9] Julian Steward has noted that it was also customary for Sheep Eaters to use this archaic terminology: "Both the Lemhi and the mountain dwellers called themselves Agaidika, Shoshoni, or Nü:wɜ, but the latter distinguished themselves as Tukadika."[10]

The similarity between the "Nü:wɜ" term of identity and the "Ne-Moy" ethnic identifier on Clark's map certainly suggests that the source for the name was probably Colter—whose route through the

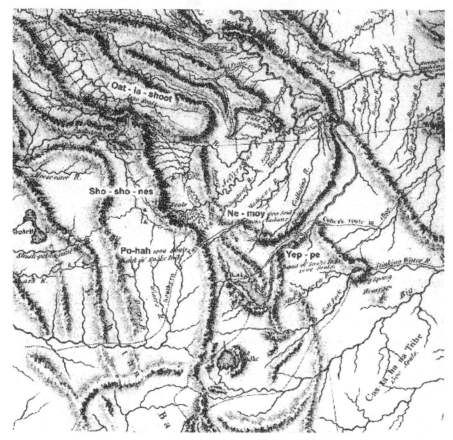

Figure 2.1. A portion of Samuel Lewis's engraving of William Clark's 1814 map showing the locations of Indian groups in the Yellowstone region. The Ne-moy and Yeppe were probably Mountain Shoshone groups. The Oat-la-shoot represent a Salish-speaking tribe, and those designated as Po-hah were Bannock.

region in 1807–8 is marked on the map—and that the Indians he encountered were Sheep Eaters. Colter is also the likely source of the name of another Indian group—the "Yeppe" "Band of Snake Indians" "1000 Souls"—located on the 1814 Clark map in the Beartooth Mountains region to the north and west of Cody, Wyoming. Because no historically known bands of Snake Indians were called the Yeppe, the identity of this group has always puzzled researchers. One possibility is that *Yeppe* was another name for an ancestral subgroup of the Shoshone known as the Yupe or People of the Timber.[11] It is also possible that the term is derived from *yap*, the Shoshone word for root vegetable.

The maps made by George Drouillard identify groups of Mountain Crow Indians—known to have been the Sheep Eaters' eastern neighbors throughout the historic period—near Cody, Wyoming, and along Rock Creek near its junction with the Clark Fork of the Yellowstone River in Montana. Especially interesting is a group located near the junction of the Stinking Water (Shoshone River) and the Bighorn River where Lovell, Wyoming, is today. Drouillard's notations describe the group as the "e-cup-scup-pe-ah (who speak the same language with the Oots-lash-shoot) amount to 280 lodges of dressed leather or 2,240 souls."[12] Since Drouillard had served the Lewis and Clark expedition as a sign language interpreter for groups of Salish-speaking Flathead Indians called the *Oat-la-shoot*, we can rely on his ability to recognize that language when he heard it. It is likely, then, that the "e-cup-scup-pe-ah" tipi dwellers at the mouth of the Stinking Water in 1807 belonged to either Flathead or closely related Pend d'Oreille groups, whose homelands were more to the north and west in Montana. Evidently these groups had repositioned themselves and were using resources south of their customary territory to avoid pressure from raiding parties of mounted Blackfoot, who had been supplied with guns by the French.[13]

The combination of information from Drouillard's two maps and the 1814 Clark map, coupled with what is known about the diversification of Mountain Shoshone groups after the arrival of the horse in the region, provides a picture of the ethnic and cultural landscape during the historic period. We have seen that there was fluid movement of peoples known now as Flathead, Pend d'Oreille, and Mountain Crow throughout a tristate area at the junctions of the Idaho, Montana, and Wyoming borders, to whom Mountain Shoshone groups—some equestrian and some not—related through trade and the exchange of ideas and resources. But what is known about the origins of the Mountain Shoshone? Maps and historic records place them in the region during the historic period, but what about their prehistoric past? At the moment, at least, there are almost as many answers to this question as there are archaeologists working in the region.

THE GREAT ARCHAEOLOGICAL DIVIDE

In 1958, when linguist Sydney Lamb published an article on the prehistory of Great Basin languages, he could never have imagined the uproar it would cause among archaeologists working in the region.[14] Lamb's simple premise, based on changes in vocabulary and estimates of word loss through time, was that Numic-speaking Shoshone groups had migrated from their homeland in the Southwest in a three-pronged formation across the Great Basin areas of California, Nevada, and Utah. The relevance of Lamb's proposal to an understanding of Sheep Eater prehistory is that the latter had presumably moved along the central prong of his model from a starting place near Death Valley National Monument and settled in what became their homeland in the area surrounding Yellowstone National Park. He proposed that the Shoshone's northeastward migration began about AD 1000 and that groups arrived in Wyoming around AD 1200.

For a number of archaeologists, Lamb's model made a lot of sense because archaeological surveys and excavations indicated that the distribution of Shoshone pottery and possible Shoshone rock art followed the same route at approximately the same time. Perhaps the most compelling support for Lamb's projections came from Owens Valley, California, where archaeologist Robert Bettinger and his colleagues had developed models complementing Lamb's temporal trajectory. The models were based on archaeological evidence of a reduction in the number of Shoshone sites—beginning in about AD 1000—in the core Shoshone region, which would be expected if a large-scale Shoshone out-migration had indeed occurred. Cultural anthropologists also supported the Lamb model, particularly the highly respected Swedish anthropologist Åke Hultkrantz, who was one of the foremost authorities on Sheep Eater ethnohistory. Hultkrantz concluded from the archaeological evidence that Shoshone groups had arrived in Wyoming less than 1,000 years ago.[15]

Although the Lamb model became the most widely accepted account of the prehistory of the Wyoming Shoshone, not all archaeologists agreed with its time frame. Among those who believed that the Shoshone had ancient roots in Wyoming and Idaho—going back perhaps 5,000 years—was Smithsonian Institution archaeologist Wilfred Husted, who based his conclusions on excavations at Mummy Cave, a deeply stratified site west of Cody, Wyoming. Another counterargument to the Lamb model resulted from the work of Gary Wright, an archaeologist who did extensive research in Yellowstone and Grand Teton national parks. Based on the archaeological record in northwestern Wyoming, Wright argued that there was no evidence of a Shoshone presence in the region until approximately AD 1600. Here the matter stood until about a decade ago: the majority of northern Plains archaeologists believed that their evidence supported the Lamb model based on historical linguistics, a small group of archaeologists thought that the Shoshone had an ancient presence in the north, and an even smaller number argued that the arrival of Shoshone groups in the region was nearly concurrent with the Euro-American entrada.[16]

Support for the Lamb model started to unravel when archaeologists began to find sites in a wide variety of settings that appeared to contain Shoshone artifacts that were older than AD 1200, the date that Numic-speaking groups were supposed to have arrived in the region. Several of these excavations were the work of Idaho archaeologist Richard Holmer and his colleagues, who had decided that the best way to determine what really happened in the past was to begin with secure historical knowledge and work backward in time.[17] Using a method that archaeologists call the *direct historical approach*, they began to excavate at a reliably documented Shoshone site that appeared on maps from the historic period. Further confirmation of the site's authenticity was provided by several of Julian Steward's Shoshone consultants during discussions in the 1930s about the locations of their former villages.

In the upper levels of what became known as the Wahmuza site, Holmer found beads and musket balls, intermixed with some stone tools. As he dug down through layer after layer, despite changes in the form of many artifacts, he discovered that all the levels—going back 3,500 years—contained a particular stone tool that he called a Wahmuza projectile point, thought to have been used on a lance. Holmer reasoned that the presence over a long time period of identical Wahmuza points represented the presence of a lengthy, continuous, unbroken cultural tradition. According to the logic of the direct historical method, because the surface materials were known to be associated with a Shoshone camp, the underlying layers represented the same cultural tradition.

At the Legend Rock site, south of Cody, research led by archaeologists Danny Walker and Julie Francis provided corroborative evidence of the time depth of the Shoshone prehistoric presence in the region. Legend Rock is an extensive petroglyph site with a mixture of different rock art styles, but the most abundant type—assigned to the

Dinwoody petroglyph tradition—has been shown to have a clear-cut and unambiguous association with the Sheep Eater Shoshone.[18] When Walker and Francis subjected a sample of charcoal overlying a Dinwoody petroglyph at Legend Rock to radiocarbon dating, the analysis produced an age of 2000 BP. When these data are combined with a variety of other relative and chronometric dates from excavations at the site, the Dinwoody petroglyph tradition appears to be 3,000 to 4,000 years old.[19]

Also little more than a decade ago, another important group of sites began to be found in Wyoming. Initially discovered in the sidewalls of ditches that had been cut as part of energy-related pipeline projects, these sites contained the remains of saucer-shaped, oblong structures that were partially dug into the ground. At first these features were called *pit houses*, but because many of them did not have the well-defined walls and entryways of the typical Southwestern pit house, archaeologists reversed the word order and began to call them *house pits*. These features contained storage and roasting pits dug into the floors but few artifacts, although the occasional manos and metates that were present suggest that the occupants' diet contained significant amounts of processed vegetable products (Figure 2.2).

House pit sites are found throughout the basin of western Wyoming, frequently positioned on the ends of finger ridges from which they overlook the floodplains below. Along Beaver Creek, south of Riverton, sites tend to be concentrated into two groups: ones dated to between 4,000 and 3,000 years before the present and more recent ones that are between 1,600 and 1,000 years old. In both groups, house pits are usually round and measure two to three meters in diameter. Some floors contain basin-shaped pits with the remains of charcoal but little else. Others have more cylindrical roasting pits with layers of heat-cracked rock, charcoal, ash, and soil, as well as the remains of prickly pear cactus and bones from cottontail and jackrabbits. The cactus may have provided a moist environment for cooking other foods, but—aside from the rabbits—archaeologists have yet to figure out what was prepared in the pits.[20] House pit sites are found archaeologically in the Great Basin to the south and west of Wyoming but not to the east on the Great Plains, and although this distribution does not necessarily mean that they can be reliably associated with the Shoshone, they represent an important component of the total picture.[21]

MUMMY CAVE

We mentioned Mummy Cave in passing when referring earlier to the research of Wilfred Husted, and now we want to describe this remarkable archaeological site in more detail. It is located at an elevation of 6,300 feet on the north fork of the Shoshone River, a few miles downstream from the East Entrance to Yellowstone National Park. Containing thirty-eight separate occupation layers that range in

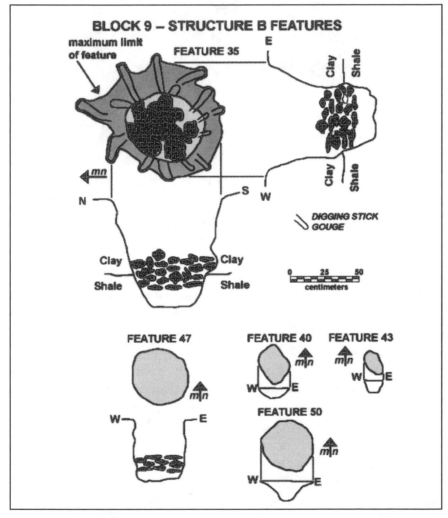

Figure 2.2. House pit features at the Sand Draw Dump site near Riverton, Wyoming. Note the digging-stick scars in the sidewalls of the largest pit. The function of these pits is not well established, but they were likely used for seed storage, although some may have been used for roasting root vegetables. Illustration by Danny N. Walker.

Figure 2.3. Mummy Cave, located along the North Fork of the Shoshone River, east of Yellowstone National Park. The cave is situated so that very little water reaches the interior. Over the hundreds of years of its use by hunter–gatherers, dryness allowed the more perishable artifacts left behind, such as feathers and basketry, to be preserved. Illustration by Davíd Joaquín.

age from Layer 1, the oldest—with a date of 9000 BP—to the most recent, Layer 38—which dates to sometime around AD 1500—it was excavated by Husted and his colleague, Robert Edgar, under the auspices of the Buffalo Bill Historical Center.

If you were to ask archaeologists to name the two most important properties of the perfect site, more often than not they would immediately say, "Number one, a protected setting providing excellent preservation and, number two, great time depth." In the case of Mummy Cave, nature provided the sequestered location and protection from the elements, which may have had something to do with the decisions of hunter–gatherers to take shelter there again and again (Figure 2.3). Archaeologists exposed layer after layer of cultural material to a depth of more than 33 feet below the surface, and at no time was there any evidence of a break or interruption in the use of the cave. Although the density and depth of the deposits do not mean that prehistoric

Figure 2.4. A view of the excavation at Mummy Cave in Wyoming. The excavation eventually reached a depth of more than 33 feet. This extraordinary site contained stratified archaeological remains ranging from a few hundred years to more than 9,000 years in age. Photograph courtesy of the Buffalo Bill Historical Center, Cody, Wyoming; P.29.1.25.

hunters and gatherers lived continuously in the cave throughout an entire year, they do indicate periodic occupations during nearly every one of the 9,000 years the site was in use.

Another intriguing discovery is that the vast majority of the animal bones found in the deposit came from bighorn sheep. Very few elk bones and no moose or bison bones were found during the entire excavation. Deer bones are present, but bighorn sheep outnumber them by a ratio of ten to one. An inescapable conclusion is that the people intermittently occupying Mummy Cave were preferentially hunting and eating bighorn sheep.[22] Of course, there were no labels on the sheep remains saying, "Sheep Eater Shoshone ate me," but other evidence, particularly the mummified human remains in Layer 36—the third level below the surface, which has a radiocarbon age of 1230 BP—supports Sheep Eater utilization of the uppermost layers of the cave (Figure 2.4).

Dryness in the cave in general, but especially in Layer 36, played a role in the preservation of coiled basketry, wooden arrow shafts, feathers, fragments of cordage, and other artifacts that usually decay in sites in wetter locations. The recovery of so many artifacts has meant that many manufacturing techniques offering considerable insight into the toolmakers themselves—such as the steps involved in making compound arrows—could be studied.

Another possible linkage between Great Basin Shoshone and Sheep Eaters is suggested by some of the projectile points in Layer 36 that are very similar to the Rose Springs projectile points (also called Rosegate) identified by David Hurst Thomas at Gatecliff shelter in Nevada.[23] Some of the Rosegate-like projectile points in Mummy Cave are delicate, corner-notched tools that are exceptionally well made from the highest-quality chert or agate. So much effort was invested in making them precisely according to form that they are sometimes referred to as "gem quality." Their pristine state may indicate that they were ceremonial items used as amulets or in medicine bundles. Support for this possibility comes from some of the Dinwoody rock art figures that have exactly the same corner-notched projectile points dangling from their arms or hanging around their necks.

Husted and Edgar have observed that Rose Springs projectile points are known to occur outside the Great Basin, and therefore their presence in a site is not proof positive that their makers had Shoshone great-grandparents (Figure 2.5). Nonetheless, when the artifact assemblage in Mummy Cave's Layer 36 is considered in its entirety, it is identical to assemblages from sites in Nevada that are indisputably associated with Shoshone groups. On the basis of this similarity, in our opinion the cultural materials in Layer 36, which are dated at 1,200 years before the present, are very likely the remains of groups that were ancestral to Wyoming's Shoshone people. Accordingly, throughout this book we have used the artifacts from this layer in our descriptions of typical Sheep Eater tools.

Cultural continuity is also suggested by the resemblance between the artifacts in Layer 36—except for projectile-point types—and those in Layer 30. This earlier layer contains McKean projectile points, dated at 4,400 years ago, and Great Basin artifacts such as coiled basketry, netting, cordage, grinding stones, worked wood, and leather scraps. Husted believes that Layer 30 is "ancestral to succeeding

Figure 2.5. Rose Springs projectile points excavated from Mummy Cave. These well-made corner-notched points are distributed across Wyoming, but they tend to be found in greater numbers in the western half of the state and into the Great Basin. Photograph courtesy of the Buffalo Bill Historical Center, Cody, Wyoming; P.29.1.21.

assemblages and complexes in Mummy Cave and comparable assemblages on the western Plains identified as Shoshoni."[24] The correctness of this claim for the great time depth of a Shoshone presence in
the Yellowstone area will have to be determined by future research.

A UNIFYING VIEW

What do archaeologists do when they are faced with apparently con-
flicting data? Sometimes they squabble until someone digs a new
site and uncovers evidence that clarifies the conflict; or sometimes
someone else examines the existing data and offers a novel interpre-
tation of the disputed patterning, and a new "square one" is defined.
We think that the controversy surrounding the origins of the Wyoming Shoshone is best dealt with using the latter approach, because
more than one of the proposed scenarios may be correct. We can start
with the population decline in the Shoshone core area of California
that Robert Bettinger has identified and interpreted as evidence for
the dispersal of the Shoshone in a migration referred to as the "Numic
Spread." This patterning may actually have resulted from the departure of a *second wave* of Shoshone groups, who left the Great Basin
and joined their relatives—descendants of the *first wave* of immigrants,
whose repeated occupation of Mummy Cave has been documented
by Husted and Edgar—already living in Wyoming and Idaho. Not
only is there precedent for an original and then a follow-up migration
to the same territory by members of the same ethnic group, this practice was common in the Yellowstone Park region. On the Plains, segments of both the Crow and the Apache nations migrated in precisely
the same way.

Stating the preceding scenario in historical terms, we think the
archaeological evidence suggests that a group of Shoshone—including persons who became the Mountain Shoshone—with ancient roots
in the Great Basin, arrived in Wyoming and Idaho as much as 2,000 to
3,000 years before the present. Several millennia later, another group
of Shoshone left the Great Basin and arrived in the Yellowstone area
sometime around 1000 BP Confusion arose in the archaeological ranks
when, as the sequence of discovery would have it, researchers initially
found evidence of the later migration and concluded that it represented the *only* migration.[25] We suggest that, in fact, there may have
been multiple migrations.

There is some evidence to suggest that the *multiple wave* hypothesis may be supported by the Shoshone's own cultural traditions. Gary Wright and Jane Dirks believe that the myth about how the cottontail rabbit killed the sun is used by the Shoshone as a historical parable to describe their migration to the north.[26] They present a strong case that the cottontail represents the relocating Shoshone, who solve various problems as they adapt to new environments. At one point in the story, cottontail rabbits encounter "their uncles"—the brush rabbits— who ask the cottontails to marry their brush rabbit "sisters." In this part of the myth, the cottontails appear to be a metaphor for another wave of migrating Shoshone, who arrive and are reunited with their metaphorical brush rabbit Shoshone relatives.

LOOKING AHEAD

In the next chapter, we will describe the landscape and habitats through which mobile groups of Sheep Eater hunters and gatherers moved as part of their annual round. The much-abused adjective *awesome* accurately describes this montane environment and its many resources, and it is an equally appropriate summary term for the intelligent and resourceful way in which Sheep Eaters adapted to life in such a rigorous climatic setting.

3

||||

Purple Mountain Majesties: The Landscape and Habitats of Sheep Eater Territory

THE INTELLIGENT AMERICAN WILL ONE DAY POINT ON THE MAP
TO THIS REMARKABLE DISTRICT WITH THE CONSCIOUS PRIDE THAT
IT HAS NOT ITS PARALLEL ON THE FACE OF THE GLOBE.

—*Hayden* (1872)

If images of the geologic history of Sheep Eater territory could be generated by computer and screened very rapidly, the epic sequence would constitute the mother of all ecodisaster films— *Volcano* meets *Earthquake* meets *Twister*. There would be no human characters in this drama; their places would be taken by cataclysmic earthquakes, enormous volcanic eruptions, and geothermal outbursts. The opening sequence would focus on plate tectonics and depict the time between 100 and 50 million years ago when the Pacific plate crashed with such ferocity into the North American plate that the earth's surface crumpled, faulted, and was thrust upward, forming the Rocky Mountains. Forces in the Earth's core projected magma toward the surface, creating—over a fifteen-million-year period—volcanoes whose lava flows solidified to form the Absaroka Mountains. Episodes of vulcanism continued, and one particularly violent explosion 600,000 years ago is estimated to have been hundreds of times the size of the 1980 eruption of Mount St. Helens. Among the features it left in its wake was a gigantic caldera, a portion of which—following other geologic dynamics—became Yellowstone Lake, whose 100-mile shoreline makes it a dominant feature of the landscape (Figure 3.1).[1]

During the past two million years, at the same time that the Earth was contorting and belching up lava, worldwide periodic oscillations in climate resulted in the formation and dissolution of huge glaciers in

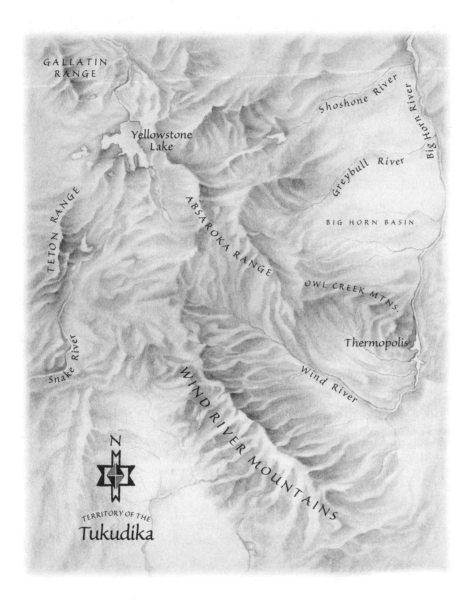

Figure 3.1. A map of Sheep Eater territory circa 1835. The area within Yellowstone National Park and southeast into the Absaroka and Wind River mountains was used most intensely by Sheep Eaters, although other Indian groups regularly moved through this region and exploited its resources. Illustration by Davíd Joaquín.

areas of high latitude and elevation. The most recent glacial maximum occurred about twenty-five thousand years ago, at which time a massive sheet of ice covered much of North America, including the Yellowstone area, masking its topography and swathing even its mountain peaks in unimaginable amounts of ice. As the buildup of snow and ice increased, glaciers moved across the landscape, scouring out sediments in their paths and creating new landforms such as deep valleys and abruptly ascending hills. As glaciers receded, they left behind boulders and porous formations of rubble transported from miles away. The latter deposits acted as sponges for meltwater, which accumulated and was transformed into steam at those places in Yellowstone—along fault lines particularly—where the Earth's molten interior approached the surface.

There are no villains in this epic, but there is a natural sound track produced, then and now, by geothermal processes that could easily be used to set the stage for the entrance of an army of nightmarish monsters in a horror film. The geysers, hot springs, and steam vents (called "fumaroles") concentrated in the Yellowstone area are so abundant that they represent the majority of such features in the world, and they regularly rumble, roar, boom, whistle, whoosh, and reverberate, often with deafening effect.

In this fast-forward view of the natural processes creating the region's landforms, we would watch as the Earth's surface was reshaped by two powerful erosional forces—wind and water—that carved away geologic formations in one place and deposited the sediments downstream or downslope in another. Repeated episodes of erosion wore away the outlines of tall peaks and swept away sediments in valleys, creating canyons and gorges. Many features of the Yellowstone landscape today bear names reflecting the forces that created them: Boiling River, Firehole River, One Hundred Springs Plain, West Thumb Geyser Basin, Mud Volcano, Sizzling Basin, Ragged Hills, Sour Creek Dome, and Hellroaring Creek, to name just a few.

As all the preceding dynamic, earth-shaping processes were taking place, the response of the biological world of Yellowstone Park and its surroundings was orchestrated by the dual processes of adaptation and natural selection. For much of that long period of upheaval and change, we have very little idea of what specific plant and animal communities emerged and succeeded each other. The tissues of living things are much less durable than the minerals forming the substrate upon which they were dependent, so it is only seldom that a slice of an ancient ecosystem is preserved. Such a glimpse into the arboreal mix of 35 million years ago was made possible by mudflows that accompanied volcanic eruptions near the park's Lamar Valley. Forests of temperate-zone species such as redwoods, magnolias, and dogwoods were encased by mud, lava, and ash and remain today as a petrified forest on the valley's Specimen Ridge.

The eighteenth- and nineteenth-century physical world inhabited by the Sheep Eaters was far removed from the primeval events of our disaster epic and was essentially identical to the contemporary environment. This means we can reliably describe the resources it offered to indigenous groups 200 years ago, as well as the challenges it posed. Although the region continues to be dominated by jagged mountain peaks, it also contains expansive mountain plateaus and broad, grassy river valleys. Differences in elevation can be abrupt, though; a person traveling across relatively flat terrain can suddenly discover him- or herself at the edge of an escarpment that drops away for thousands of feet. The large amounts of water falling annually in the form of rain and snow respond to gravity by concentrating in rushing cascades and waterfalls that often fall from thousand-foot-high sheer cliff faces. Yellowstone Lake is only the largest of the region's many bodies of water, some of which are small, glacially formed pothole lakes, whereas others are more amorphous marshes and wetlands.

Altitude is the determining factor in what we tend to think of as the landscape and its scenery. Most of the terrain in Sheep Eater territory is above 7,500 feet, but there is considerable biological variety even with such a high altitudinal baseline. Regions closer to the baseline contain completely different ecological zones and a mix of resources not found at higher elevations. Some eroded basins appear botanically sterile and consist exclusively of clays and mineral pigments, while river valleys often support thick stands of deciduous cottonwoods, willows, and box elder trees. In a place with so much diversity in geographical setting, there are also varied and abundant habitats for plant and animal species. Approximately 80 percent of the Yellowstone region is forested, dominated by lodgepole pine at higher elevations and Douglas fir at lower ones. In less heavily forested areas, shrubby plants, grasses, and wildflowers are prolific and provide forage for bighorn sheep, bison, and elk; species of grasses, rushes, and sedges provide habitat for waterfowl in wetland areas.

The ecosystem diversity of mountainous regions offers many advantages to hunters and gatherers. The presence of a variety of accessible niches provides foragers with numerous food choices and insulates them from the potentially disastrous effects of focusing subsistence activities on only a few resources, the supply of any one of which might be sharply and unpredictably reduced. If, for example, an insect infestation affected a heavily exploited food species in one area within Yellowstone, Sheep Eaters would have had the option of shifting to another food species whose supply remained unaffected and still bountiful.

The location of Sheep Eater territory at the intersection of three major culture areas provided advantages not offered to many hunting and gathering groups. To the northwest were the large villages of salmon-fishing peoples on the Columbia Plateau; to the northeast and east were mobile groups of mounted hunters who exploited the faunal resources of the High Plains and Great Plains; and to the south were bands that occupied various ecozones in the Great Basin. From their position at the crossroads of these culture areas, the Sheep Eaters were able to trade mountain resources—primarily valuable animal skins and furs—and to learn about new social or ideological innovations.

Points of intersection also have their disadvantages. There is always the possibility that outlanders frequenting the area will come with unfriendly intent. History records incidents in which visitors to Mountain Shoshone territory not only obtained important resources like obsidian but raided and plundered Sheep Eater camps as well. Even though the Sheep Eaters were mobile and did not maintain permanent villages—which made them less vulnerable than sedentary groups—women and children were often captured and forced into servitude or sold into slavery.[2] Sacajawea's abduction (discussed in chapter 2) occurred after travel by horse had become a feature of western life that enabled horse-owning Indians to cover greater distances in shorter periods of time. Nevertheless, the tradition of outsiders' traveling by foot to the mountains in search of important resources was an ancient one.

Though it is generally true that mountainous landscapes can present difficulties for the traveler, just how big an impediment they represent depends very much on how much gear is being transported and what the starting points and destinations are. For Euro-Americans, the great Rocky Mountain chain loomed as one of the major hurdles to be overcome in their settlement of the West. Their passage from east to west was through terra incognita, and they were accompanied by vehicles and animals that were poorly suited to the terrain.

In contrast, the Sheep Eaters traveled on foot through territory that they knew well, carrying many fewer possessions. The mountains in and around Yellowstone National Park were laced with trails that the Sheep Eaters and other Indians used extensively (Figure 3.2). In the latter half of the nineteenth century these trails were traveled so frequently by Idaho's Bannock Indians on their hunting expeditions to areas east of the park's current boundaries that the network is often referred to as the Bannock Trail, even though for centuries many different Indian groups used the trail system.

Sheep Eater movements through the mountains were often along a north–south route, corresponding to the orientation of the river courses that flow out of Yellowstone Lake. Today, the site of Mummy Cave is on a main tourist highway connecting Yellowstone National Park to points east, but this asphalt-covered road runs parallel to an ancient Indian trail that followed the North Fork of the Shoshone River between present-day Cody, Wyoming, and the park. Less obvious is a mountain trail running south along Eagle Creek for about 30 kilometers, at which point it forms a junction with the Thorofare Trail. In times past, the Thorofare Trail was the equivalent of an interstate highway traversing the heart of Sheep Eater territory, connecting the Wind River Mountains to the south with the Absaroka Mountains to the north. From its intersection with the Eagle Creek Trail, one could continue south and connect to a network of mountain trails leading to the Wind River valley. Another option would have been to turn north onto the Thorofare Trail and follow it along the eastern shore of Yellowstone Lake to its junction with the rivers flowing north from the park.

There is little evidence that Sheep Eater territory included the Pryor Mountains in southern Montana near the Wyoming border or the Bighorn Mountains further to the east. Some researchers have claimed an association between the Sheep Eaters and the Bighorn Medicine Wheel—an 80-foot circle of stones on the western peak of Medicine Mountain in north-central Wyoming—but the evidence of any connection is weak and based on conjecture.[3] If the presence of Dinwoody petroglyphs is used to establish the extent of Sheep Eater

Figure 3.2. A map of the Indian trails traversing Yellowstone National Park. Not only did the trail system connect the east and west sides of the park, but, importantly, it also created routes between the south and north sides. Users of wheeled vehicles think of mountains as barriers, but to the Sheep Eaters, the trail system provided the equivalent of interstate highways linking important destinations. Illustration by Davíd Joaquín.

territory, their domain would include the Absaroka Mountains, the Wind River Mountains, the Owl Creek Mountains, and adjacent Wyoming basins. No Dinwoody petroglyph sites are known in the Pryor Mountains, and the figures are extremely rare to the east of the Bighorn River.

To the west, Sheep Eaters apparently ranged as far as the Beaverhead Mountains along the Montana and Idaho border, although how often and for what duration are uncertain. Estimating the overall size of Sheep Eater territory has to be approximate, but one would begin with the total area of Yellowstone National Park, which is 3,472 square miles, or slightly smaller than the State of Connecticut.[4] As we know that the park represented only part of Sheep Eater territory, a reasonable estimate of their total range would be somewhere between five thousand and six thousand square miles. If one visualizes the geometry of mountainous terrain, however, that estimate includes only the hypotenuse of each vertical feature and ignores the expansion of the area that would occur if the actual topography were measured.

Looking Ahead

Of course, as we noted in the prologue, the Sheep Eaters shared this large area with numerous other mobile Indian groups, and in subsequent chapters we will describe the use they made of the land and its resources as well as their interactions with their neighbors. In the next chapter, however, we move to a different domain—the world of first causes and of beliefs—whose beings and energies gave meaning and direction to the lives of individual Sheep Eater men, women, and children.

4

||||

Living among the Powerful Spirits

EVERYTHING IS ALIVE AND WE FORGET THAT. PRAYER IS THE ONLY
WAY WE'RE GOING TO LIVE ON.

—*Corbin Harney, Western Shoshone spiritual leader (Harney 1995:xix)*

Once upon a time, which in this instance means more than two millennia ago when Latin was the Romans' spoken language, the word
primitivus meant "the first or earliest of its kind."[1] Two related meanings,
"ancient" and "original," also reflect the fact that *primitivus* expressed
qualities related to time, origin, and sequence and was therefore a
neutral term with none of the value-laden baggage that adheres to its
English derivative *primitive*.

Anthropology's genesis in the Europe of the Victorian era meant
that many of the attitudes constituting the zeitgeist of that socially
stratified, stuffy, squeamish, hypocritical, and predatory period
formed the lenses through which other cultures were initially viewed.
In fact, the first comprehensive treatise—by Edward B. Tylor—enun-
ciating the aims and subject matter of anthropology as understood in
1871 was called *Primitive Culture*.[2] Although the word *primitive* is now,
thankfully, banished from the anthropological lexicon, until the last
quarter of the twentieth century the word was used liberally and inap-
propriately to describe foraging and horticultural peoples as well as
many aspects of their lives.

In the century and a half since Tylor's seminal work, the belief
systems of non-European, small-scale societies have been examined,
categorized, and described by ethnographers and other professional
culturologists. Most researchers have attempted to provide a comprehensive body of data about the groups they have studied because a
society's worldview, its explanation of its origins, and its concept of
humanness are fundamental to an understanding of its lifeways. Along

the way, anthropology as a discipline has shed many of its prejudices and learned to recognize that the belief systems of small-scale societies represent a sophisticated integration of concepts of a structured universe, spiritual tenets, and practical knowledge about how to thrive in many different settings in the physical world. Ceremonies and practices—often called *rituals*—are perceived as ways to concretize beliefs and, through repetition, to reinforce traditions that bind people together, celebrate their survival, and usher individuals through important life stages such as birth, puberty, marriage, and death.

We approach the subject of Sheep Eater beliefs and their expression in daily life with the greatest respect and also considerable empathy. One of us (Loendorf) has stood on mountaintops in the Beartooth Range and sensed a timeless, enveloping power. To have been born and to have lived intimately—as Sheep Eaters did—in a world of such energy, beauty, and physical challenge would have been unthinkable without an explanatory connection linking human beings to the forces of nature. Fortunately, it is not necessary to rely on empathy, imagination, and personal experience for insight into what Sheep Eaters might have believed. Thanks to the Swedish scholar Åke Hultkrantz, who devoted much of his life to the study of the Shoshone worldview, it is possible to sketch here some of the important figures in their universe and some of the ways in which individuals connected to the generative principles embodied in their spiritual world.

The Relationship between Humans and Spirits

Like many other hunters and gatherers, the Sheep Eaters did not make a distinction between the natural and supernatural worlds. This paradigm—called *animism*—accepts that the entities that today are classified by science as inanimate are actually living beings. In this worldview, strangely shaped rocks, animals, and human beings are all "animated" or given life by an indwelling spiritual power. One could say that Sheep Eater religion was ecological in focus, for the spirit entities embodied in meteorological forces and various animals were seen as controlling the dynamics of their mountain environment. The Sheep Eater universe consisted of a layered spiritual hierarchy: at the apex or zenith were the "sky people," below them were the "ground people," and still lower were the "water people." Physical phenomena were also hierarchically ordered, with the sun and lightning at the pinnacle and rattlesnakes occupying the bottom rung of the cosmos.

Spirits were not all equal: the strongest—those of the *toyawo*, or mountain medicine—lived "in the wooded mountain areas of the Yellowstone National Park, the Absarokas, the Wind Rivers, and possibly the Big Horn Mountains."[3] Shoshone bands living at lower elevations also believed that the strongest *puha* (power) existed in the mountains. Consistent with this spiritual hierarchy, the Sheep Eaters were recognized as "living among the powerful spirits" and absorbing some of their power. When, in the 1870s, Sheep Eater groups were moved to reservations, they were regarded as particularly powerful medicine people.

In the seamless world of matter and spirit, Tam Apo, or "Our Father," was an omnipotent Supreme Being who was closely related to the sun; in fact, he created the sun, also a superior being.[4] When praying, Sheep Eaters faced the sun, although their prayers were actually addressed to Our Father. Hultkrantz was told by Sheep Eater consultants that the "Our Father" figure predated any contact with the white man's religion, a claim that is supported by the inclusion of an ancient Father Dance in their ritual life.

Sheep Eaters believed that lightning and thunder were emanations from equally important, powerful spirits. Lightning was closely associated with thunderbirds, spirits that could be represented by eagles, although they more often assumed the form of a hummingbird.[5] Some claimed that this fast-moving little spirit was actually a small brown bird that only appeared to have hummingbird plumage, but whatever its true coloration, the thunderbird was thought to be able to shoot lightning from its eyes. Screech owls were also sometimes associated with lightning, but they were a benign species compared to the malevolent *wokaimunbitsch*, a large, owl-like bird that was believed to steal and eat people. This massive bird talked and behaved like a human being, but at night it hovered around campfires, swooping down to grab people in its large talons. The *wokaimunbitsch* sometimes took captives to its lair and fed them to baby *wokaimunbitsch*, but more often it simply ate them.[6]

Other "sky people" included ravens, crows, and magpies, which could give people the power to find lost objects, and cranes, which had important *puha* enabling them to travel very fast. Within the hierarchy of powerful spirits, "ground people" such as fearsome grizzly

Figure 4.1. Petroglyph of a Dinwoody-style water ghost spirit. The figure stands more than a meter tall on an east-facing boulder on the banks of a mountain lake. Water ghost figures are most common at lower elevations, but they may be located near any body of water. Photograph by Lawrence L. Loendorf.

bears, crafty weasels, and powerful bighorn rams (whose horns were placed in offering trees at trap sites) had potent medicine. *Tundzoavits*—or rocky-skinned ghosts—were giant 12-foot-tall ogres weighing 500 pounds, most of whose tough skin was made of stone, although their faces and hands were soft. Male and female rocky-skinned ghosts lived in caves, from which they emerged and snatched people. They were able to travel across the landscape in pursuit of victims, which gave them an advantage over similarly predatory water ghosts.

Further down the Sheep Eater spiritual hierarchy were the "water people," a variety of ghostlike creatures classified under the general heading of *pandzoavits*, or water ghosts (Figure 4.1). These creatures included the *pa:unha*, or "water-babies"—squat, heavy-set creatures inhabiting springs, creeks, rivers, and lakes. Other, larger water ghosts had big hands and feet, enabling them to snatch people who came close to the water's edge. The special mission of the female water ghost Pa waip was to coax men into the water, often on the pretext of a sexual liaison, after which she captured and drowned them. Water ghosts had various techniques of enhancing their range and power. Pa waip, for instance, often dispatched her amphibious assistant, the turtle, to perform errands on land, and other water ghosts shot their victims using magnificent horn bows and arrows whose points were invisible except to a person who had water ghost power.[7]

Spirits in all three domains of sky, ground, and water were known to travel. Some Shoshone thought that spirits took a terrestrial route when they came down from the mountains in the winter, paralleling the seasonal movements of animals like bighorn sheep and the Sheep Eaters who followed them. Other supernatural creatures, like the many kinds of water spirits, took a different route to and from the mountains. The *pandzoavits*, for example, not only were powerful

Figure 4.2. Petroglyph panel of a water ghost woman with attendant canid-like animals. Note that she holds her bow in one hand and a rattle in the other. The figure, which stands nearly 1.5 meters tall, is located near Thermopolis, Wyoming. Two other similar figures are found in the vicinity of this example, which suggests that the area was especially favored by the female ghosts. Tracing by Linda Olson.

enough to make the water in hot springs boil but they were thought to travel through an underground hydrological network linking geysers in Yellowstone Park to hot springs at places like Thermopolis, Wyoming. Other spirits traveled from lake to lake though interconnecting streams and rivers, while yet another group was able to move through rock formations using a system of connected fissures and caves. Despite their mobility, spirits had a home territory, and it was there that they were most likely to be encountered (Figure 4.2).

Within this matrix of powerful forces and potent creatures, the Sheep Eaters believed that each person had three types of "soul." The *suap*, or "ego-soul," was embodied in breath; the *mugua*, or "body-soul," activated the body while awake; and the *navushieip*, or "free-soul," could leave the body during dreams and trance states. The first two souls were closely related because breath and heart represent physiological functions that are essential to remaining alive. When a person died, the *mugua* left the body through the top of the head, taking the *suap* with it. In contrast, the *navushieip* was not related to the state of the body but, rather, was free to wander. In a powerful dream or trance state known as *puhanavuzieip*, the free-soul would look for a guardian spirit to incorporate into the individual's life, acting as an ally and providing important kinds of protection. Spirit helpers could come from any of the sky people, the ground people, or the water people that a free-soul encountered as it traveled throughout the Sheep Eater spirit world.

THE VISION QUEST

As it was believed that spirits from the three domains left their likenesses on rock surfaces in the form of petroglyphs, Sheep Eaters—especially men—often went to rock art sites to connect with their power.[8] It was claimed that the sound of these potent creatures pecking their images on the rocks was audible, especially in the wintertime, but that when a person approached, the spirits quit pecking. The supplicant's quest for power followed an established practice: first, he bathed in a lake or stream, and then he painted a little red pigment on his chest and forehead, smudged in cedar smoke, and placed himself in front of a panel of rock drawings. There he sat throughout the night and perhaps for several more days and nights, wrapped in a blanket, awaiting a visit from the spirits (see Plate 5).

A sufficiently large number of spiritual visitations have been recorded to permit a generalized description of the usual sequence of events. First, there was a visit from a *nynymbi*, or "little person," who led the supplicant on a journey directly into the rock surface through holes or crevices that at first seemed impassable. Once inside the rock, the human–*nynymbi* pair passed by a frightening series of ogres or monstrous creatures. As each of the creatures was encountered, the "little person" would instruct the supplicant in the behavior appropriate to such a meeting, but at some point the little person would leave the supplicant to fend for himself. Now alone and terrified, he was often confronted by a creature that seemed at first to be an animal, and then a man or animal composed of parts of different animals, such as an owl with human arms, or a rattlesnake with the legs of a weasel. At other times these creatures—who gave the supplicant supernatural power and defined the conditions and regulations for owning and using the power—could take on a more naturalistic form, so that, for instance, a spirit bear might look just like an anatomically correct bear.

The spiritual passage we have described is very similar to the vision quest ritual that was simultaneously prevalent among Plains Indian groups, although Sheep Eater supplicants sought their power at rock art sites far more than other Plains groups did. In this respect they were more like the Salish-speaking tribes to the northwest, although the Salish identified rock art sites with individuals or families and believed that drawings and engravings were the records of their visionary dreams rather than images made by the spirits themselves.[9] This important difference meant that—to Sheep Eaters—petroglyphs were self-portraits of the spirits that could be used to identify the pantheon of cannibal owls, thunderbirds, and water ghosts that gave their power to supplicants.

Medicine and Healing

A Sheep Eater who had successfully completed a spiritual quest and now possessed supernatural power was recognized as a *púhagant*—or a medicine person—and could use his or her power in different ways. Some individuals used their power to become superb warriors, aided by the ability to make their bodies as hard as stone and therefore invulnerable to arrows and bullets. The power gave other persons the knowledge needed to cure the sick. Sheep Eaters believed that many illnesses were caused by invisible arrows that were shot into their bodies by bad spirits. In these instances, the healer would press a tubular pipe against the victim's skin at the site of the entry and would suck out the bad medicine.

Archaeologists have found one complete and six reconstructed tubular stone pipes, as well as the fragmentary remains of five others, manufactured from steatite, sandstone, serpentinite, and other soft stone, at the base of a petroglyph panel near Thermopolis, Wyoming.[10] The pipes, which are constricted at one end and range in length from two to eight inches, have maximum diameters ranging from less than one inch to slightly more than two. Archaeologists believe that the pipes were deliberately broken, and, because the fragments were found grouped together, they speculate that they had been stored as a group on at least two different occasions, perhaps in a hide bag.

Waldo Wedel, longtime Smithsonian Institution archaeologist, examined several of the pipes and has suggested they had been used by shamans as sucking tubes. The location of the pipes at the base of a petroglyph panel certainly suggests their use in a healing context, as does the fact that none of the pipes exhibits nicotine stains or other evidence that they had been used for smoking. One pipe was filled with red ochre, and several were incised with linear designs, including representations of swans, cranes, or other waterbirds. The petroglyph panel under which the embellished pipes were found includes a large Dinwoody-tradition figure whose big hands and feet protrude from behind water lines surrounding the figure. Standing nearly five feet in height, the figure holds a bow and arrow and a rattle in its left hand, and a projectile point dangles from its left elbow.[11] The genderless figure is almost certainly a representation of a *pandzoavits*, or water ghost, who used its bow to shoot arrows into its victims. A shaman with *pandzoavits* power would have been the only person who could see the arrows inside the victim and, using a sucking tube, would have been able to remove the magical arrow and cure the patient.

Togwotee, the well-known Sheep Eater who acted as a guide for President Chester Arthur's excursion through Yellowstone National Park (Figure 4.3), possessed *pandzoavits* power that he apparently used for malevolent rather than curative purposes. Sheep Eater informants told Åke Hultkrantz that many Shoshone had feared Togwotee's abuse

Figure 4.3. Togwotee, a nineteenth-century Sheep Eater medicine man and historical figure. Togwotee Pass, west of Dubois, Wyoming, is named for this prominent Sheep Eater. Illustration by Davíd Joaquín, based on a photograph of Togwotee.

of his power and had been hopeful that a day would come when it could no longer affect their lives:

> [Togwotee] used to carry a doll that was clad in buckskin and tied to his necklace. He used his power to injure people, for example, by depriving them of [their] navushieip [free-soul]. His doll represented pandzoavits. Many good men and women were killed with this medicine. There was only one way of overcoming Togwotee and thus curing his victims: to call for a medicine-man who had still stronger medicine.
>
> Now Togwotee was living in the vicinity of Dubois [Wyoming]. After many appeals from people, a Ute medicine man promised to out maneuver Togwotee. The Ute arrived at Fort Washakie [Wyoming], rolled up his sleeve and sucked his arm, with his gaze fixed in the direction of Dubois [about 50 miles northwest]. In this way he deprived Togwotee of his medicine. The Ute sucked the medicine into his body, both the necklace and the doll.
>
> He then vomited up the two objects and held them out in his hands, so that all those standing round about could see them. At his request he was now handed by my grandfather an old muzzle-loader used in buffalo hunting. With a knife he cut the doll into

little pieces, loaded the gun with powder, stuffed the doll into the barrel of the gun, and fired. People could then hear the shriek of a child. The Ute said, however, that this was Togwotee's own voice, and he also said that Togwotee's *puha* was now destroyed and that Togwotee himself would now fall ill little by little, turn blue and waste away. This actually happened. The name of the Ute medicine-man was Little Doctor, and he was known as a very clever medicine-man.[12]

Contemporary studies of shamanism tend to emphasize the positive role played by shamans, but the story of Togwotee's demise illustrates that not all medicine was directed to life-enhancing ends. In fact, ethnographic studies have shown that in many societies in which shamanism is practiced, repeated struggles have occurred between individuals who try to use their power for nefarious purposes and persons opposing such use. It was after the Sheep Eaters had moved out of the mountains that Togwotee became such a fearful figure in Shoshone society, and his malign influence reflects the power and respect that lowland Shoshone groups had for mountain medicine.

Sheep Eater society was sufficiently egalitarian that women as well as men could obtain *puha* and become a *púhagant* by going to the petroglyphs and sleeping on the rocks beneath them. John Trehero, a highly respected Shoshone medicine man, has stated that *puha* will come to a woman in a dream and tell her that she will be cured. Trehero used an example from his own family to illustrate that women can also be *púha-gant*: "My mother was a mighty *púhagant*; she just touched the sick person once with her hand, and then he was cured."[13]

In Sheep Eater daily life, religion and medicine were so tightly interwoven that it is difficult to distinguish between where one began and the other ended. A curing ritual was as much a religious invocation as it was a healing event. Calling on a guardian spirit to assist with the medicine was only part of the ceremony, however. The practitioner also used a variety of plants and minerals to help the patient return to health. Knowledge of nature's pharmacopoeia might, in fact, come from the guardian spirit, but more often it was passed down from one generation to the next. In the case of John Trehero, both he and his mother were powerful *púhagants*, and he undoubtedly learned a great deal about herbal and other medicinal remedies from his mother.

Remedies were closely guarded secrets, and although it might be possible to learn the species of a particular plant best suited to treat an illness, the dosage was seldom revealed. It was common knowledge, however, that the most potent medicinal herbs came from locations near rock art sites or from the mountains in the heart of Sheep Eater territory. Proximity to the source of many healing plants was another reason that Sheep Eaters were so highly respected as shamans and healers.

One plant in particular—the deadly *toyatawura*—is repeatedly described as an extremely potent medicine.[14] Power came to the person brave enough to visit the plant and dig up a bit of its roots. Collection was a challenge, though, for *toyatawura* could never be picked in direct sunlight or in the dark of night, when its power would cause it to emit sparks. Prior to collecting the plant, a medicine person was required to lie nearby on the ground and pray to the plant for assistance. Sheep Eater consultants have explained that "you should pick it at sundown. You mustn't fool with it when it is awake."[15] Even a few pieces were considered so powerful that they were kept on a stick outside the house, high above the ground.

Toyatawura was never carried as a personal accessory until its owner wanted to use its power. Often the plant's spirit would assume a human form and come in a vision to the person who possessed a piece of it. The spirit might direct the person to paint his or her face red, white, or black or to paint stripes on the forehead and would also explain how to use the medicine in many different ways. Some men used *toyatawura* to make themselves invulnerable, and it was said that a man who had this power could catch the enemy's arrows or bullets before any damage was inflicted. Others would put the medicine in the tracks of an animal or another human and then say, "I want to catch the deer" or "I want him to die."

Of all the medicines, however, *toyatawura* was known for its strength as an aphrodisiac, conferring the *puha* to control the opposite sex. According to Shoshone consultants, a man (*waípepuhagant*) or woman (*tïnapöpuhagant*) with this *puha* "could make you come close, draw you with their power."[16] Described as having red, yellow, and blue flowers, the powerful but demanding *toyatawura* is always found high in the mountains, a location contributing to the belief that Sheep

Eaters possessed power because they lived in the region where *puha* was strongest.

MORE THOUGHTS ABOUT PETROGLYPH SITES

In light of the association of altitude with power, it is difficult to explain the prevalence of petroglyph sites—where power was also concentrated—at lower elevations. Also somewhat mystifying is the fact that no rock art sites have yet been recorded in Yellowstone Park, as the area's many thermal features were known to have been the domain of powerful forces. There may be a practical explanation for the distribution of petroglyph sites, however, having to do with the materials and technique of production. The surfaces of many rocks develop a dark patina over time, and petroglyph images are made by pecking designs through the covering layer and exposing the lighter, underlying stone. Of the rock surfaces available in Sheep Eater territory, sandstone formations have a less resistant crust, making them especially suitable for petroglyph inscriptions. These rocks, however, are not found in the higher elevations of the Wind River and Absaroka Mountains, so Sheep Eaters would have had to travel some distance to pursue their spiritual quests.

Another intriguing feature of Sheep Eater rock art is the almost complete absence of images of bighorn sheep. This omission is puzzling in light of the centrality of sheep in their daily life and the fact that hunters used magic to coax them into traps and, with apparent ritual intent, placed their skulls in the branches of trees at trap sites. There may, however, be another explanation besides the simplistic assertion that there was insufficient supernatural connection between sheep and humans to result in petroglyph creation. Shoshone groups in California, who ate more rabbits than sheep, made hundreds of bighorn sheep petroglyphs, which rock art researcher David Whitley argues were part of a rainmaking ritual. If, in fact, Sheep Eaters also ascribed rainmaking power to bighorn sheep, it makes sense that the petroglyph repertoire of Sheep Eater Shoshone would not include rain-inducing symbols in the Wyoming mountains, where annual precipitation is high and there are few severe droughts. Whitley also thinks that the vast majority of the California sheep petroglyphs were made post–AD 1300, when conditions in the region were quite dry.[17]

Given what is known about hunter–gatherer mobility and the

ongoing transfer of information across large regions, it is not far-fetched to suggest that there was contact between Shoshone groups in Wyoming and California, particularly among shamans, who were known to travel great distances to provide their services or to obtain new power. The role of shamans as mediators between the supernatural and natural worlds would have extended to rainmaking, a service that, should Wyoming Sheep Eaters ever have required it, could have been met either by requesting the presence of a California Shoshone shaman or by sending their own shamans to California to acquire rainmaking power.

Curiously, the few existing Sheep Eater bighorn petroglyphs are distorted, highly stylized depictions of the animals. In engravings on rock surfaces in the Torrey Valley southeast of Yellowstone Park, images of sheep have long, curving horns extending the length of their backs and spiral tails twisting upward toward the sky. One unusual figure in the Thermopolis region has the body of a small sheep with a long, vertical neck ending in a bizarrely shaped head. This unnatural looking figure has attributes that make it seem likely that it was associated with trance-inducing activities.

SHEEP EATER DANCING

In many of the world's societies, patterned, rhythmic movement has long been an expression of the nexus among spiritual beliefs, healing, kinship connections, and seasonal celebrations of various kinds. Today we call this activity *dancing* and do it for strictly recreational purposes, but to Sheep Eaters the word would have encompassed much more than an enjoyable group pastime undertaken for its own sake. In the interactive world of spirit and matter, people danced and sang to create harmony between themselves and the forces of nature, to celebrate the beings with whom they shared their universe, to ensure abundance, and to grow strong. There is very little detailed information about the specific ways that Sheep Eaters maintained the balance in their world through dancing, but by piecing together separate bits of evidence, we can reconstruct some of their corporate expressions of community.

On special occasions Sheep Eaters performed various kinds of circle dances. These were linked to the seasons of the year so that in the spring, for instance, dancing was focused on helping the grass flourish and the young game animals grow strong. A circle dance sometimes occurred in a brush corral, but even when there was no enclosure, a juniper pole marked the center of the circle. Participants initially lined up in alternating male–female pairs, although if a woman did not like the two men on either side of her, she could change position. Holding hands, dancers moved one foot to the side and brought the other to meet it (sidestep–together, sidestep–together) in unison around and around in a circle. Children might form an inner circle of their own and dance with the adults.[18]

During Robert Lowie's research at the Ross Farm Agency in 1907, Mountain Shoshone consultants provided him with part of a circle dance song:

Ma'zambi a	un-du'a wa'sipi	un-du'a-tsi,
Mountain-sheep,	her son, mountain-sheep's	son,
du'mbi	ma-to'owEn.	
on the rock	goes out.	
E'nga-m-bo	pa go'nait	wu'kum-bai	yo'ina,
A red ball	cloud	wind has	(?)
pado'nobina.			
go outside.			

(At this point, several of the singers knelt on the ground.)

Bi'a-gwina	umbi-oi	un-du'atsi	pa'wucorotogin.
Eagle	white (?)	her son	(?)
Ta'ham	bi'agwina	bi'oi	du'atsi.
Our	white-	eagle's	son.[19]

The musicologist Judith Vander, who has studied the Wind River Naraya songs at the core of the Ghost Dance tradition, has refined Lowie's translation of the circle dance song based on her own research.[20] Vander suggests that a better translation of the word ma'zambi a is "ewe bighorn sheep" and that the second reference to mountain sheep (wa'sipi) can also refer to other big game such as deer, antelope, and elk. Although Lowie was somewhat hesitant in his translation of the word umbi-oi as "white," Vander thinks that it may refer to the white eagle tail feathers that shamans used in healing.

Vander points out the song's earth–sky duality that is expressed in its references to young terrestrial animals in the first line and to clouds, wind, and birds in the remainder of the verse. The sequence of images from sheep on their rocky slopes to an eagle in the windy sky traces the trajectory of the Sheep Eater spiritual pantheon in which an eagle is at the zenith of the universe. The placement of petroglyphs of birds and flying figures at the pinnacle of the Sheep Eater worldview also reflects this preeminence.

A dance with a similar sidestepping movement was called the *apunukan*, or "father dance," which was apparently performed to ward off diseases such as smallpox. Like the circle dance, the *apunukan* shares affinities with the Naraya songs of the Ghost Dance that were strongly present among residents of the Wind River Reservation at the end of the nineteenth century.[21] A back-and-forth dance was performed by many Northern Shoshone groups, and it is likely that this dance was popular with Sheep Eaters, too.

We are left with educated conjecture when it comes to the complete range of Sheep Eater dancing, but because many of the purposes that were satisfied by this corporate effort were shared with their Shoshone relatives—the desire to cooperate with the forces of nature, the expression of social cohesion, the need for healing—it is likely that we can glimpse, in the more fully documented groups of the Wind River Reservation and elsewhere, a reflection of Sheep Eater aspiration and its satisfaction through ceremony.

POSTSCRIPT

The history of the American Indian in the last 500 years records a sequence of tragic intrusions on the lands, natural resources, lifeways, and very existence of the estimated eighteen million residents of North America prior to the arrival of Columbus. Government regulations and prohibitions have interfered with the rights of descendants of the First Americans to practice their religion, as have restrictive land claims and similar efforts to turn sacred sites into commercial ventures such as ski resorts. Modern technology has defaced landscapes to such an extent that, as one of Hultkrantz's consultants said, "the spirits are not as common today as they were in the old days. The power lines and poles especially have scared them away. They have retreated for good to the mountains."[22]

LOOKING AHEAD

In the next eleven chapters we will reverse the clock and return to the timeless past when Sheep Eater groups were uncontested in their use of the land and resources in the Yellowstone region. We will describe the shelters they built, the tools they made, the clothes they wore, and the animals and plants on which they subsisted. Their engagement with the material world depended, however, on the families with whom they shared life in all its many facets and the bonds they forged with one another, which we discuss in the next chapter.

5

||||

Weaving the Social Fabric:
Sheep Eater Relationships with One
Another and the Outside World

One of the most fascinating aspects of the study of human societies is the variety of ways in which people have structured their relationships to one another. For well over a century, ethnographers have observed and recorded life in hundreds of small-scale societies around the world. In the many instances in which tribal peoples were no longer able to maintain their traditional lifeways, anthropologists have interviewed their descendants, who had been taught the values and practices of their now-departed elders. Sometimes an ethnographer's report was published and widely read (for example, Margaret Mead's *Coming of Age in Samoa*, first published in 1928), but often it remained in manuscript form on the shelves of an academic archive, rarely if ever consulted and sometimes not even cataloged.[1] Periodically, when researchers would become interested in either a specific or a general question such as "What were the marriage conventions of the Agta?" or "What groups in sub-Saharan Africa practiced secondary disposal of the dead?" they would have to spend months or years tracking down all the sources of information on their research topic.

Cross-cultural comparison—the term for shifting the research focus from an individual society to the cultural characteristics of a large number of societies—was made much easier by the work of George P. Murdock, an anthropologist interested in looking at similarities and differences in human behavior around the world. In the 1940s, Murdock and his colleagues began collecting and classifying a massive amount of previously hard-to-find information about social groups. The fruits of this labor were eventually coded, indexed, and made available in two immense databases, the Human Relations Area

Files (most often referred to by its acronym, "the HRAF") and the Ethnographic Atlas (1962–80), which was later republished as the *Atlas of World Cultures*.[2] Researchers consult the HRAF database and the *Atlas* in order to look at patterns in human behavior relative to any of a number of different environmental, social, and geographical variables, with the hope that they will see regularities and connections in their data that they will then attempt to understand.

For example, the archaeologist Lewis Binford has recently published a comprehensive analysis of hunter–gatherer behavior in which he presents evidence in support of—among other things—polygyny (a form of marriage in which one man has two or more wives) as a strategy for increasing the female labor force:

> Another feature to be considered when thinking about the relationship between division of labor and polygyny is the coordination of male and female labor during the bulk processing of food for storage.... In such a situation, temperature determines the time that is available for processing many meaty foods. The higher the temperature, the more imperative it becomes to process food resources at the same time that they are being procured. When groups establish simultaneous labor parties, the males are usually involved in procurement and the females in processing.[3]

Now, Binford is not implying that polygyny occurs *only* in groups whose subsistence depends on simultaneous male procurement and female processing of bulk food resources for storage. His conclusions are part of a step-by-step series of generalizations leading to sophisticated and controversial archaeological theory building that is beyond the scope of this chapter. We are using this example to point out that there are sufficient co-occurrences of analytical triplets such as polygyny, availability of bulk resources, and division of labor to make one think—hmmm, there seem to be some very good reasons that certain people have organized their family life in ways that may seem strange to a twenty-first-century reader.

As we describe what is known about Sheep Eater social organization, we want readers to keep in mind that all societies structure their marriage conventions, design their kinship networks, and ignore or celebrate different life stages as part of an integrated effort to sustain life by adapting to their physical and social circumstances. In the case of the Sheep Eaters, it must be remembered that until their life was disrupted by the trappers, land speculators, and military vanguard of the western migration of Euro-Americans, they had developed and successfully preserved for centuries a way of living with one another and their neighbors within the territory they occupied.

SHEEP EATER KINSHIP UNITS

As might be expected of a person who coupled a knowledge of hundreds of different social groups with an interest in societal similarities and differences, George Murdock has provided a classic definition of the family: "The family is a social group characterized by common residence, economic cooperation, and reproduction. It includes adults of both sexes, at least two of whom maintain a socially approved sexual relationship, and one or more children, own or adopted, of the sexually cohabiting adults."[4] If we were to superimpose Murdock's abstract familial template over the occupants of a Sheep Eater domicile, there would be a perfect fit. Mom, Dad, and the kids formed the family nucleus, and they could be joined by an additional wife, one or more blood relatives, and perhaps a few friends or acquaintances. Sheep Eater social organization corresponds to what anthropologist Carling Malouf has identified as a *kin and clique*, a social unit that is by no means confined to the Sheep Eaters but was, in fact, the social configuration of other Shoshone groups, as well as neighboring peoples like the Flathead and the Pend d'Oreille in pre-horse times.[5]

An individual Sheep Eater kin and clique varied in size and composition from year to year, although the parent–child nucleus usually remained the same. As Malouf notes, there were no social or political pressures on the members of a kin and clique to maintain a permanent relationship with a particular group of individuals. Friends or acquaintances might change their affiliation for practical reasons or as a matter of preference. A quarrel or the prospects of a better opportunity for food in another region might result in the departure of some members, who would often meet up and rejoin the group the next year.[6]

Sheep Eaters did not have the clans, lineages, secret societies, age-grade groups, or men's or women's societies that are often a feature of life among groups living in much larger agricultural communities. Puberty rites and any preparations for and rules governing a girl's first menstruation were handled by the kin and clique. There was also no special ceremony to celebrate a boy's first hunting success. These simple protocols met the Sheep Eaters' needs for many years, and it was only after the introduction of the horse at the beginning of the eighteenth century that some Shoshone combined their kin and clique units into larger, more highly structured hunting bands.[7]

BORN, BRED, AND WED

If you had been born a Sheep Eater, your birth would have taken place in a special hut, set apart from the family shelter.[8] Anticipating your imminent arrival into the world, your mother would have knelt and grasped an upright pole for support as she pushed you into the waiting hands of a midwife, who sat behind and steadied her. During the delivery process, your father would have wandered the hillsides, praying for your safe journey. Once it was announced that you had arrived, he would give away any game he had recently killed or his most recent winnings at games of chance. For the first month of your life, you and your mother would remain secluded in the birth hut, during which time your father would bring firewood to keep the hut warm but would not come inside to see you. Your mother would help you become accustomed to your cradle, which had a woven willow frame, shaped like a large teardrop, and was covered with soft buckskin. You would be strapped to the cradle, at first for short periods and later for hours at a time.

When you and your mother rejoined the other members of your family, you still would not have a name. Sheep Eater children did not receive names until they were "old enough to laugh."[9] Once a name was bestowed, it was seldom changed, although nicknames might be earned and then replaced numerous times throughout life. Like many Shoshone, Sheep Eaters were reluctant to tell their names to others, especially in a public setting.

Boys and girls played together during the years before a girl's first menstrual period and before boys reached puberty, and both boys and girls helped with household chores. Girls helped their female relatives dig and process root vegetables, while boys practiced hunting. Boys made toy bows and arrows at an early age, and by the time they were eight, they were already pursuing small game with rocks or willow bows and arrows. Girls had buckskin dolls and cradles, and they

Figure 5.1. Sheep Eater children playing a game of cat's cradle. By passing the string back and forth, players made traditional designs that included forms representing humans and animals. Illustration by Davíd Joaquín.

set up miniature lodges and played house. Boys were especially fond of playing football, a game in which they kicked a rawhide ball filled with grass toward a distant goal. Several boys would compete, and—as the goal might be more than a mile away—when one boy tired, his partner would take over. It was against the rules to touch the ball with the hands, so if it got stuck in the brush, it had to be removed with the feet or a stick.

Another popular game was cat's cradle, played with buckskin strings (Figure 5.1). Robert Lowie observed the Salmon Eaters making figures that they named "boy," "woman," "fish trap," and "rabbit snare." An "antelope" figure was designed so that as the string was loosened and tightened, the animal gave the appearance of moving. Although there is no specific information on Sheep Eater string figures, we can imagine children making one called "bighorn sheep" that would have moved when tugged on or pulled.

Although in many small-scale societies a variety of customs, rituals, and taboos surrounded the onset of menstruation, among the Sheep Eaters a girl's first menstrual period was treated matter-of-factly. On the first morning of menstruation, a strong woman who was known to have light flow was called on to wash the girl and offer prayers asking that the girl would also bleed little throughout her life. She was then escorted to a small wood-frame lodge similar to the birth hut. There was little furniture except for a sage-bark mattress, but a small fire in the center of the hut provided warmth. A girl would stay in the hut for ten days during her first period but for only three days during each subsequent period. She was not allowed to eat meat during her menses and had to subsist on roots and water. When it was time to leave, she bathed, painted her face with red ochre, dressed, and returned to the other members of her kin and clique.

Like many of the world's societies, Sheep Eaters were known to follow traditional cross-cousin marriage rules. According to this kinship system, Person A was expected to marry a first cousin who was the child of the *father's sister* or the *mother's brother*.[10] Marriage to the children of the *mother's sister* or the *father's brother* (who have the same biological relationship to Person A as the approved first cousins) was absolutely prohibited, but for a very good reason. It was common practice—although not required—in instances in which Person A's father died, for the widow to marry her dead husband's brother (a practice that anthropologists refer to as the *levirate*) or, if Person A's mother died, for the widower to marry his dead wife's sister (the *sororate*). In fact, a child often referred to the mother's sister as "mother" and the father's brother as "father," and their children were considered Person A's brothers and sisters. These designated—as opposed to strictly biological—maternal and paternal relationships were of such importance that it would have been considered incestuous for cousin-brothers and cousin-sisters to marry one another.

Like parents everywhere, Sheep Eater mothers and fathers tried to ensure that their children made good marriages. A young woman's father, concerned for his daughter's future security and well-being, would choose a good hunter from among the eligible young men who had the appropriate kinship connection to be her mate. The young man would visit his intended's camp, and, after several visits, they would spend the night together in the same shelter. Despite the proximity, sexual intercourse would not occur, and the young man would return to his own camp early the next morning. If a satisfactory relationship developed, in time the couple would express their intention to live as husband and wife simply by presenting themselves together openly. No bride-price or any exchange of gifts was required to solemnize the marriage. Throughout the "becoming acquainted" period, which might take a year or more, the young man would hunt and bring game to the bride-to-be's family. After marriage, the couple might stay with the bride's family for a few years, but once they had children they would usually establish their own kin and clique or return to the kin and clique of the husband's father.

We have just presented the ideal matrimonial scenario, but marriages could also be initiated in other ways. Sometimes a young man who was attracted to a girl would begin to hang around her kin and clique. If he was considered an acceptable mate for the girl, he might be allowed to stay, but if the family decided that he was not husband material, the older women would chase him off with their digging sticks. Sometimes a man would enlist his friends to help him abduct a girl from her kin and clique, although often her family would resist and foil the attempt. Abduction was not considered an acceptable way to get a wife, and even if an attempt was successful, there was always the possibility that the young woman might escape and run home. In such a situation, the man seldom attempted to carry off the girl a second time.

A DAY IN THE LIFE

When the nineteenth-century poet James Russell Lowell observed that "no man is born into the world whose work / Is not born with him. There is always work," he could have been describing how the new day looked to male and female Sheep Eaters when they got up in the morning.[11] There were many, many things to do to keep a family fed, clothed, warm, and clean; most of the duties were assigned to the members of a kin and clique on the basis of their gender. We have already mentioned that men and boys were responsible for hunting and fishing and that women's dietary contribution consisted of digging for root vegetables, but berries, seeds, and pine nuts were also important food resources collected by women. Depending on the season, the vegetable products produced by women's labor supplied as much as 75 percent of the daily diet, although the percentage of meat and plants shifted to roughly 50–50 when groups were in the mountains where bighorn sheep and fish were abundant. If the calculation is in terms of protein and carbohydrates, however, it is important to remember that although pine nuts are classified as plants, they are very high in protein, so the protein-to-carbohydrate ratio of the Sheep Eater diet was always high.

Nonetheless, an equal proportion of meat and plants in the diet does not mean that men and women shared equally the labor required to care for a family. Women had many other responsibilities, among them preparing meals, working hides, and drying fish, as well as their duties as the primary caretakers of children. Men's work also included other tasks not directly connected to subsistence, among them making horn bows and other more specialized tools, procuring chipped stone and steatite, and manufacturing tools from these materials. But, as in many societies that are identified as egalitarian, in which there were no class distinctions and no one individual was more important than another, equality was not synonymous with parity in terms of labor investment. In Sheep Eater society, women did most of the day-to-day work in the kin and clique, and their work "was never done." Another perspective on women's activities comes from the fact that, even though two or three Sheep Eater kin and cliques would often cooperate in the construction of large fishing weirs or in a communal hunt, in most critical situations the family unit did not rely on help from outside sources, except in times of illness or stress, when help from a shaman or medicine man might be solicited.

When quarrels developed between individuals not part of the nuclear family, a resolution was easily arranged: the aggrieved parties simply moved away and joined another kin and clique. On the other hand, arguments between members of the immediate family were not as easily resolved. If irreconcilable differences persisted, divorce was an option, and once children had reached an age at which they could travel on their own, they were also free to leave and join relatives elsewhere.

As Time Goes By

As cold temperatures and falling snow began to make life uncomfortable in the high mountain forests and meadows where Sheep Eaters spent the summer, kin and cliques would begin to move their camps to lower elevations, positioning themselves in and around the winter bedding areas of bighorn sheep. In Wyoming, a favorite locality was the Wind River valley near Dubois—known as "the warm valley"— but an alternate site was next to one of the tributary streams flowing out of the Absaroka Mountains into the Bighorn River, north of Thermopolis. Several kin and cliques often camped near one another, and, if the snow was not too deep, men might assemble for communal bighorn hunts. Sometimes, but not often, the winter was especially mild and the bighorns stayed at higher elevations, prompting Sheep Eater groups to camp nearby.

The most difficult daily task was collecting wood, which could be time-consuming, especially in the coldest weeks of winter. Men and older children sometimes helped out, but most of this work was done by women, who would have to spend several hours each day collecting sufficient wood to keep the family warm for the next twenty-four hours.

As spring approached and the snow began to melt, winter camps broke up, and individual kin and cliques began the trek up into the mountains, where sheep were already looking for the first fresh, green grass. The melting snow and warming earth made it possible for women to use their digging sticks to uncover the bulbs of sego lilies and spring beauty, as well as other root vegetables as they became accessible. Some kin and cliques might decide to stay at lower elevations and participate in a spring trading rendezvous, held in May or June, before heading into the mountains.

By summer, the kin and cliques were living in the high mountains near streams and lakes. At this time of year fishing was the primary pursuit, although women continued to collect root crops. It was in July 1835 that Osborne Russell encountered a Sheep Eater kin and clique of six men, seven women, and eight to ten children (see chapter 1) in the Lamar Valley of Yellowstone National Park.[12] This is a reasonable size for a midsummer kin and clique because the volume of hunting and meat processing at this time of year would not have required extra people. At least three or four of the men and women were probably married, and one or two of the men may have had more than one wife. The research of anthropologist Demitri Shimkin suggests that the other adults in the group might have included two or three unmarried men and an aged female relative or a divorced woman who was cared for by the group.[13]

In August, Sheep Eater kin and cliques moved their camps to the mountain slopes covered with pine trees, whose pine cones contained nutritious nuts that were ready for harvesting. While women collected and processed pine nuts, men would hunt for deer and replenish their supplies of obsidian and chert, some of which they would use to make their own stone tools and some of which they would keep in reserve to trade (more details about male and female food provisioning appear in chapters. 12–13, and obsidian sources are discussed in chapter 11). In September and October, when collecting baskets and pouches were full, some groups would begin their descent from the mountains early enough to take part in the fall trading rendezvous, whereas others remained behind until the bighorns were forced down by winter snowstorms.

TRADING VENTURES

In September 1866, trapper and gold prospector A. B. Henderson encountered a large group of Sheep Eaters in the Absaroka Mountains southwest of Cody, Wyoming, near the head of the Greybull River. According to Henderson, there were sixty individuals, a number of dogs, and one old mule, all of which were "loaded down to the guards" with sheepskins and marten furs.[14] Sixty Sheep Eaters traveling together suggests that three or four kin and cliques were on their way to one of the two trading rendezvous that took place each year in Sheep Eater territory. François Larocque, a Northwest Fur Company representative, attended one such fall trading event held on the Yellowstone River in 1804 near present-day Billings, Montana. In his excellent account of the participants, Larocque identifies Sheep Eaters and perhaps other Shoshone, as well as Flathead Indians, who had come to Montana to trade with a group of well-traveled Crow Indians.[15] Larocque had met the Crow at a Hidatsa village on the Missouri River in North Dakota and then accompanied them on their return trip to home territory on the Yellowstone.

It is not known whether the fall trade fair had ancient roots or if it began after the Crow moved to Yellowstone River country in the fifteenth and sixteenth centuries, but there is archaeological evidence supporting an annual spring trading rendezvous that apparently began at least 2,000 years ago.[16] In the historic period, a spring trade fair attended by Indians and white trappers is known to have taken place on the Green River in southwestern Wyoming, where there was abundant grazing for the herds of horses that Ute and Comanche traders brought from Texas and New Mexico. Although the Green River locality became well known as a good place for the spring rendezvous, the get-togethers occurred in several different locations. The junction of the Salmon and Snake rivers in Idaho was one popular meeting place because it had good year-round salmon fishing, and visitors could be confident that there would be plenty of food while they conducted business. At this location, Shoshone groups met and exchanged goods with Nez Perce and perhaps other Plateau tribes. At meetings in western Wyoming, which may have occurred in Jackson Hole or on the Wind River, primarily Shoshone groups got together and exchanged the products available in Wyoming's desert areas for resources found only in the mountains.

The articles that Sheep Eaters brought to trading sessions—tailored clothing, sheep- and other animal skins, horn bows, obsidian preforms—were of fine quality and were much sought after by their trading partners (Figure 5.2). In the luxury goods category there were robes constructed from the processed hides of two wolves that were sewn together to make a warm covering.[17] Hunters also brought other hard-to-get animal skins, such as those from mountain lions, which might have been tanned and traded with no further alteration, although they were sometimes made into quivers for arrows. Ermine tails, popular as adornments on clothing for special occasions, were routinely included in the Sheep Eater trading inventory.

By contemporary capitalist trading standards, the Sheep Eater approach to deal making was dangerously selfless. Trappers reported that the Indians simply threw their tanned hides and skins on the ground and asked for whatever amount the trapper felt was a fair price. Naturally, the trappers were excited by the Sheep Eaters' apparent naïveté and would take advantage of them by offering in return goods of vastly lesser value.[18] What the trappers did not know was that Sheep Eaters were practicing a form of exchange identified by anthropologists as *balanced reciprocity*, according to whose rules the trappers were expected to honor their indebtedness at a later time. Kin and clique exchanges were conducted in terms of this principle, so when tanned skins were placed on the ground and a trapper offered an

Figure 5.2. Sheep Eaters showing their wares at a trading rendezvous. Horn bows were among their most prized trade goods, but other items included obsidian preforms, tanned animal skins, and clothing. Illustration by Davíd Joaquín.

amount less than their actual value, the Sheep Eater assumed that if his family needed food during the coming year, he could rely for support on the trapper who was indebted to him. There are no records, however, indicating that trappers were ever available when their Sheep Eater trading partners needed help, and it is likely that—after a number of instances of what turned out to be severely *imbalanced* reciprocity—Sheep Eaters would have demanded a more equitable exchange.

In a world in which "shopping" has replaced "trading," a premium is placed on the efficiency of the purchasing transaction. Holding up the line in the supermarket in order to exchange news about one's family would provoke irritation and, eventually, complaints. In contrast, trade between Sheep Eaters and other Indian groups was a complicated, drawn-out engagement in which more than goods were exchanged. At a trading rendezvous, information changed hands, new people might be introduced into social networks, and marriages and cooperative hunting sorties might be arranged. Although these engagements might sometimes be intimidating to the individuals involved, they contributed novelty, fresh ideas, and opportunities to the mountain-dwelling Sheep Eaters.

LEADERSHIP AND CONFLICT

Leadership in Sheep Eater society was informal, which means that there were no hereditary leaders and that leadership positions did not pass from generation to generation within families. Charismatic or successful individuals, who were known as "headmen," made the day-to-day decisions, while a group of adults was consulted about what to do in exceptional situations. Headmen earned their reputations by consistent performance or, if they were particularly powerful shamans, by using their supernatural powers to make informed decisions. Headmen were consulted about or asked to lead game drives and vegetable-gathering forays or to lead a ceremony, but their preeminence ended at the conclusion of the corporate activity. Older persons who knew places where plant and animal resources could be found were valued members of a kin and clique, but they were never elevated to prestigious positions.[19] Although it is likely that these leaders were more often men than women, women undoubtedly played a significant role in determining the schedule for collecting and harvesting important plant resources like camas and biscuit root and deciding the sequence of locations to be visited.

WARFARE

The history of warfare demonstrates repeatedly that human groups resort to aggression and violence against their neighbors in order to control access to resources perceived to be essential to their existence and as a way of retaliating for perceived injustices. For most of the Sheep Eaters' existence, they were so well adapted to their natural setting, so self-sufficient and independent, and so free from competitive pressure that, unlike their neighbors on the Plains, there were no circumstances in which raiding or aggressive behavior would have been rewarded. This very reasonable lack of engagement is partially responsible for their reputation as "cowards," although that epithet reflects the value system of nineteenth-century U.S. military personnel, who tended to evaluate Indians in terms of their willingness to "stand their ground like a man and fight back." When threatened or attacked, a common Sheep Eater defense was to retreat and hide in the mountains, whose terrain they knew better than any enemy did. The U.S. Cavalry was flummoxed by Indians who chose to disappear into mountain recesses, where they held the tactically advantageous high ground and put the troops at lower altitudes at a disadvantage.

In rock art panels in the region, the bellicose "shield-bearing warrior" figures so widely distributed across the Plains states and the Colorado Plateau—where they are linked to known warring groups—are totally absent from the Dinwoody petroglyphs associated with Sheep Eaters. This significant omission suggests that the large, body-covering shields so common elsewhere, and routinely depicted in other rock art, were not included in either the Sheep Eater material inventory or the rock art panels because these items were unnecessary in a society that used evasive action rather than warlike tactics to ensure physical security.

LOOKING AHEAD

In this chapter we have explored what is known about Sheep Eater family composition as well as the ways in which members of this basic unit were connected to others to form a social fabric that gave structure and meaning to the activities of daily life. In the next chapter, we will focus on a different kind of human structure—not the household but the house. We will consider Sheep Eater dwellings in terms of their formal properties and their settings, the degree of comfort and protection that they offered, and the kinds of items that people made, used, and stored or discarded when they moved on.

6

||||

Sheltering Sheep Eaters: A House for Each Season

In the waves of exploration and exploitation that swept over the lands west of the Mississippi River following the Lewis and Clark expedition, some travelers had commercial intent and represented the economic interests of nations on both sides of the Atlantic. Others became "mountain men," shedding the raiment and customs of their upbringing, and learning—often from indigenous foraging peoples—to be self-sufficient. Still others came to experience for themselves and report on for others the vastness and grandeur of the landscapes. Some observers commented, often with condescension, on the exotic and colorful tribal groups who did not take afternoon tea, wear silk ascots, or affect the social refinements of Victorian England.

One intrepid visitor to the West was Isabella L. Bird, the daughter of an English parson, whose gentle upbringing would never have predicted that she would become a world traveler and renowned travel writer. Venturing alone in the latter half of the nineteenth century to such faraway places as Malaysia, Tibet, Kurdistan, India, Japan, China, and Hawaii, she spent several months in Colorado in 1873. She traversed on horseback the area between Estes Park and Pike's Peak and confided in her letters to her sister in England—later collected and published in *A Lady's Life in the Rocky Mountains*—the rigors and curiosities of life on the American frontier.

Bird's observant eye was also drawn to others of her caste, one of whom she described witheringly:

> Bob Craik...came in to supper with a young man in tow, whom, in spite of his rough hunter's or miner's dress, I at once recognized as an English gentleman....This gentleman was lording it in true caricature fashion, with a Lord Dundreary drawl and a general execration of everything; while I sat in the chimney corner, speculating on the reason why many of the upper class of my countrymen—"High

Toners," as they are called out here—make themselves so ludicrously absurd. They neither know how to hold their tongues or to carry their personal pretensions.[1]

Ms. Bird's "Lord Dundreary" may be a thinly disguised reference to Thomas Wyndham-Quin, the Fourth Earl of Dunraven, a big-game hunter and sportsman who was traveling in the northern part of Yellowstone Park not long after the previous remarks were written. If Dunweary and Dunraven were one and the same, he kept his sense of superiority to himself when he recorded the following:

> Our path...crossed a low divide into the valley system of the Fire Hole, or east fork of the Madison River. Before crossing the divide we passed a few old wigwams, remains of encampments of Sheepeaters. These were the last indications of Indians that we saw....A few wretched Sheepeaters are said to linger in the fastnesses of the mountains about Clarkes Fork; but their existence is very doubtful; at any rate they must be a harmless, timid race.[2]

Less restrained in his execration was William Baillie-Grohman, another well-born Englishman who spent a significant part of the latter half of the nineteenth century hunting and roaming in the Rocky Mountain West. After visiting a number of Sheep Eater houses, he sniffed: "Sheepeaters' 'teepees' or lodges are without exception the most miserable human dwellings I ever saw; and considering their very great altitude, consisting of piled-up stones, and lean-to roof of slender pine trunks, their inmates, wretchedly clad, as they undoubtedly were, must have suffered intense cold."[3]

The English stately home was apparently uppermost in Baillie-Grohman's mind as the model of acceptable housing, but had he known more about hunter–gatherer peoples he would have realized that brick-and-mortar dwellings not only were incompatible with a life defined by mobility but consumed human energy best spent in other pursuits. A high investment in permanent shelter became necessary when populations increased, mobility was restricted, and, ultimately, the landscape was parceled out to lineages that now owned it and needed to defend their ownership rights. The effort that foraging peoples devoted to housing was, on the other hand, proportionate to their need to protect themselves from the elements and to be able to respond flexibly to the availability of resources in their territories. In the temperate zone in general, housing tended to be more ephemeral during the warmer months, when mobility was often highest, and to be more substantial when lower temperatures and snow made travel more difficult and protection from the cold necessary.

We know that Baillie-Grohman's assumption that Sheep Eaters were "wretchedly clad" is incorrect (see chapter 8), but what about the aspersions that he casts on their domiciles? It is true that pre-horse Shoshone groups in general were not known for fine housing, compared to the large, elegant tipis of their Plains Indian neighbors. As Robert Lowie has pointed out, they lived in small, conical-shaped, brush-covered structures whose "crudity" led to their being referred to as the "Bad Lodge People" in Indian sign language.[4] (This generalization by non-Shoshone Indians reveals that not only Euro-Americans indulged in cultural stereotyping.)

SHEEP EATER HOUSES

Sheep Eaters lived in a forested environment and made two similar kinds of structures using the raw materials available to them. The most common type was made by arranging deadfall timber logs into a freestanding, conical-shaped dwelling known as a *wickiup*. The second type was built in much the same way except that the deadfall timbers were arranged in a semicircle inside a low rock foundation wall, with the tops resting against the back wall of an overhanging cliff face or rock shelter. All the Plains and Plateau tribes, including those that frequently traveled through Yellowstone Park, made similar houses for temporary shelter when they were hunting or raiding, but structures at their main camps were more substantial. The Sheep Eaters, on the other hand, had no other kind of housing (Figure 6.1).

Two features made Sheep Eater wickiups different from those of other tribes. The first is that they were made of an exceptionally large number of eight- to ten-foot poles that were fitted very tightly together, which made them weatherproof.[5] It was not unusual for a Sheep Eater wickiup to be composed of 75 to 100 poles, although the norm was to use about half that many. Some Sheep Eater wickiups were covered with grass or brush; when it was available, giant wild rye grass (*Elymus condensatus*) made a good thatch for the outer covering.

Figure 6.1. A Sheep Eater man seated outside a wickiup. A distinguishing feature of wickiups is the large number of poles used to construct the shelter, which was used primarily for sleeping. Food preparation and cooking took place outside. Although this structure is in the open, shelters were also built in caves and rock overhangs for use during inclement weather. Illustration by Davíd Joaquín.

The second unique feature was first recorded by archaeologist Jake Hoffman while documenting the remains of Sheep Eater wickiups in Yellowstone National Park.[6] He notes that long, heavy, deadfall logs had been positioned so that they rested on the apex of each structure, where they exerted pressure that helped hold the house upright in a windstorm. Most Sheep Eater wickiups have now collapsed and deteriorated or been destroyed by forest fires, so it is not possible to determine if the leaning pole was invariably present or used only when the structures were set up in inclement weather.

According to Philetus Norris, the second superintendent of Yellowstone National Park, freestanding wickiups were once fairly common in the "sheltered glens and valleys" of Sheep Eater territory. In Norris's 1880 annual report, he describes the remains of a Sheep Eater site on the divide between Hoodoo Creek and Miller Creek, where a single wickiup was still standing amid the collapsed remains of more than forty others. According to longtime Yellowstone Park photographer Jack Haynes, this site was still extant in 1924:

> In the fall of 1924 in company with Superintendent Horace M. Albright, Samuel T. Woodring, chief ranger, and Ed Bruce I saw a large, ancient Indian camp ground northeast of Parker Peak across the gully between there and Hoodoo Peak. It was on the bank, sheltered by the southern ridge and about 1/4 mile west of the rim of the gully. The area consisting of three or four acres was covered with tepee poles—hundreds of them—flanked at the west by a grove [of] aspen trees.[7]

Haynes describes the site—initially visited in 1894 by his father, Frank Jay Haynes, accompanied by Captain George Anderson and George Whittaker—as the largest in the park.

In 1977, archaeological enthusiasts Stuart W. Conner and Kenneth J. Feyhl, from Billings, Montana, visited the region and recorded artifacts at a locality known as the Parker Peak site (48YE506), but they found no evidence of fallen wickiups.[8] It seems likely that in the intervening eighty-three years, the collapsed wooden poles had deteriorated and eventually decomposed in the relatively wet conditions. Nonetheless, the nineteenth-century historical record of this site confirms the prevalence of freestanding Sheep Eater wickiups and their use as summer dwellings.

In the southwestern corner of Montana, to the west of Yellowstone Park, two wickiups were found at Pass Creek (Figure 6.2).[9] One of these structures was collapsed, but the other is still standing and has a diameter of 3.7 meters and an interior height of 2.5 meters. Its forty-three remaining poles, some of which are longer and appear to be similar to the heavy leaning poles noted by Hoffman in the wickiups in Yellowstone Park, are supported by a tripod foundation. The two Pass Creek wickiups are especially important historically because Henry Hildreth, a local rancher who settled in the area in 1890, remembers their use by the Northern Shoshone.[10]

Figure 6.2. A conical-shaped wickiup at the Pass Creek site in Montana. Wickiups were made by all the western Indian tribes, but those of the Sheep Eaters contained more poles in their walls and traditionally had long leaning poles that stabilized the structure. Photograph courtesy of Carl Davis and Sara Scott.

Figure 6.3. The remains of a Sheep Eater lodge inside Wickiup Cave, Montana. This structure may have had an outer thatch covering made of rye grass. Note the long leaning pole that stabilizes the structure. Photograph courtesy of Carl Davis.

At Wickiup Cave, another site in southwestern Montana near the border with Idaho, archaeologist Carl Davis recorded a typical Sheep Eater cold-weather dwelling built of timbers, branches, pine boughs, and rocks (Figure 6.3).[11] After two long poles had been braced against the back wall of the rock shelter, more than thirty additional timber poles were leaned against the framework, enclosing a semicircular area that was 17 feet in diameter and 10 feet high. Many of the poles were burned on the ends, suggesting that they had been felled or cut to the required length using fire. Smaller tree branches and pine boughs had been interwoven into the structure's walls for heat retention and protection from wind and moisture. A rock wall had been constructed by stacking limestone blocks to a height of two feet around the exterior of the structure, leaving an opening that served as an entryway. In a variation on this house type also found in Sheep Eater territory, the entire perimeter of a fairly small rock shelter had been enclosed with a low rock wall, and an upper wall was constructed from closely fitted poles. In such a design, the roof of the overhanging rock shelter would have offered protection from snow and rain, while the log and branch wall would have kept out the wind and cold.

Inside the structure at the Wickiup Cave site, a four-foot by eight-foot bedding area had been outlined with rocks and lined with layers of pine boughs and giant wild rye grass to soften the sleeping surface. No interior hearth was found, but extensive digging by relic hunters was evident and may have destroyed such a feature. At other sites in the region, the outlined bedding area was lined with rock slabs under which a layer of hot coals was laid each evening before the family retired.[12] The warmth generated by the coals kept the slumbering adults, children, and dogs—all snuggled together under sheepskin blankets—toasty warm during the coldest of nights. The only drawback to such comfort would have come in the morning, when it was someone's unpleasant duty to get up in below-zero temperatures to start the day's fire.

By the time Carl Davis began his excavation at Wickiup Cave, it was clear that the site had been looted by persons in search of mementos from the past. Davis invested a lot of energy tracking down pilfered artifacts and found a number of them in local collections. He was able to recover about thirty small, triangular arrow points, some with side notches and others with side and base notches, as well as a third group of unnotched triangular forms. One triangular point was still attached with wrapped sinew to a broken arrow. Other arrow fragments are similar to the compound arrows recovered from Mummy Cave.

The Wickiup Cave assemblage included cutting, scraping, and drilling tools, among them a typical long, narrow Shoshone knife with an extensively resharpened blade, shaped like a willow leaf and measuring 17 centimeters long by 4 centimeters wide. Two bone awls, one made from a bone splinter and the other from the scapula of an unidentifiable mammal, were also recovered from the deposit. Davis had more difficulty recovering the ceramics taken from the site, apparently examples of the flat-bottom Intermountain ware usually identified as Shoshone.

DAVE LOVE'S MYSTERY SITE

Most known rock shelter sites in the region are located at ground level or slightly above it, so access to them would have been comparatively easy. Some, however, are situated high enough on a cliff face to have posed a challenge to those attempting to approach. Only a few such sites have been explored, none of them by archaeologists, but local hikers and climbers have told of finds made in such caves. Perhaps the most intriguing discovery was made by the world-renowned Rocky Mountain geologist J. David Love, a man who spent countless hours traveling on horseback through the Absaroka and Wind River mountains studying the geology. While exploring an area on the southern side of the Absarokas, Love found a rickety, two-pole ladder leaning against a cliff face. In a story straight out of "Jack and the Beanstalk," Love reported that when he looked up he could see that the ladder led to a ledge and that, by traversing the ledge, it was possible to reach a second ladder ascending to another ledge, on which yet *another* ladder led to a third and final ledge, where there was a cave.[13]

Love recalls that curiosity and a sense of adventure urged him to try to explore the cave, but the effort would have been difficult because the rungs of the lowest ladder, presumably made of rawhide, had completely deteriorated and he would have had to improvise a means of ascent. Love's discovery occurred in the pre–cell phone era, when a fall or other accident in so remote a location would almost certainly have meant a solitary death, so he decided not to risk the climb. He did look around at the foot of the ground-level ladder, where he found a white quartzite knife that he made a point of mentioning later when he talked about the site, because the raw material was foreign to the region.

The cave is in a remote area with very difficult access, and Dave Love never organized a team to investigate its contents. Many years later he took one of us (Loendorf) to a ridge several miles away, from which—using a spotting scope—it was possible to see caves and leaning logs, but whether one of them was the site Love had found is a mystery. A serious effort to explore the area would require time, organization, and money, all of which have been used for other endeavors. If there have been any twenty-first-century visitors to the site, they have kept their experiences to themselves, so whatever lies at the top of Jack's Absaroka beanstalk remains a mystery.

DEPREDATIONS AT FLAMING GORGE RESERVOIR

It is unfortunate that Wickiup Cave is the only Sheep Eater dwelling site that has been properly investigated by trained archaeologists because much more can be learned about the past from a systematic excavation than from just digging up interesting artifacts. Sometimes sites are protected from curious nonprofessionals by their inaccessibility, but subsequent human actions can place their integrity and contents at great risk.

Consider the caves and rock shelters located high on the sandstone cliffs along the stretch of the Green River running between Utah and Wyoming. In 1958, construction began on what was to become the Flaming Gorge Dam, which impounded the Green River and created 207,363 acres of reservoir and recreational facilities. During the ten-year construction period, a group of explorers waited patiently—boats ready—for the water level in Flaming Gorge Reservoir to rise. When the water was high enough to allow the group to approach the once-isolated caves, its members were able to paddle to the entrances and retrieve a woefully large number of artifacts. In one cave, for example, they found a bundle of twisted cordage snares with wooden catch pins that had been cached there several centuries earlier by a former cave occupant. We know about the snares because, in time, they were presented for examination to Danny Walker, a skilled archaeologist at the University of Wyoming, who concluded that they had been used to capture small game such as gophers and ground squirrels. Of course, it is not possible to prove that the snares Walker examined had been left at the site by Sheep Eaters, for Flaming Gorge is considerably south of their normal range.[14] What is certain is that Sheep Eaters used very similar snares, as did other regional Indian bands, and had the site been excavated rather than mined for its contents, a much more definitive assessment of the snares' provenance could have been made.

LOOKING AHEAD

Sheep Eaters left more behind at the sites they occupied than just structures or disarticulated building materials. Their mobile way of life also precluded the transport of very heavy steatite bowls made and used for cooking and storage. In the next chapter we will discuss what is known about the distribution of steatite raw material and the techniques that Sheep Eaters employed to make—without the benefit of metal tools—the distinctive, multipurpose vessels that have been found in the archaeological deposits in their territory.

7

Chip and Chisel versus Make and Bake: Steatite and Ceramic Vessels in Sheep Eater Country

Despite the inclusion of uncooked meat disguised with an ambiguous name (such as steak tartare) on the menus of many upscale restaurants, most human carnivores prefer to eat their animal protein roasted, baked, fried, grilled, steamed, or boiled. Around one million years ago our hominid ancestors discovered the many uses they could make of fire, which included warmth in cold settings and protection from animal predators. Burned, cracked animal bones in archaeological sites around the world are testimony to their additional insight that cooking some of the foods they ate was, to quote a contemporary culinary priestess, "a good thing." Not only did heating meat help reduce the likelihood of bacterial infection associated with consumption, but some cooking techniques transform the chemical structure of meat and make it softer to chew.

For most of human history, cooking food did not involve the many different kinds of receptacles and utensils that we take for granted today. Specialized implements such as sauté pans, chafing dishes, and turkey basters became part of the paraphernalia of food preparation only after humans had become sedentary, meals had become scheduled events in which most family members participated, and all the many tasks associated with cooking took place in specialized protected areas that we now call kitchens. During the millennia in which humans were highly mobile foragers, meat and vegetables were dried; smoked; buried with fuel, fire, and hot stones in earth ovens; or placed in baskets or skin bags along with water and red-hot rocks and allowed to boil. As populations increased and the area exploited by mobile groups became more circumscribed—"reduction in range size" is how archaeologists frequently refer to this phenomenon—the places where people exploited resources and camped were reused much more fre-

{ 76 }

quently. Routed foraging—or returning periodically to the same place—resulted in many changes in human lifeways, one of which was the introduction of a new kind of cooking vessel, a solid stone pot made out of a mineral called "steatite" (STEE-uh-tight). Steatite pots were capable of withstanding direct heat from a fire, but they were frequently large and very heavy, which reduced their portability. Often they were left as "site furniture" at the places to which people knew they would soon be returning.

The prehistoric use of steatite vessels has been documented in many places around the world, from the Near East to Bulgaria, from Finland to Africa. Ethnohistoric accounts in California show that Gabrieliño Indians on Santa Catalina Island quarried steatite and then traded the finished pots (and perhaps the raw material itself) to groups to the north and east. In eastern North America between 4000 BC and AD 1, utilitarian use of steatite occurred in Ohio, North Carolina, Maryland, and Virginia, and the raw material can often be traced to deposits in the Appalachian Mountains from New England to Georgia.

An early description of the use of a steatite vessel in Sheep Eater country was recorded in 1805 by François Larocque, who had met with Lewis and Clark on the Missouri River and later traveled to the Yellowstone River near Billings, Montana. According to Larocque, "I traded eight Beavers with the Snake Indians in whose possession I saw a kettle or Pot hewn out of solid stone. It was about 1 ½" thick and contained 6 or 8 quarts."[1]

Lewis and Clark themselves marveled at the ability of the Shoshone to make pots out of stone, but a great deal more is now known about steatite (which is also sometimes called soapstone) and its properties than in the nineteenth century.[2] For instance, it is a comparatively soft metamorphic stone that originated as a loose mixture of sands and silts at the bottom of ancient oceans or seas. Throughout eons, the weight of the overlying water and sediments caused the sands and silts to compact into a harder substance. In many places in the world, ancient ocean floors have been thrust upward by pressures related to the dynamics of plate tectonics occurring below the surface of the Earth's crust. These forces often resulted in episodes of orogeny, or mountain building, during which the Earth's surface was uplifted and tilted, exposing the undersides of adjacent rock. It is in such exposures in the mountains of Idaho, Montana, and Wyoming that Sheep Eater Indians found and quarried the steatite they used to make their stone pots.

The use of the term *soft* to describe steatite is perhaps a bit misleading. Although the mineral has a rank of "1" on Moh's Scale of Hardness, which reflects the fact that a human fingernail can leave a scratch on an untreated steatite surface, it is also very dense and, surprisingly, less porous than marble, slate, limestone, and granite. Because a dense surface is a nonstaining surface, steatite is the material of choice for countertops in chemistry labs and, increasingly, in trendy kitchen makeovers. As for steatite's thermal properties, not only is it an excellent conductor of heat, but it hardens when exposed to fire, and then is not easily altered.

Making a steatite pot is not for the faint of heart; the task is labor-intensive, even with steel tools from the neighborhood hardware store. But, were there such a group as Sheep Eater "reenactors" who, inspired by Civil War buffs and their painstaking replication of life as Union Army soldiers, decided to make their own culinary equipment, square one would involve gearing up and heading out to locate the raw material. Steatite outcrops are often found high in the mountains, and, depending on the starting point, the journey might take a couple of days. Of course, the distance to travel is reduced if one already lives in the mountains, but there are no steatite outcrops in Yellowstone National Park, so Sheep Eaters who camped there had to look elsewhere.

Steatite is known to occur in about twenty-five sites in Montana and Wyoming. Two or three of these are in the region around Dillon and Virginia City, Montana, and include some sources that are currently commercially mined. One of these outcrops is undoubtedly the source of the "green pipestone" known to early trappers and identified by Jim Bridger on an 1851 map. Twenty more sources have been identified in the Wind River and Absaroka mountains to the south of Yellowstone Park, some of which contain material that was transported, perhaps by glacial activity, from the original site of upthrust to a new location. Eight or ten of the sites, however, are primary outcrops whose beds of steatite are exposed in situ. Tens of thousands of broken steatite shards cover the ground around these outcrops, evidence of the intensive quarrying and manufacturing of pots that occurred there. Another steatite source is in the Bighorn Mountains,

Figure 7.1. A Sheep Eater woman and her heirlooms. A group of steatite pots of different sizes sits in front of the woman and her daughter, who would one day inherit the pots. These pots would have been considered personal property and were not used as trade goods. Illustration by Davíd Joaquín.

south of Tensleep, Wyoming, and there are probably other deposits in the area that remain undiscovered. There are, for example, rumors of a site on the Beartooth Plateau, above Red Lodge, Montana, but its location is yet to be pinpointed.[3]

The trek to a steatite deposit would be followed by the product-testing phase of the endeavor. As is the case for many other kinds of minerals (diamonds come to mind), the structure of steatite is not always uniform. The presence of flaws and fractures can produce unexpected breakage, so it is essential to find a solid piece of stone.

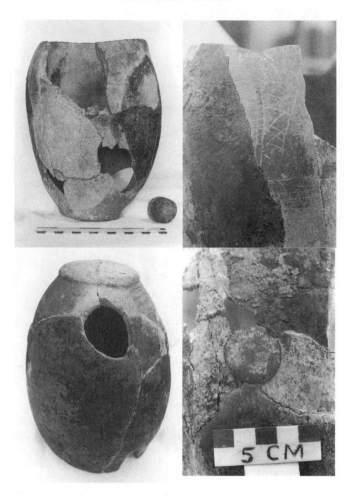

Figure 7.2. Four views of a flat-bottom steatite vessel found west of Cody, Wyoming. As the pot's walls thinned, steatite plugs shaped like corks were inserted into the holes. One of these plugs still fits the hole. An incised pattern of crosshatched lines decorates a portion of the exterior wall. The larger scale is 15 cm. The vessel is in a private collection. Photographs by Lawrence L. Loendorf.

Successful procurement favors a unit of material that is still embedded in the outcrop, although detached steatite boulders, if they are large enough, can also be used. Working with a still-attached segment of an outcrop has the advantage of providing a natural anchor for the emerging pot that keeps it stable as its shape is defined by forceful chiseling and percussion.

On some steatite outcrops, the pattern of partially formed pots interspersed with holes where pots have been removed resembles a crude row of teeth, like on a jack-o'-lantern. These remnants suggest that the pot-making technique involved shaping the vessel by first cutting away the steatite around a unit that was designated as a blank and then defining the outside of the pot-to-be. Once the outside surface assumed a desirable shape, the inside was hollowed out, leaving walls that were one to two inches thick. Finally, the pot was detached from the outcrop by cutting it away at the base.

The finished product was a heavy, thick-walled vessel that could hold several quarts of liquid. It was transported and then used without much further refinement of its shape or surface. In the course of years of use, a pot's walls would gradually become thinner and develop a black luster from fire and grease, so that an old, well-used pot could have walls that were less than a quarter-inch thick. Steatite pots took on the identity of heirlooms and were passed from mother to daughter through several generations (Figure 7.1). Daily use over so many years frequently produced holes in the thinnest walls that were repaired by trimming away any irregularities in the shape and filling the newly circular opening with another piece of steatite, shaped like a cork (Figure 7.2).

Sizes and Kinds of Stone Pots

Early trappers and explorers report that some Sheep Eater steatite pots were capable of holding as much as two or three gallons (256 and 384 ounces, respectively), but as no pots with these dimensions have ever been found, the accuracy of the estimates is suspect. One possible explanation for this error in judgment may begin with the fact that stone pots start their "use-life" with thick walls, a characteristic that makes them large overall but with a smaller capacity than a ceramic vessel of comparable size that has comparatively thin walls and, therefore, greater capacity than a steatite pot of similar outside dimensions.

Because the best way to determine the capacity of steatite pots is to measure them, Richard Adams, while a graduate student at the University of Wyoming, did just that.[4] As part of his study of their manufacture and use, he concluded that the majority of pots held about one quart (32 ounces) of liquid. One of us (Loendorf) had the opportunity

POT NUMBER	SHAPE	WEIGHT	HEIGHT	WALL THICKNESS	INTERIOR DIMENSIONS	VOLUME	FEATURES
95-4-2:SH 368i-1	large; globular; flat bottom	~5 lbs	16.5 cm	2–5 mm	22 cm diameter	129 oz with hole plugged; 135 oz if intact	polished surface; hole in one wall; broken rim
95-44-1:H8F-1	large; straight walls; flat bottom; elliptical	50 lbs	outside: 33.3 cm; inside: 12.1 cm	10–15 mm	18 × 25 cm (elliptical)	64 oz with broken rim; 120 oz if rim intact; ~240 oz if completely hollowed out	broken rim; inside only one-third hollowed out
85-32	classic flowerpot form	33 lbs (35 lbs if complete)	27 cm	variable; 12 mm in one place	18 × 20 cm (slightly asymmetrical)	slightly less than 128 oz if rim complete	broken and partially reconstructed; crude flat bottom indicates made by stone tools
Pot A	straight walls; flare- to oval-shaped mouth	9.5 lbs	20 cm		14 × 14.5 cm	40 oz	closer in size to average flat bottom steatite pot
97.12	small; flat bottom	4.8 lbs	11.8 cm		11.5 × 12.5 cm	20 oz	
Pot B	flat bottom; similar in size to 97.12						locked in display case and could not be measured
Pot C	small; flat bottom	6.9 lbs	10 cm	2.0–2.5 cm	12.5–13 cm	24 oz	
Pot D	rounded; flat bottom; low walls		9 cm		19.5 cm diameter	40 oz as is; 48 oz if rim not broken	break in rim

Table 7.1. Steatite Pots in the Collection of the Wind River Historical Center, measured by Lawrence L. Loendorf

to add to this body of data by examining the excellent sample of steatite artifacts—most of which had not been studied—in the collection of the Wind River Historical Center in Dubois, Wyoming (Table 7.1). As part of the research, the height, weight, circumference, and wall thickness of a number of specimens were measured, and the observations were summarized. Overall, the seven pots examined ranged in capacity from 2.5 cups (20 ounces) to 16.9 cups (135.2 ounces), with an average capacity of 7.9 cups (63.2 ounces). If the one unfinished pot (95-44-1:H8F-1) with an estimated capacity of 30 cups (240 ounces) is included in the sample, the average capacity is 9.7 cups (77.6 ounces), or roughly double the average capacity of the pots measured by Richard Adams.

CERAMIC VESSELS

Ceramic pots have also been found in Wyoming and Montana, and for years these discoveries have provoked discussions among archaeologists about whether they are sufficiently distinctive to be classified as the pottery made by Shoshone Indians (Figure 7.3). This discussion really became focused in the 1950s, when Waldo Wedel, a highly respected archaeologist at the Smithsonian Institution, was completing an excavation at a site near Cody, Wyoming. As Wedel was preparing to return to Washington, D.C., Don Marquess, a local Wyoming resident, brought him a pot that had been found under a rock overhang along Goff Creek, about ten miles from the East Gate of Yellowstone National Park. The pot, which was in four pieces, had apparently been cached for safekeeping by its owners under the low rock overhang until they returned to the site. Wedel was able to put the pieces of the pot back together and then take measurements. The restored vessel was 26 centimeters high and had a flat circular base that measured 10.5 centimeters in diameter. Just a few centimeters below the rim, the walls flared outward to a maximum diameter of 25.5 centimeters. The upper body of the pot was very dark gray, but around the middle it was more buff to tan. Crushed granite had been used as the temper. Wedel compared the Marquess pot to others that had been found in the region and suggested that it had probably been made recently by Shoshone potters.[5]

A few years later, Jake Hoffman, an archaeologist working in Yellowstone National Park, found the better part of another flat-bottom pot

Figure 7.3. An Intermountain tradition (Shoshone) pot from the Crocket site in southern Idaho. Note that it has a flat bottom and is the same general shape as Sheep Eater steatite vessels. The distribution of Intermountain pottery covers a wider area than steatite vessels that are found in traditional Sheep Eater territory. Courtesy of the Herrett Center for Arts and Science, College of Southern Idaho.

on the shore in the West Thumb section of Yellowstone Lake.[6] This pot had been discovered in an excavation that included a few other artifacts, among them a spherical disc of pottery that measured 25 millimeters in diameter, an obsidian corner-notched projectile point, a quartzite end scraper, an obsidian chopping tool, and a mixture of obsidian, chert, jasper, and quartzite flakes. The small pottery disc is a rare artifact, but the stone tools are common at sites in the region.[7]

The West Thumb pot, which has a slightly flanged base, appears to have been made by hand modeling, as there is no evidence that coiling or paddle-and-anvil techniques were involved in its production. The exterior of the pot was covered with shallow striations that Hoffman thought might have been made by wiping the unfired pot with grass or some other fibrous material to smooth it. The color varied, ranging from gray, to black, to reddish brown. The pot was in too many fragments for complete reconstruction, but Hoffman was able to estimate that it had been 25 centimeters high, with a base diameter of 13.2 centimeters and a mouth diameter of 20.5 centimeters.

The shape, size, and color of these two pots are so similar that they almost certainly came from the Intermountain ceramic tradition, a classification that most archaeologists have identified as Shoshone in origin. Pots in this tradition exhibit little variation: a few have lips that are rolled over onto the outside surface like those found on antique milk pails, and others are simply rounded and unfinished at the lip. Flanged bases vary somewhat and are found on some vessels but not on others. The shape of Intermountain pots is usually compared to contemporary flowerpots whose straight walls flare outward. The vessels are unpainted and are not decorated with surface patterns common elsewhere, such as cord marks, punctates, or other stamped impressions. They are also poorly fired, easily broken, and seldom found as complete specimens.

Because some steatite pots also have flat bottoms and are the same general shape and size as the Intermountain ceramic vessels, the two have been identified as variants of Shoshone containers. Waldo Wedel made this comparison when he reported the Marquess pot and also described three steatite pots from the mountains in the vicinity of Yellowstone National Park.

A Comparison of Steatite and Ceramic Pots

In the 1970s, Thomas Marceau, a graduate student at the State University of New York, Albany, became interested in the geographical distribution of steatite pots in Wyoming, particularly in whether steatite pots with flat bottoms were found at sites that also had Intermountain pottery. Marceau's research uncovered a number of interesting facts: (1) Intermountain pottery vessels were distributed over a much larger area than steatite vessels were; (2) steatite pots were usually found at higher elevations than ceramic ones; and (3) steatite pots and artifacts were older than flat-bottomed pots in western Wyoming. It is interesting to look at these facts in light of more recent discoveries.[8]

Marceau's study identifies fifty sites that contained steatite vessels and artifacts. Using a point on the Continental Divide about midway between Yellowstone Lake and Jackson Lake as the center of the distribution, he found that within a radius of 100 miles, sites with steatite vessels were about 2.4 times more common than sites with Intermountain pottery. The ratio of steatite to pottery vessels was about the same when the radius of the geographic area was expanded to between 100 miles and 200 miles from the arbitrary center, but at distances from the center that were greater than 200 miles, ceramic vessels were four times as common as steatite. Using statistics to test the randomness of the distribution, Marceau concludes that "when the distribution of steatite vessels is compared to that of their ceramic counterparts, the assessment that steatite bowls are generally restricted to western Wyoming, particularly the high country of northwestern Wyoming, cannot be attributed to chance."[9]

Marceau's study has been criticized on methodological grounds, particularly his apparently arbitrary placement of the center of the distribution between Yellowstone Lake and Jackson Lake in the Grand Teton National Park. In evaluating his decision, however, it is important to remember that although there are no known steatite outcrops in Yellowstone Park where the raw material could have been quarried, Marceau identifies fourteen steatite pots that were found inside the park boundaries (although Loendorf's own tally of this sample has identified only ten pots). In addition, at a single locality—the Lawrence Site (48TE509) on the north shore of Jackson Lake—ten complete steatite pots, one cup, one platter, one broken vessel, one unfinished bowl, and one steatite pipe fragment were recovered.[10] As steatite pots were so common in these two localities, Marceau's decision to place the center of his area of analysis roughly between Jackson Lake and Yellowstone Lake makes perfect sense.

Loendorf took another approach to the question of steatite bowl distribution by developing a geographical unit based on the locations of known steatite quarries. An area containing three steatite sources was defined: the outcrops near Dillon, Montana; those in the Wind River Mountains, south of Dubois, Wyoming; and the quarry area in the Bighorn Mountains, south of Tensleep, Wyoming. When a dot was placed on the map at the midpoint between these three locations, it fell within Yellowstone National Park (which is not markedly different from the center of Marceau's study area), demonstrating that the results of his comparison are changed very little by using quarries as geographical points of reference.

In the meantime, the number and variety of steatite vessels that have been discovered continue to grow. Richard Adams had the opportunity to look at steatite vessels in small museums and private collections across western Wyoming, and, in the process, he recorded the locations of a dozen sites not included in Marceau's study. In the years since Adams was identifying extant specimens, four complete pots and another platter, now kept in the Dubois Museum, were found in the Wind River Mountains. Other pots or fragments of pots not analyzed by either Marceau or Adams are now in the collections of small museums like the Mountain Man Museum in Pinedale, Wyoming, which brings the total of steatite pots that are now in protected circumstances to approximately one hundred. Valuable archaeological information, such as the location where some vessels were found, has not been recorded in detail, but it is known that most are from the Wind River Mountains. It is also acknowledged that Marceau was correct: the original distribution of these pots is not nearly as extensive as that of Intermountain pottery.

Marceau's study looked not only at the horizontal distribution of steatite and ceramic pots but also at the elevations where each type of vessel was found. His research shows that a significantly greater number of Intermountain pottery vessels (7.3 to 1) were found at elevations below 5,000 feet. Further, the contrast between the number of ceramic pots at low elevations and the number of steatite pots at or above 8,000 feet is extreme. Marceau found twelve upland sites with steatite vessels for every one site with an Intermountain pot, and, if we include the sites with steatite pots found in the Wind River Mountains in the years since Marceau did his research, this ratio would jump to 16 to 1. Clearly steatite pots are more common at higher elevations than are ceramic ones. By adding this information to the study of their distribution across space, we can confidently say that steatite pots are most frequently found in the higher mountains of northwestern Wyoming.[11]

THE SEARCH FOR A TIME FRAME

One of the questions most frequently asked about steatite pots is, "How old are they?" Marceau concludes that steatite vessel sites are older than sites with ceramic vessels, and although we tend to agree with him, at present the data are inconclusive. Many different factors play into the dating process, foremost among them the physical properties of an object on which a date is based. Although radiocarbon dating of organic materials—charcoal, for instance—usually produces an accurate estimate of a sample's age, a nonorganic object such as a potsherd with mineral temper and no plant or animal residue on the surface, or an object made of steatite, is dated by reference to other items of known age.

Archaeologists have been able to date many ceramic types because they have been found in deposits with burned bone or wood remnants that produce a reliable radiocarbon date. The ages of other ceramic styles have been based on judgments about whether their forms or other stylistic attributes resemble those of ceramics of known age. These attributes must be unambiguous before the style can be assigned to a particular period in a regional chronology. The classification "Intermountain pottery" is, unfortunately, not based on recognizable, exclusive attributes, and it is therefore difficult to assign pots or fragments with generalized features to this or any other particular time period. In fact, many potsherds that have been identified as Intermountain ware may actually be representatives of another pottery type.

One steatite pot whose age has been determined by radiocarbon analysis of the sooty contents adhering to its interior walls was less than 200 years old.[12] Of course, this date is based on an analysis of the food residue produced the last time the pot was used. Because the steatite pot may have been an heirloom that had been kept for several generations, its actual age could be as much as 300 or 400 years. Unfortunately, the vast majority of the steatite pots in museum collections were found and removed by hikers or artifact collectors before their archaeological context could be studied and any artifacts with which they were associated could be dated.

Another problem is the scarcity of steatite vessels in the few sites in the region that have been excavated. The Mummy Cave site in Wyoming, just east of Yellowstone Park, contained 1,100-year-old steatite beads but no pots. Birdshead Cave, a site in the Owl Creek Mountains at the south end of the Bighorn Basin in Wyoming, contained steatite pot fragments in association with an iron fragment. The proximity of these artifacts to each other has been used by some archaeologists to justify the conclusion that all steatite pots were made fairly recently. But as Marceau has pointed out, the upper levels of the Birdshead Cave deposit were not, in fact, distinct; they had been mixed, a situation that led the cave's excavator, Wesley Bliss, to question whether the association of steatite and iron fragments was all that firm.[13]

Nonetheless, at the time of publication, only a few steatite pots have been dated, and the results point to a recent origin. In contrast, the oldest pottery in Wyoming has been determined to be 500 years old, while in Montana and Idaho the earliest ceramics are anywhere from 800 to 1,000 years old. Although definitive dating techniques appear to have answered one question, at least for now, the question remains whether Intermountain pottery was made by the Shoshone or by some other group.

LOOKING AHEAD

To a large extent, the picture of Sheep Eater lifeways that is presented in this book reflects activities and behaviors that were documented by a range of visitors to the Yellowstone area over the past 200 years, during which Sheep Eaters were known to be engaged in food procurement, processing, and cooking in their steatite pots. Further discussion of the antiquity of these vessels must be deferred until such time as more information on the subject is available. Meanwhile, in the next chapter we will drawn again on accounts by witnesses who recorded in their journals and memoirs just how splendid the fully outfitted Sheep Eaters appeared to those who were fortunate enough to encounter them.

8

||||

Fleeced and Greased: Sheep Eater Clothing and Presentation of Self

Myths and legends describing the exploits of so-called Little People are a feature of the folklore of most western Indian nations, including those in Wyoming and Montana. According to many stories, the little folk were expert hunters, but being diminutive, they were often easy prey for eagles.[1] Tales have continued to evolve, sometimes incorporating details meant to enhance credibility, as in the accounts that purport to describe a cave where someone found "perfectly formed" dwarf-size mummies. The burials, of course, are always sent to a local university or to the Smithsonian for analysis, only to have both the specimens and the research results mysteriously disappear.[2]

Joseph Medicine Crow, a remarkable historian who has collected accounts of the Crow Indians over the past seventy years, has suggested that, through the years, the Little People have become confused in the popular imagination with the Sheep Eaters.[3] Why there should be a conflation of legendary figures and historically documented peoples like the Sheep Eaters is unknown, but there are many instances in the historical record in which the beholder's eye has been shown to be in need of corrective lenses. The transformation of Sheep Eaters—in actuality a robust people of medium height who had adapted to their mountain terrain by developing the large lung capacity typical of persons living in the Andes and Himalayas—into "pygmies" represents a terrible distortion of the facts.[4]

The archaeological evidence of Sheep Eater stature, we have to report, is not as definitive as we would like, primarily because the human burials that have been excavated in known Sheep Eater territory do not contain materials or characteristics that can be confidently identified as particular to any one ethnic group. There are, however, human remains from at least three individuals for which a good argument about their Sheep Eater ethnicity can be made. The first is a burial found in 1963 in an extremely dry cave in the mountains west of Cody, Wyoming. There, postburial conditions caused the body to desiccate, preserving its flesh and hair and promoting the belief that it was a mummy. As it is traditional in archaeology for sites to be named for their location, or the person who discovered them, or their most noteworthy artifact or feature, it is not surprising that for the past forty years this site has been called Mummy Cave.

The preserved body had been wrapped for burial in a sheepskin robe with the hair on the inside, and because public interest in the remains was strong, it was initially placed on display at the Buffalo Bill Historical Center in Cody. After a time, interest in the exhibit waned, and the body was transferred to a storage area that housed other items in the museum's collections. After reposing in relative peace for twenty years, in 1987 the "mummy" came to the attention of several medical doctors who were members of the Paleopathology Association, a scholarly organization that conducts research on diseases, disabilities, and causes of death in prehistoric populations. Radiographs, multidimensional tomograms, and CT scans produced images of the body's entire anatomy, from the skull to the extremities, and allowed researchers to make observations on the age, sex, stature, and physical condition of the remains.[5]

Reports describe the Mummy Cave individual as a 5'5" male who died in his mid- to late thirties. His joints show no evidence of arthritis, nor is there any indication that he died from a traumatic injury. Analysis of the stomach contents reveals that he had eaten both meat and plant foods shortly before his death. The body was found lying on its right side with its knees flexed against the chest, facing the back wall of the cave. It had been buried in a shallow pit scooped out of the cave floor and was enclosed by a low rock wall. Dirt had been thrown over the body, and, over time, a thick deposit of cultural debris had accumulated on top.[6] The remains have been radiocarbon dated to between AD 670 and 890. Although no grave offerings were found with the body, the cultural level in which it was recovered included very distinctive corner-notched arrow points, along with a variety of chipped-stone tools used for cutting, scraping, drilling, and engraving. Bone and antler tools were also found in the same level, associated with perishable items like feathers and basketry.

The Mummy Cave burial is similar in size and physique to human remains recovered at other locations in Wyoming; these burials include three individuals from Yellowstone National Park that were discovered in the course of construction projects. One of them—referred to as the Condon burial because David Condon, a park ranger and naturalist, studied it—belonged to a 5'5" adult male of medium build who died in his late thirties or early forties.[7] Another burial has been identified as a woman, 5' to 5'1" tall, who died between the ages of forty and fifty. Both the male and female burials include dog skeletons, and a variety of chipped-stone tools had been placed in association with the male body.

The convergence of two types of evidence—the location of these burials in traditional Sheep Eater territory and the fact that Sheep Eaters are known to have been buried with their dogs—supports the claim that these are Sheep Eater burials.[8] The individuals were neither puny nor elfin but, rather, were people of medium height with relatively robust bodies. There was even the occasional statuesque Sheep Eater, such as the medicine man and guide Togwotee, who in 1883 led President Chester Arthur and his party on a tour through Yellowstone National Park. At 6'2" Arthur was one of the country's tallest presidents, and he topped Togwotee in height by a mere two inches.

It is important to remember that human morphology, particularly stature, has reflected directional change throughout the history of the human species. The average height of nineteenth-century European males, for example, was less than their twenty-first-century progeny, but it was remarkably consistent with contemporaneous Sheep Eaters. Statistics indicate that the average Victorian-era gentleman was 5'5", the same as Harry Houdini, Pablo Picasso, Nikita Khrushchev, and Denver Nuggets guard Earl Boykins—none of whom have had to endure the embarrassment of being referred to by the P-word.

Sheep Eater Style

Personal adornment is one of the characteristics that distinguishes human beings from their hominid ancestors—and from other mammalian species, for that matter. Although elephants given paper and crayons by their zookeepers have sometimes produced interesting sketches, their artistic expression has not been known to include embellishment of their own bodies, unless we include Babar and Celeste and their sailor-suit-wearing offspring. But if a parade of everyone from Adam and Eve to the supermodel darlings of our day were to traipse by, arranged in terms of the simplicity or elaborateness of their dress and presentation of self, Sheep Eater men and women would definitely not be among the minimalist ranks—those dressed in "basic black" or its equivalent—nor would they be found at the over-the-top end of the fashion spectrum.

Sheep Eater hairstyles tended to be simple. By looking at historical photographs we can see that men and women had straight black hair that they parted in the center. Although they started to braid their hair after moving out of the mountains, originally it was allowed to fall to about shoulder length or slightly longer. Both men and women might have short bangs, and sometimes the remaining hair was pulled back into a ponytail or tied into two equal queues on either the side of the face.[9] Women would sometimes put red paint along their parts, and men often wore feathers tied loosely in their hair.

Mountain Shoshone body decoration would be considered fairly conservative, at least in comparison to the colorful displays by human peacocks at rock concerts and shopping malls today. The men were clean shaven, and neither men nor women pierced their noses, ears, or other body parts. Tattooing was not prevalent, although circles on the forehead or cheeks were occasionally made by puncturing the skin and filling the wounds with grease and soot. Both men and women decorated their faces with red paint made from mixing ochre and grease, and young girls sometimes made facial patterns with bluish black or white clay-based paint.[10]

Then as now, beads were a popular form of self-adornment. Both men and women wore beaded necklaces, pendants, and hair ornaments, and seven beads or pendants recovered at Mummy Cave reflect some of the variation in decorative items. Two flat disk beads about three-quarters of an inch in diameter are made of semitranslucent green steatite, and one is incised with parallel horizontal lines as added decoration. A dark green steatite pendant about one and three-quarter inches long has a hole on one end and is incised with six horizontal lines on one side and seven on the other. A tubular bone bead, three-quarters of an inch long, has an incised line around the middle. Two flat bone pendants, each one-inch long, have holes near one end, while a flat, oval-shaped piece of mother-of-pearl—one and three-sixteenth inches long by one-half inch wide—has holes in both ends.[11] The mother-of-pearl would have come from a local freshwater species, but the Sheep Eaters also had access through trade to shells from California and Oregon.

Some of the best sartorial commentary comes from the journal of Meriwether Lewis, who noted that the Sheep Eaters used feathers for personal decoration. This practice is difficult to confirm archaeologically because feathers are often too fragile to survive the postburial process. Sometimes, though, it is possible to determine whether those that have been recovered in archaeological deposits were used for decoration or a more practical purpose. For example, feathers in Layer 36 at Mummy Cave appear to have been trimmed in preparation for use as part of the fletching of an arrow. Lewis also reported that elk tooth beads, fish bone beads, and bear claw necklaces were popular adornments; women and children apparently preferred to wear elk teeth, whereas men seemed to favor the larger, more imposing bear claws.

The most unusual items of personal adornment found on the human remains at Mummy Cave are ear bobs or "medallions," each made of a piece of rabbit fur that had been gathered at the center with loops of sinew and then fluffed out into a circle, four inches in diameter. They looked very festive, like the fancy bows that often provide the final flourish on gift packages. Several twisted loops of rabbit fur were also attached to the medallion, which was itself then tied around an ear with a loop of sinew.[12]

DRESSING THE PART

The name *Sheep Eaters* was conferred on the Mountain Shoshone because of the perception that "you are what you eat." But the Tukudika could just as well have been called the *Sheep Wearers*, for although they used the hides from more than a dozen animals when making the elements of their wardrobe, it was bighorn sheep hides that were prized for men's shirts and women's dresses.[13] This is primarily because they were the correct thickness and color for making fine buckskin and also because they were relatively easy to transform into clothing. More often than not, Sheep Eaters trapped bighorns and then killed them with clubs, so the hides had few arrow holes or other humanly caused imperfections that a tailor would have to work around. Sheep Eaters processed more hides and made more clothing than they needed, and,

Figure 8.1. A Sheep Eater woman scraping a hide. Bighorn sheep hides are the right thickness for making excellent clothing. The Sheep Eaters used a tanning process that produced superior hides much sought after by neighboring tribes at trading encounters. Illustration by Davíd Joaquín.

because they were renowned as world-class furriers, their appearance with their wares at regional trading fairs was eagerly anticipated.

In the time-honored, multistage process of turning a sheep's hide into a finely tailored garment, which involves both physical manipulation and the application of chemicals, women were the primary artisans (Figure 8.1). First, the skin was removed from an animal carcass and placed on a large tripod frame, where it was left at least overnight.[14] The next day—or whenever the woman responsible for tanning the hide was ready—it was placed on a forked stick, skin side out, and leaned against a tree. At this point, any remaining bits of flesh and fat were removed, and the hide was then submerged in a nearby creek for several days. When it was decided that the hide was "ready"—an intuitive judgment based on years of experience—it was put back on a forked stick and again leaned against a tree, this time with the hair side out. The hair was then removed with a handheld scraping tool called a *teshoa*, made from a split-cobble flake, by pulling the tool across the hide like a drawknife.[15] After another soaking in the creek, the hide was spread on the ground with what had once been the hairy side upward, and the artisan pounded the surface with a large round rock, sometimes for the better part of a day.

All that elbow grease had a softening effect on the hide, but it still required an additional overnight soak to prepare it for the finishing touches. The next day the hide was again placed on the frame, given a final scraping with the sharp edge of a *teshoa* to remove any remaining tiny surface veins, and then coated with one of nature's finest and most accessible tanning agents—animal brains. The application of the acids and emulsified oils in brains breaks down a hide's tough fibers and gives the skin the supple, durable properties desirable in clothing. Whereas other Indian groups used only one sheep brain at this stage of processing, Sheep Eaters were well known for using two for each hide.[16] The lubricated hide was then placed in the sun, which accelerated the absorption of tanning agents, and then, finally, placed in water overnight for the last time. In the morning, it was fastened to a tree at one end and twisted to squeeze out as much water as possible. When nearly dry, the hide was attached to the tree at the remaining end and stretched into shape. Once a hide had been prepared correctly, it would never revert to rawhide and was ready for use, although sometimes it might be smoked, which produced a golden bronze color and, it was claimed, made hides waterproof.

The end product of all this processing was called *buckskin*, whether the hide had originally belonged to a sheep, an elk, or a deer. The finished hide was often folded along the backbone, and the legs were cut off to leave a rectangular piece that was well suited for clothing. The leg pieces themselves, as well as other scraps, were cut into thin strips and used as thread, as was sinew from the shoulder area of the sheep or deer.

Now the artistry involved in designing and tailoring clothing could begin. Using a bone awl that would have been made from one of several different animal bones, a seamstress would punch a series of holes through two pieces of buckskin and push through a thread to make a running stitch along the seam. An elk astragalus, or heel bone, was popular as the raw material for an awl because it is T-shaped, which made it easier to hold and push through the hides. Bone awls in the upper layers of Mummy Cave included one made from a split piece of bighorn sheep tibia that had circles and lines incised on it for decoration. Another was made from a large bighorn ulna that had a hole through the butt end, and several others came from unidentified mammal scapulae.[17] Women would have carried two or three of these awls, each sharpened to a needlelike point, in a buckskin pouch on their belt.

There are few examples of Mountain Shoshone apparel in museum collections, but fortunately, Meriwether Lewis (whose attention to frontier costume makes him the Elsa Klench of his day) included in his journal a detailed description of the clothing worn by the Shoshone he met in 1805. Although Great Basin Shoshone were noted for their minimal investment in personal attire, Lewis considered Sheep Eater garments to be some of the finest worn by any of the western tribes.[18] He was especially impressed with their tippets, or fur cloaks, which were so skillfully made of tanned, luxurious skins that it is likely that even Queen Victoria would have considered them regal raiment.

The tippet collar was made from a single otter skin, trimmed to about four or five inches wide, with the nose and eyes forming one end, and the tail the other, a style later popularized by chic matrons in the 1930s and 1940s. The body of the tippet was made from 100 to 200 ermine skins (the white winter pelt of the least weasel), from which a strip down the back was cut, rolled, and sewn around a yucca cord, each ending up about the size of a large porcupine quill. The ermine "quills" were then joined together in twos or threes and attached to the lower edge of the otter collar. Further embellishment included ermine tail tassels that were sewn to show off their black tips and abalone shell disks that were attached to the center of the collar. The completed tippet was a majestic rather than everyday garment that would have outshone the ceremonial regalia associated with the House of Lords. Although it was designed to be worn by men over their shirts, falling over the shoulders almost to the waist, the circumstances calling for such fancy wear have not been described, leaving posterity somewhat in the dark about this aspect of Sheep Eater attire (see Plate 6).[19]

If time travel enabled us to tour a frontier emporium devoted to Sheep Eater clothing, in the men's department we would find shirts made of the dressed skins of deer, antelope, bighorn, and elk. Lewis's journal tells us that elk hide shirts were the least common and bighorn shirts the most prevalent. A shirt was collarless and fitted loosely around the chest, which sometimes required that it be made of two or more skins, depending on the girth of the wearer. The animal's tail would have been left on the hide and was usually folded and allowed to hang loosely down the back of the garment. More often than not, side seams were fringed, fringe serving both as decoration and to wick off water that would otherwise soak through the hide.

Strips of dressed hide were sewn into a yoke at the shoulders, to which the body pieces and sleeves were attached, and were often decorated with porcupine quillwork. Quillwork also embellished the side seams to within five or six inches of the armhole, at which point the sides were left open. Tubular sleeves were attached to the shoulders and yoke and were left open to the elbow, below which they were tightly fitted to the forearm. This design allowed the wearer to pull his arms through the open side seams to remove the shirt. The bottom of the shirt was either fringed or trimmed with the forelegs and neck of the animal, if these had been left on the hide during processing.

Men also wore a set of leggings, each legging being made from an entire buckskin hide that was sewn into a tubular shape. At the waist, each hide's tail and back legs were wrapped around a belt, which held up the leggings, while the neck extended down the back of the wearer's calf, sometimes as far as the heel or even touching the ground. Although the Basin Shoshone did not use coyote skins for any purpose because of their mythological relationship with these canids, coyote skins on which the fur remained and to which quillwork decoration had been applied around the ankle were often used by Sheep Eaters for winter leggings.[20] Breechcloths or loincloths were apparently optional gear but, when used, were made from antelope or sheep hides. Those men whose wardrobes did not include undergarments would pull up their leggings high enough to conceal their private parts.

We live in an age in which the garments worn by women far exceed in variety and range of formality those worn by men, but a tour of the women's department of our mythical emporium would demonstrate that Sheep Eater women's clothing was characterized by

Figure 8.2. A woman's buckskin dress with a bird foot hanging from one shoulder and claws hanging from the other. Note the projectile point—a talisman—fastened at the neck. Collected in the Utah Territory between 1871 and 1879. Catalogue No. 19828, Department of Anthropology, Smithsonian Institution.

simplicity in design and purpose (Figure 8.2). Women wore loose dresses ornamented with quillwork and constructed very much like men's shirts, except that they had an attached lower panel extending to the knees (see Plate 7). A yoke was dispensed with, and the front and back sections of the garment were sewn together at the shoulders. Side seams were open under the arms so the wearer could pull her dress on over her head and then slide her arms into the sleeves through the openings. This design also provided women with easy side access for nursing babies. In our Sheep Eater emporium there would have been no lingerie or sportswear sections, because women wore neither underclothing nor leggings.

For warmth, both men and women wore robes made from a variety of tanned skins with the hair still on them. Elk, deer, antelope, bighorn, and bison skins were all used, although Sheep Eaters were most fond of robes made from two wolf hides. As wolves were difficult to track and kill, Sheep Eaters prepared their hides with the greatest of care, making robes that were considered the finest examples of Sheep Eater handicrafts.[21] Given their access to an abundant supply of bighorn hides, Sheep Eaters probably made many robes from this species. We know that the human burial in Layer 36 of Mummy Cave was wrapped in a bighorn sheep robe, which suggests that these robes were so important that they were taken to the afterlife.

Less commonly used animals included beaver and marmot, but highly prized robes were also made from strips of rabbit skins that were twisted and woven into poncho-like capes and worn for all occasions. Major Howard Egan, who lived among the Shoshone from 1846 to 1878, describes the practical properties of these robes: "When hung around the neck the person so clothed can stand in a hard rain or snow storm and not one drop of wet will pass through the robe. They are wind and rain proof and almost cold proof."[22] Fragments of tightly twisted rabbit fur strips in Layer 36 of Mummy Cave demonstrate that rabbits were accessible and probably captured in large numbers during forays into the lower-altitude basins of their range.[23] Another possible source of rabbit fur might have been trade with other Shoshone, who spent a greater part of the year in the lowlands.

Robes were worn like a cape, left open in warm weather and belted to keep them closed in the coldest weather. Because robes were used for bedding at night, they were not decorated with quillwork, although pieces of red-colored bighorn hide in Mummy Cave suggest that the skin of some robes may have been dyed.[24]

In the accessories and footwear department, we would have found men's caps made from coyote skins, lined with fur and cut so that they protected the ears.[25] Headbands were made of fox skin but were worn infrequently. Footgear included moccasins cut from tough badger skins or sometimes from elk hides, although softer deer-hide moccasins were also worn. A pair of Sheep Eater boots, made between AD 670 and AD 890, was found in Mummy Cave cached beneath a grinding stone, as though the owner intended to return and use them another season (Figure 8.3). One of the boots was in better condition than its mate and was fitted with a bent U-shaped stick insert to help retain its shape.[26] The foot section of the boot had been made from four pieces of bighorn sheep hide with the hair intact.

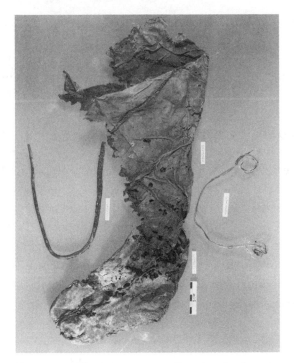

Figure 8.3. A boot or moccasin found in the deposits at Mummy Cave. This example and its mate, which was in poorer condition, were apparently stored in the cave and never retrieved by their owner. Photograph courtesy of the Buffalo Bill Historical Center, Cody, Wyoming; P.29.1.38.2.

To replicate this boot today, one would sew the sheep hide pieces together along both sides and down the center of the sole and vamp in the following sequence: first, sew together the edge and sole seams with the hide sides inside, then turn the pieces hide side out and sew the longitudinal vamp seam from the outside. The hair, now inside, will provide warmth and help cushion the wearer's foot from the seam running down the length of the sole. The final step is to make the boot's shaft, or upper section, by folding a sheep hide so that the fleece side is out and then sewing it into a tube that is then attached to the foot portion with a running overhand stitch. The finished boot is completely fleece lined and, looked at from the outside, has a hide "shoe" for durability and a fleece shank for warmth and style. Once on the foot, the shank would be wrapped with a two-ply twisted buckskin lacing for a snug fit.

Even though such a design would provide good protection for the foot in cold snow-packed conditions, grass boot liners found in the same cultural level as the boots at Mummy Cave appear to have been used for added warmth. Living year-round in mountainous terrain makes it likely that Sheep Eaters would have considered boots were more often a better type of footwear than moccasins, although summer boots would have been made of hairless buckskin, minus the unnecessary thermal properties of fleece.

For those readers interested in speculations about the tracks these boots would have left, we know that the toe-to-heel seam on the sole would have divided the tracks in half and left what might be called a "broken track" print. During the attempt by Lewis and Clark to find a route over the Rocky Mountains, they were told about a group of fierce mountain Indians called the "Broken Moccasins," who had the reputation of living in caves like bears, eating roots, and stealing horses (for food) from all who passed their way.[27]

Looking Ahead

Dressed in their practical yet elegant tailored fur-and-skin garments, Sheep Eater men, women, and children were prepared to cope with the rigors of their environment. They were accompanied in all life-sustaining activities—and sometimes on that great journey to the world beyond—by their dogs, whose contribution to Sheep Eater life we will discuss in the next chapter.

9

||||

Barkeology, or, What We Know about Sheep Eater Dogs

Humans and dogs have been best friends for 15,000 years, so conclude researchers studying the evolutionary history of the ancestors of Spot and Lassie. Several different analyses of canine mitochondrial DNA—one a worldwide sample of more than six hundred domestic dogs—indicate that groups of hunters in East Asia were the first to selectively breed wolves, whose offspring came in from the cold to a life within the circle of the human family.[1] In return for a share of the daily provender and a place by the fire, members of the newly emerging species *Canis familiaris* became less aggressive and more docile, obeying commands that they sit, stay, and fetch. Recent research also suggests that as part of the domestication process, dogs developed the ability to interpret human actions and signals with more sophistication than either wolves raised in captivity or, more surprisingly, chimpanzees, humanity's closest living relative.[2]

The effort involved in breeding, training, and feeding prehistoric dogs was unlikely to have been altruistic. According to Jennifer Leonard of the National Museum of Natural History, there must have been some "advantage to having this domestic animal at [such an] early time period."[3] The range of services provided by dogs in the distant past, as well as during the nineteenth-century Sheep Eater era, demonstrates that the celebrated bond between the human and canine species may have had as much to do with their being business partners as friendly companions.

Sheep Eater dogs worked for a living, so it is not surprising that, fully grown, they were large and robust animals. Their coloring revealed that there were wolves in their family tree, not only long ago but also more recently. The clan's resemblance to wolves has been described in numerous historical accounts, including that of John

Richardson, who wrote in 1836 that "the wolves and the domestic dogs of the fur countries are so much like each other, that it is not easy to distinguish them at a small distance.... The offspring of the wolf and the Indian dog are prolific, and are prized by the voyagers as beasts of draught, being stronger than an ordinary dog."[4]

Frederick Kurz traveled in the region in 1851, and he, too, noted that these dogs "differ very slightly from wolves, howl like them, do not bark, and not infrequently mate with them."[5] Kurz's sketch of several dogs, one of them pulling a travois, is the only remaining eyewitness image of a member of this tough breed, which the artist noted was able to haul travois loads of 70 pounds and to carry packs weighing as much as 50 pounds.

Sheep Eater Dogs

Neither the archaeological nor the historical record offers a good account of the ongoing contribution made by wolves to the gene pool of the domesticated dog, but it is well known that Indians intentionally made their dogs accessible to wolves for breeding on the northern Plains.[6] This may have had something to do with the fact that members of the Canidae family, to which both wolves and dogs belong, run on their toes instead of on their heels like other carnivorous species, such as bears, an adaptation that enables them to run down and capture their prey.[7] Reinvigoration of their dogs' cursorial abilities would have been strong motivation for Sheep Eater hunters periodically to introduce lupine genes into the bloodlines of their four-legged partners (Figure 9.1).

Although Sheep Eater dogs are no longer extant as a breed, possible skeletal examples were discovered more than twenty years ago in human burials in Yellowstone National Park. Faunal analyst William Haag has studied dozens of Indian dogs from various parts of North America, and his examination of the Yellowstone Park skeletons established that, in life, the dogs ranged in height from medium to tall, placing them between coyotes and wolves on a scale of stature. Their frame was robust and supported a large head that was comparable in width to that of a wolf.[8] When Danny Walker, an archaeologist and bone expert at the University of Wyoming, examined the same skeletons, he discovered a characteristic that Haag did not record. Walker noted that the tips of the dogs' teeth had been ground down or

Figure 9.1. A typical Sheep Eater dog and its master. These large, part-wolf dogs were very important to the Sheep Eater way of life. Horses were not well suited to the high mountainous terrain occupied by the Sheep Eaters. Illustration by Davíd Joaquín.

knocked off, presumably by their owners, which would have effectively kept the dogs from chewing through leather trappings and would have controlled their biting.[9]

Ethnographic and historic descriptions of the behavior of North American Indian dogs are not always complimentary. One colorful account by the American fur trapper Warren Ferris describes a Pend d'Oreille camp near Deer Lodge, Montana, in 1832. Ferris complains that the dogs would steal every scrap of unattended food and eat anything made of leather. He was so exasperated trying to fend off the scoundrels that he threw his axe at them. Retrieving his axe, he discovered "a scurvy cur, coolly trotting off with my saddle bags, which the rascal had stolen from within the protection of the tent. It is needless to say that I pursued and recovered them, but ere I could return to my post, I perceived three large fellows marching leisurely homeward, with a bale of dried meat, weighing not less than forty pounds."[10]

Ferris writes that the members of the Pend d'Oreille camp were reduced to a starvation diet and survived primarily on roots. Their dogs' behavior indicates that they were similarly nutritionally deprived and probably received only scraps of leftover, poor-quality food. Unfortunately, Ferris's account of human and canine misfortune is not that unusual in the historical literature of the nineteenth century.

In contrast, the quality of life and behavior of Sheep Eater dogs have been described in much more glowing terms, particularly by Osborne Russell, who recorded his encounter with a small group of Sheep Eaters in Yellowstone National Park in 1835.[11] The group consisted of six men, seven women, and eight to ten children, accompanied by thirty dogs. This is a ratio of more than two dogs to every adult and represents many mouths to feed. Russell also noted that the dogs appeared to be well fed, well behaved, and contented and that the mood of the camp was calm. Because it is well known that Sheep Eaters customarily fed their dogs before they themselves ate, there must have been enough food in camp to satisfy all appetites. Working dogs had to be healthy dogs, particularly because their labor was essential to Sheep Eater survival, so it is no wonder they were served first at dinnertime.

Russell made his observations only three years after Ferris had described the impoverished Pend d'Oreille in the same region, so it is unlikely that the difference in living standard between the two groups can be related to drought or some other vagary of nature that would have afflicted all the populations in the area equally. Historians record that groups of horse-riding and bison-hunting Indians on the Plains also suffered from starvation during this time period, which justifies the conclusion that by residing primarily in the mountains and exploiting without significant competition a hunting niche focused on bighorn sheep, Sheep Eater groups were able to maintain their well-being when other hunters, dependent for subsistence on other resources, were not.

What does history tell us about the job description of a Sheep Eater dog? First, like dogs everywhere today—whether in an apartment in the inner city or on a farmstead in New England—they were day and night watchmen. Imagine the uproar that thirty dogs would have made when aroused. Then as now, their vocalizations would have served a protective purpose, warning of the approach of another tribe's war party or driving off wild animals such as grizzly bears and mountain lions. Interestingly, with the increase in the past decade of grizzly bears in the Absaroka Mountains, there has been a significant increase in the number of outfitters and hunting guides who keep dogs in camp for warning and protection.

Sheep Eater dogs also represented skilled labor. The travois that they learned to bear usually consisted of a two-pole rig that was attached to them by a harness and supported a willow basket (Figure 9.2). This was not as elaborate as the device used by other tribes who had horses that could pull heavier loads. Sheep Eater children were not carried by a dog travois, presumably because of the possibility that, in response to the sight and smell of a prey animal such as a rabbit, the dogs might lose control and give chase, losing the child in the process. There is, in fact, a Crow Indian tale about just such an event in which the lost child is rescued and raised by the Little People, whom we mentioned in chapter 8.[12]

Dog travois was not suitable for travel through rough mountain terrain, and, at the margins of such areas, the travois would have been unhitched, and the load transferred to a pack. Poles may have been stashed by standing them upright against the limbs of a tree for use on another trip through the area. Poles, probably from horse travois, can be found standing like this in Yellowstone Park on the edges of the Lamar River valley, where transferring the loads in preparation for the trek off the Absaroka plateau would have been anticipated by travelers who were familiar with the terrain. The Lamar Valley is open, relatively flat, and easy to negotiate, and it may have been a traditional place to abandon the travois for the packs and vice versa, depending on which direction the party was traveling.

Trappers and travelers who visited Crow, Flathead, Nez Perce, and other western Indian groups in the 1800s all report that the use of dog travois survived into the historic era even among horse-riding tribes.[13] For those families not affluent enough to own and maintain horses, dog transport represented a cheaper alternative, especially for lighter loads such as carrying wood near camp. And, as Frank Roe has pointed out, dogs were more adept than horses at movement in heavy winter snow, and they could add their body warmth to the family bed on those nights when temperatures were below zero.[14]

In the 1930s Demitri Shimkin learned from a Sheep Eater informant that dog packs consisted of rawhide envelopes, or *parfleches*, that were lashed directly to a dog's back with a rawhide binding that was

Figure 9.2. A Sheep Eater dog pulling a dog travois. Illustration by Davíd Joaquín.

Figure 9.3. A Sheep Eater dog carrying a pack and wearing booties. Illustration by Davíd Joaquín.

strapped across the chest and under the belly.[15] Another strap went under the dog's tail to help secure the pack. In recent interviews with descendants of Sheep Eaters, one of us (Loendorf) learned that they even made rawhide booties for their dogs to wear in the winter to protect their feet from frostbite and prevent ice buildup between the toes (Figure 9.3).

Using historical accounts of various northern Plains tribes, Henderson compiled data on the size and weight of the loads that dogs were expected to carry and the distances—which varied with the difficulty of the terrain—they typically covered on a trek.[16] In fairly flat landscapes, dogs were capable of carrying 35- to 50-pound loads for up to thirty miles. After a one-hour rest, it was not unusual for a dog to be ready to hit the trail again. Carrying a pack in mountainous country required much more energy, so a pack dog could not be expected to cover more than five to ten miles a day. It was widely accepted that as long as dogs had sufficient water and did not overheat, their strength and endurance made them superior to horses. It has been reported that some Plains Indians castrated their dogs in an effort to make them more docile and tolerant of the demands associated with carrying or pulling heavy loads, but Sheep Eater dogs were apparently cooperative workers without surgical intervention.[17]

Sheep Eater dogs were not led by leashes but, rather, were controlled entirely by voice commands, and like some of the legendary dogs of the past—Old Yeller and White Fang—Sheep Eater dogs were named for their coloring.[18] When a group moved from place to place, the air must have been full of sounds evoking the more somber end of the visual spectrum ("Faster Spotted One!" "Stop Big Blackie!"). Any person who has hiked the Absaroka and Wind River mountains will appreciate the important role played by these forgotten canine bearers and offer homage to any creature or technological gadget that might assist the trek up a mountain pass.

The partnership between Sheep Eaters and their dogs was most apparent when it was time to provision the family. In fact, the image in the popular imagination of a solitary hunter and his dog has been derived from the long history of such human–canid cooperation in the hunt. Scott and Fuller have summarized some of the historical evidence for such teamwork, beginning in 1389 when a complaint was made in the English Parliament that laborers and their greyhounds were wasting too much time hunting.[19] Most of the breeds that parade with aplomb in front of judges at the Westminster Dog Show are the product of specialized skills that hunters needed their dogs to bring to the hunt. The bloodhounds' highly developed sense of smell helped them chase down wounded game. Terriers were bred to invade the dens and burrows of foxes and badgers and flush out their residents. Setters were stealthy, creeping up on flocks of birds until their startled prey took to the air, where waiting hunters could shoot them.

The men and dogs of Team Sheep Eater primarily pursued bighorn sheep and deer and, as described more fully in chapter 12, would work collaboratively to herd and then capture their prey. The terms governing the relationship between humans and their domesticated animals among groups in the Plains and Rocky Mountain regions are demonstrated by the fact that Sheep Eater dogs were well rewarded for their labor with generous portions of the meat they helped their owners obtain. On the other hand, Plains equestrian tribes kept an estimated six to twelve dogs per family—about 30 percent less than Mountain Shoshone—because their dogs, who had the same nutritional needs as Sheep Eater dogs, were not active participants in provisioning families and so did not earn their keep to the same extent.[20]

A different kind of reason for having fewer canids in their camps was offered by a Plains Shoshone group to Captain William A. Jones during his travels through the Wind River Valley in 1873. Jones, the leader of a U.S. engineering expedition to find a suitable route into Yellowstone Park, considered it unusual that the Plains Shoshone had so few dogs in their camps but was told by a group's medicine man that the nightly barking of many dogs would drive away the spirits of the departed.[21]

The respect that Sheep Eaters had for their dogs' intelligence and prowess is exemplified by the fact that two of the canine skeletons from the excavation in Yellowstone Park described earlier were buried with an adult male and one accompanied the burial of an adult female. That both men and women were interred with dogs suggests that both genders greatly valued the contribution that dogs made to all aspects of life and thought of their company as essential to the afterlife. This bond was forged early, as Sheep Eater children played with pups and raised them as friends whom they loved throughout their lives.

Dogs in Burials and Petroglyphs

The interment of people accompanied by their animals has a long history. In Israel, dogs appear to have been placed intentionally in human burials as long ago as 12,500 BP, during what is called the Natufian period, and a recent discovery on Cyprus of the deliberate placement of a large cat in a human burial accompanied by an unusual number of grave goods has been dated to approximately 9,500 years ago.[22] More recently, in the equestrian cultures of the Plains, it was also not unusual for a warrior to be buried with a favorite horse. Among the Blackfoot, for example, as many as twenty horses were put to death at their owner's funeral, although it was rare for a horse to be sacrificed upon the death of a woman.[23]

Most of what is written about Sheep Eater lifeways is based on secure knowledge, but the contention that images resembling dogs in many of the panels of the Dinwoody petroglyphs are in fact to be interpreted literally is somewhat problematic. James Stewart was the first researcher to point out the similarity between these four-legged figures and Sheep Eater dogs as described in the ethnohistoric literature. Stewart contends that lines attached to the engraved dogs represent leashes, and—apparently because wolves and coyotes do not have the habit of lifting their tails—he cites the upraised tails on some petroglyph quadrupeds as additional evidence that the figures represent domesticated dogs.[24] It is probably unwise to attach too much credibility to this speculation because the presence of what we consider to be anatomical and behavioral characteristics of living animals may actually have been a means for depicting supernatural occurrences. Nevertheless, the figures do look like dogs, and the petroglyphs are almost certainly the work of the Mountain Shoshone.

Looking Ahead

As we have seen, Sheep Eater families and their dogs worked as a team. Dogs acted as an early-warning system by barking at the approach of visitors to camp, they carried heavy packs when families were on the move, and they were partners in the hunt. In the next chapter we will discuss another essential component of the Sheep Eater hunting effort, the bighorn bow, and describe its virtues and manufacture.

10

The Call of the Bow: Sheep Eater Bow Making and Its Superior Result

WITH AN ELK-HORN BOW, THEY SOMETIMES DRIVE AN ARROW
COMPLETELY THROUGH A BUFFALO, ITS PROPELLING POWER BEING
GREATER THAN THAT OF THE YEW BOW.

—*Alfred Jacob Miller, noted fur trade artist, making an observation
about Shoshone horn bows in 1837 (Miller 1951:60)*

August 29, 1911, was an exceptional day in the history of American anthropology. Outside a slaughterhouse near Oroville, California—a town about sixty miles north of Sacramento—workers discovered a hungry, exhausted, middle-aged American Indian man, dressed in rags and speaking a language that no one could understand. After spending two days in jail, during which accounts of his exotic background and current circumstances made headlines in local and San Francisco newspapers, he was escorted by anthropologists Alfred Kroeber and Thomas Waterman to the anthropology museum at the University of California.

During the next four and a half years, Kroeber and his colleagues learned to communicate with the man, who told them that he was the last living member of his Yahi band. As was the case for almost all other groups of indigenous Californians, Yahi Indian populations had dwindled from the combined effects of Euro-American diseases, starvation resulting from incursions into Indian hunting territory, and outright genocidal attacks. Realizing that it was traditional for Indians not to reveal their own names, Kroeber and others at the museum began to call their guest "Ishi," the Yahi word for "man."

People who knew Ishi described him as gentle, good-natured, and eager to teach his guardians and the public alike about Yahi lifeways.[1]

He was gracious and welcoming to the many families who visited the museum on Sunday afternoons specifically to see him. He developed a particular friendship with Dr. Saxton T. Pope, an instructor in surgery at the University Medical School and a lifelong woodsman, who treated Ishi's persistent cough. Pope has written that "from the first weeks of our intimacy a strong friendship grew up between us, and I was from that time on his physician, his confidant, and his companion in archery. He often asked if I were not part Indian, which, although it is not a fact, I naively admitted I was."[2]

Pope's father was an army surgeon whose postings in remote areas of the southwestern frontier provided the boy with a childhood that, as he later described, was focused on outdoor life, often with Native American companions with whom he shared the "call of the bow." "I, too," Pope wrote, "shot the toy bows of boyhood; shot with Indian youths in the army posts of Texas and Arizona. We played the impromptu pageants of Robin Hood, manufactured our own tackle, and carried it about with unfailing fidelity."[3]

During his collegiate and early professional years, Pope's time and energy were consumed with academic study, followed by marriage and the demands of establishing a medical practice. Meeting Ishi, though, revived his passion for woodcraft and archery, and, after learning from Ishi the Indian way of bow making, Pope and his friend often went hunting together. Another person drawn into their circle was archery enthusiast Art Young, with whom Pope continued to travel widely, camp, and hunt with a bow long after Ishi died of tuberculosis in 1916 (Figure 10.1).

So confident were Pope and Young in their bow-making and hunting skills that in 1920 they used bows and arrows in Yellowstone Park to shoot and kill six grizzly bears, now on permanent display at the California Academy of Science.[4] On a six-month safari to Africa in the mid-1920s, their staggering list of trophies included Thompson gazelle, reedbuck, waterbuck, wildebeest, kongoni, eland, jackals, hyenas, assorted small game, and—the biggest prize of all—several African lions.[5] These two adventurers became legendary in the world of competitive archery, establishing scoring standards that were named in their honor and continue to be used by archers to determine world-record trophy animals.

As surfers chase the perfect wave, so archers search for the perfect bow, and Saxton Pope was no exception. But before we can describe his research and the preferences he developed, we need to present an abridged version of the terminology of archery as a complement to the illustration of a bow and its parts in Figure 10.2. Most bows are fairly simple devices. They are said to have a *back* (the part of the bow facing away from the archer) and a *belly* (the part facing toward the archer). A *bowstring* is attached at both *nocks*, or ends, of the bow. The section midway between the nocks, by which the archer holds the bow, is called the *grip*, and the parts above and below the grip are called the *limbs* or *arms*. If a bow is made from a single piece of wood or horn, it is called a *self bow*, and when it is made up of multiple attached pieces, it is referred to as a *composite bow*. Once the raw material from which the bow is to be made has been cut into long pieces ready for further refinement, the unfinished shape is called a *bow stave*. A person who has developed the skills necessary to take a bow stave and transform it into a finished implement is frequently referred to as a *bowyer*.

Figure 10.1. Saxton Pope (r.), medical doctor, outdoorsman, and authority on hunting with a bow and arrow, with his colleague Art Young. Photograph courtesy of the Pope-Young Club.

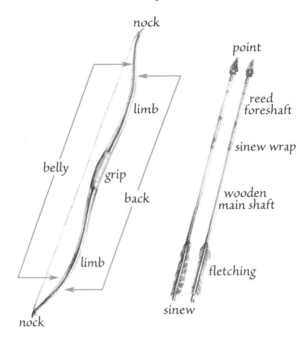

Figure 10.2. Typical Sheep Eater bow and arrows with the parts identified. Illustration by Davíd Joaquín.

Special bows are augmented by layers of sinew, in which case they are called *backed bows* (Figure 10.3). *Sinew* is the fibrous animal tissue that attaches muscles to bones and cartilage and to other muscles. The sinew most often used in bow making comes from an animal such as a deer, whose longest and most useful pieces occur on either side of the spine along its entire length. When a bowstring has been fitted into the end notch of an arrow but the archer has not yet begun to take aim, the bow's grip—relative to that arrow—is somewhere near the arrow's midpoint. When the archer pulls on the bowstring and releases the arrow, the amount of force, measured in pounds, required to draw the bowstring to its full extension is called the bow's *draw weight* or *pull strength.*

As part of Saxton Pope's exploration of the world of bow and arrow making, he tested the pull strength of many American Indian bows, as well as the penetrating power of replicated arrows in museum collections. His experiments with European wooden bows that had sinew backing convinced him that this combination of features produced the strongest bow, but because he did not include in his comparison

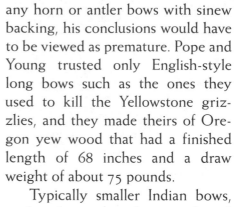

any horn or antler bows with sinew backing, his conclusions would have to be viewed as premature. Pope and Young trusted only English-style long bows such as the ones they used to kill the Yellowstone grizzlies, and they made theirs of Oregon yew wood that had a finished length of 68 inches and a draw weight of about 75 pounds.

Typically smaller Indian bows, made of wood and strengthened with sinew backing, had proved to be too weak for shooting large game, especially at distances of 40 to 50 yards. But had Pope and Young experimented with a Sheep Eater horn bow with sinew backing, they would have discovered that, at about half the length of the long bow, it would still have had 65 to 75 pounds or more of pull weight and, therefore, been competitive with their non-Indian bow of choice. Saxton Pope's books chronicle his experiences as a bowyer and marksman and remain widely cited today, in general deserving the high regard in which they are held. We have to take exception, however, to his conclusions that all Indian bows were

Figure 10.3. A sinew-backed bow with a thick, three-strand string and buckskin thong grip. This short bow, likely made by a Mountain Shoshone, is 97 centimeters long and was collected from the Idaho Territory before 1869. Catalogue No. 9044, Department of Anthropology, Smithsonian Institution.

used primarily for shooting small game such as rabbits and that the English long bow is the most effective bow ever made.

SHEEP EATER BOW MAKING

The secret underlying the impressive strength of a Sheep Eater bow was the application of sinew backing material. In fact, as replicator Bill Holm discovered with his first experimental sheep horn bow, which had only a rawhide backing, a horn bow made without sinew is not very strong and can simply shatter.[6] Sinew, on the other hand, provides strength, and its remarkable elasticity allows it to stretch in response to pressure and then snap back to its original shape when the pressure is released. In bow making, judgments about just how much of this essential material to use are critical. T. M. Hamilton learned that too many layers of sinew backing either will make wooden bow staves too strong to draw or can cause the bow to break down.[7] In contrast, horn or antler bow staves can be overdrawn and are capable of withstanding considerably higher crushing strengths because they have more elasticity from the extra sinew backing. Another factor in Sheep Eater bow strength is that the horn of the bow's belly is able to withstand more compression than wood.

One of the more comprehensive descriptions of Sheep Eater horn bows is found in the letters of Nathaniel Wyeth, a fur trader who in 1834 founded the Fort Hall trading post near Pocatello, Idaho. Writing to Henry Schoolcraft in 1848, Wyeth observed that

> they are about two feet ten inches long, and when unstrained have a curve backwards. They are of two parts, spliced in the centre by sturgeon glue, and deer-sinews, wound around a splice. The horn is brought into shape by heating and wetting, and worked smooth by scraping with sharp stones, and being drawn between two rough stones. A cross section of the bow would show the back side less convex than the front. At the centre the bow is spliced, before winding the splice, two deer-sinews, nearly entire, are strongly glued and secured by their butt ends; the small ends of them being outward at the ends of the bow. When they are strongly wound and secured, these sinews cover the whole width of the back of the bow. As a matter of ornament, the skin of a snake, commonly that of a rattlesnake, is glued externally on the back of the bow.[8]

All the mountain men, including Osborne Russell, who had helped Wyeth establish Fort Hall, recognized the power of these bows. According to Russell, the Sheep Eaters "were well armed with bows and arrows pointed with obsidian. The bows were beautifully wrought from Sheep, Bufalloe and Elk horns secured with Deer and Elk sinews and ornamented with porcupine quills and generally about 3 feet long."[9] As Russell notes, a bighorn sheep bow in good working order, with red, white, and black porcupine quills interlaced into decorative patterns—or a shiny rattlesnake skin on its back—was a thing of beauty.

Such bows were considered excellent trade items, although they were expensive and not usually for sale. George Belden, another mountain man and trapper, relates that, after considerable pleading, he was finally able to buy one for thirty-two dollars in gold, a huge sum at the time.[10] The passage of time may have led Belden to exaggerate the cost of his prized purchase, but it is well known that the bows were highly sought after at trading get-togethers.

CONTEMPORARY INVESTIGATION OF INDIAN BOWS

Alfred Jacob Miller, whose comments are quoted at the beginning of this chapter, was another traveler to the West who appreciated the effectiveness of an Indian horn bow (Figure 10.4). He painted two pictures of Shoshone hunters testing their bows and wrote that these remarkable weapons were "made of Elk-horn with sinew strongly cemented on the outer-side. Now if an Elk-horn was carried to the smartest Yankee we have, with a request to make a bow of it, the probability is, that for once, he would find it not convenient to attempt it."[11]

Despite Miller's caveat, some contemporary Yankees have attempted to make horn bows, and, to a person, these bow makers speak of them as a completely different class of weapon. For example, in 1984 W. J. "Jack" McKey, a hunter and outdoorsman from Darby, Montana, made a sheep horn bow that had the impressive draw weight of 100 pounds. McKey has written that such a bow is "a highly technical achievement [that] remains unmatched by modern sophistication to this day."[12] Tom Lucas, a well-known bowyer from Lander, Wyoming, feels the same way. By preference, Lucas's bows have a draw weight of about 60 pounds, but he explains that increasing the draw weight is as simple as adding another layer of sinew.[13] What he does not say is that

Figure 10.4. A drawing by the western artist Alfred J. Miller that shows Shoshone hunters testing their bows. Miller accompanied Sir William Drummond Stewart to the 1837 fur trade rendezvous on the Green River in Wyoming. Courtesy of the Walters Art Museum, Baltimore.

the draw weight of a Sheep Eater–like horn bow is concentrated in such a short bow length that it is very difficult to hold and aim the weapon. The only option is to pull and shoot in a single motion, hence the name "fast little bows."

Within the category of "bow, horn" the raw material provided by different horned species is not always comparable. Lucas claims that the horns of bighorn sheep make the best Sheep Eater–like bows. Experts agree that although using elk antlers produces slightly longer bows than using sheep horns, the extra length does not necessarily make the bow more effective. A number of elk antler bows from museum collections measured by Bill Holm ranged in length from 31.15 to 43.5 inches, whereas sheep horn bows in the same study ranged from 29.5 to 41.0 inches long.[14] At least one of these specimens was cut from a single antler or horn and measured 39 inches in length, but the majority were made by splicing together the horns of one sheep and fitting additional pieces across the joint.[15] No bison horn bows are known to exist, but Tom Lucas, who has made many bison horn spoons, thinks the horn is suitable for making a bow, although the process would be difficult because multiple splices would be required.

So far, only one horn bow has been found in an archaeological context. This specimen, currently on display at the Mountain Man Museum in Pinedale, Wyoming, was made from two sheep horns that were spliced at the grip. It was found tucked into a crack in the back of a cave in the Gros Ventre Mountains of western Wyoming, where for many years it had remained dry and free from rodent damage.[16] When archaeologist George Frison examined the bow, he concluded that the two conjoined sheep horns were very likely a matched pair from the same ram. In the years since the bow had been cached in the cave, the sinew backing had contracted, and, in the process, the broken joint was exposed on the bow's belly side.

In an attempt to learn more about the joint and with the cooperation of the Mountain Man Museum, one of us (Loendorf) was able to have the bow x-rayed (Figure 10.5). On the film it is clear that the grip end of one of the bow's limbs protrudes and is shaped like a tongue depressor, fitting into a slot or groove cut into the belly of the grip end of the other limb. A thin piece of horn, the width of the bow and about 15 centimeters in length, had been fitted to the back of the bow and glued across the joint. There was evidence that a second piece of horn may also have been fitted across the belly side of the joint, but it was missing. Apparently sinew had been wrapped around the joint originally, but at some time in the past a museum conservator had repaired and rewrapped the joint, in the process creating some ambiguity about just what the original joint looked like. The back of the bow was covered with several layers of 33-inch sinew, a practice common on all horn bows.

Loendorf was very curious about the age of the bow, and, again with the museum's cooperation, he arranged for three small fragments of sinew to be removed and submitted to the Rafter Radiocarbon Laboratory for accelerator mass spectrometry analysis. Before the dating process actually began, the laboratory scraped the sinew to remove its outer surface coating, immersed it in a cold solution of acid, and then gelatinized the sample. All dating techniques produce a range of possible ages for any sample, but after calculating all the permutations, it was determined that the bow dated to AD 1737, which seems

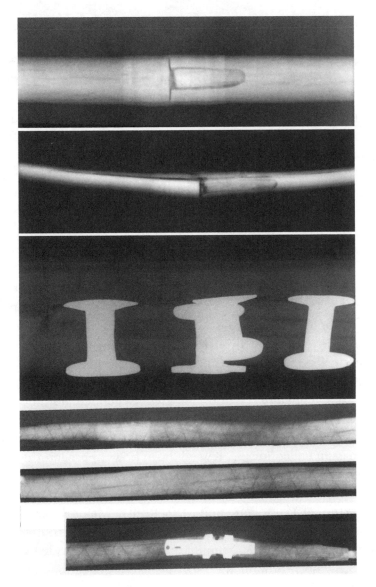

Figure 10.5. The upper two images are x-ray views of the horn bow on display at the Mountain Man Museum, Pinedale, Wyoming. The bow is broken at the joint. The upper view is from the belly side. Second from the top is a side view. Third from the top is an x-ray view of the side of the joint in the horn bow at the Montana Historical Society. The fasteners may be copper or lead. On the bottom is a view of the reinforcement in the elk horn bow at the North Dakota Historical Society. The metal is apparently part of a door lock. The bottom two bows may have been made for ceremonial purposes. X-rays made under the direction of Lawrence L. Loendorf.

reasonable and accurate. To place this artifact in its historical context, at about this time in the region's chronology—almost three hundred years ago—horses were first brought to the Wind River region.

A sinew-backed bighorn sheep horn bow in the collections of Grand Teton National Park has also been x-rayed.[17] This specimen measures 30 7/8 inches long by 1 1/8 inches wide at the grip and tapers to 9/16 inch wide and 1/2 inch thick at the nock. The x-ray of the bow joint was made by William King Peck, a medical doctor at St. John's Hospital in Jackson, Wyoming, and reveals the presence of iron nails that were used to repair a break in the bow.[18] Some unknown bowyer had drilled "two holes, about an inch apart, through which hand-forged nails had been run and crimped over the belly side. To make such a repair the sinew had to be soaked off first, then glued back in place. The final repair was to wrap the limb over the break with a thin band of sinew for about three inches."[19] Of special interest is that the x-ray reveals the bow to have been made from a single bighorn sheep horn. The bow is identified on the park's accession card as Crow or Nez Perce in origin, but the attribution is simply a guess.

Loendorf arranged for x-rays of two other horn bows, one of which is a magnificent sheep horn bow in the collections of the Montana Historical Society. The other is a less elegant elk horn bow in the collections of the North Dakota Historical Society (see Figure 10.5). The 43.5-inch Montana bow is the longest sheep horn bow known to be in museum collections. A few elk horn bows approach this length, but other sheep horn bows are 6 to 12 inches shorter. The Montana Historical Society accession card identifies the bow as coming from the collection of Major Peter and Mary Ronan. Major Ronan served as the superintendent of the Flathead Indian Reservation from 1885 until his death in 1892, and it is assumed that the bow was made by the Salish. The elk horn bow in the North Dakota collections, misshapen with age and thought to be Hidatsa in origin, is about 35 inches long.

MAKING A SHEEP EATER HORN BOW

Over the past decade as Loendorf has worked closely with Tom Lucas and followed the time-consuming steps involved in making a horn bow, Loendorf's appreciation for the craft and skill that Sheep Eater bowyers brought to their bow making has grown considerably. Lucas begins by removing both horns from a bighorn sheep skull and then

Figure 10.6. The soaking phase in the process of making a
horn bow. Hot springs and geysers in Sheep Eater territory
provided a constant source of hot water to soften the bighorn sheep horns used for bow making. Illustration by David
Joaquín.

soaking them in hot water until they are soft and pliable and relatively
easy to cut. He has learned from experience that the hotter the water,
the faster the horn will soften; moderately hot water is also effective,
but it takes longer.

Historical accounts record that Shoshone and Crow bow makers
successfully soaked and softened sheep horns in some of the many
local hot springs (Figure 10.6), but questions have since been raised
about whether the water from these sources was really hot enough.[20]
To test this point, Lucas and Loendorf immersed a pair of sheep horns

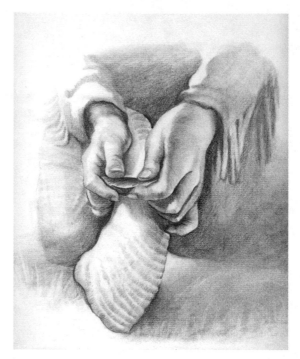

Figure 10.7. The process of cutting and shaping a water-softened horn. Razor-sharp obsidian flakes were used to cut the water-soaked horn. Readers should not assume that the process was easy, however. Making a horn bow was a relatively long and laborious task. Illustration by Davíd Joaquín.

in the 125-degree Fahrenheit water at the Fountain of Youth Hot Springs, north of Thermopolis, Wyoming. After twenty-four hours, even though the horns had acquired a white mineral coating, they had softened sufficiently to allow Lucas to whittle on them with an obsidian knife. After several hours of repeated cutting and soaking, Lucas felt that with continued patience and using only stone tools he would be able to carve usable bow staves from the processed sheep horn (Figure 10.7).

Once strips of horn have been detached from a horn core, a casing remains on their outer surface and must be removed. First, however, the horn staves need to be straightened by soaking them in hot water until they are pliable, at which point they are bound between two boards, where they remain for between seven and ten days. Lucas then carves and rasps the horn strips until he has shaped them into the two halves of the bow. The shaping process seems to work best if the horn is still damp, so after removing the staves from their board binding, it is sometimes necessary to put them back into hot water before carving and rasping can begin. Any shavings created during carving are saved for later reduction into glue.

As part of the shaping process, Lucas smoothes and straightens the pliable bow staves with his hands to take out any side curve. Because—on the hoof—sheep horn is decidedly curved and even after straightening may have a tendency to resume its normal curve, Lucas compensates by using the stave's formerly inside-the-curl surface as the back of the bow, so that when the bowstring is pulled, pressure is applied against any residual, natural curvature. Once a bow stave has been straightened and shaped, the butt or grip ends are beveled and fitted together. Lucas has tried different ways to secure the joint but has learned that the most important factors are to use good glue and to bind the joint firmly but not so tightly that the glue is squeezed out.

Lucas fits two linear pieces of shaped horn over the joint, one on the belly and one on the back of the bow, and then glues them in place. Then he applies the all-important sinew backing, which he describes in reverent tones as "remarkable stuff" that takes on a special quality when wet and pliable. He places several layers of sinew on the bow's back, being careful to overlap the ends, and allows each layer to dry completely before another is added. This process can take more than a month to complete, but when finished, the sinew buildup is nearly half an inch thick and transforms the bow into a powerful weapon with a pull strength of 60 to 70 pounds.

The bow string is made from a piece of twisted sinew with loops on each end that fit into notches at each of the nocks. There are exceptions, however, such as the Mountain Man Museum bow, whose ends are bent outward and have no notches to secure the string. Other bowyers place a small blob of pine pitch on each end to keep the string from slipping. Wyeth says that Sheep Eaters kept their bow strings loose and "those using this bow require a guard to protect the hand which holds it."[21] When preparing to fire, a hunter would hold the bow vertically and use a technique called "primary release" in which the archer draws the arrow by pinching it between the thumb and forefinger.

The Sheep Eaters and other Shoshone groups also made wooden bows from a single piece of wood that required no splicing. These self bows were usually made of locally available chokecherry (*Prunus melanocarpa*) or juniper (*Juniperus scopulorum* or *Juniperus utahensis*). The wood of the nonnative Pacific yew (*Taxus brevafolia*), which was especially prized as bow-making material, had to be obtained through trade with tribes on the plateau to the west. Juniper trees have straight, knot-free sides, so cuts could be made without interruption down the length of the trunk, and the desired piece could then be split from the standing tree. Many of these large trees, still bearing scars from the removal of bow staves several hundred years ago, have been found in Wyoming.[22]

Making a wooden bow was much simpler and required fewer steps and less elbow grease than making a horn bow. The back of a bow stave was scraped and smoothed, while the belly, especially when made of chokecherry, retained more of the curvature of the original wood. Sometimes wooden bows were backed with sinew, and at other times bow makers skipped this step. According to Shimkin, wooden and composite horn bows were functionally comparable, and both were used for hunting and warfare.[23] Horn bows were said to be more accurate and to send an arrow "faster" than wooden bows, so it is not surprising that they were considered by Sheep Eater men to be their most prized possession.

OTHER EVERYDAY TOOLS

The two distinctive kinds of knives that Sheep Eaters used for many different daily cutting tasks were much less labor-intensive to make than bows but equally diagnostic of their makers. Sheep Eater hide-skinning tools are identical in design to ones found so often in archaeological sites across the West that they are referred to as *Shoshone knives*.[24] These ovate tools were resharpened along the opposite edges of one side of a blade, a technique that produced a flat side that lay against a dead animal's flesh as the hide was removed, much like an old-time skinning knife. Demitri Shimkin describes how the unhafted butts of these knives, which could be as much as 15 centimeters long, were wrapped with sinew or rawhide so that users could hold them without risk of injury to their hands (Figure 10.8).[25] The wrapping also prevented the butt from being resharpened, and, once the knife

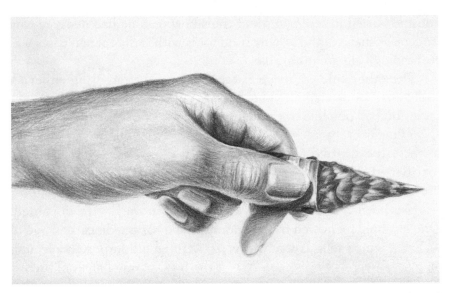

Figure 10.8. A Sheep Eater hide-skinning knife. Wrapping the butt of the knife with rawhide so that it could be held in the hand meant that resharpening the tool gave the blade concave sides but left the butt with convex sides. Illustration by Davíd Joaquín.

Figure 10.9. Three Sheep Eater hafted knives. These knives, which sometimes were notched to aid in hafting, were fitted with bone, wood, and antler handles. Illustration by Davíd Joaquín.

became buried in sediments and the sinew or hide had decayed, the lanceolate shape of the heavily used tools with unsharpened bases was archaeologically unmistakable.

The other kind of Sheep Eater knife was hafted using either an antler or a wooden handle. These tools were shaped like an old butcher knife and had notched or eared butts for ease of hafting (Figure 10.9). Over time in archaeological deposits, the handles on the vast majority of these tools rotted away, but wear scars from the rawhide thongs that bound the handles to the knives are still visible at the base of the blades. Like the ovate handheld implements, hafted knives appear to have been resharpened many times before they were discarded. One example recovered from Mummy Cave has a radiocarbon age of AD 734, which tells us that this very useful, multipurpose implement may have been, for millennia, one of the Swiss Army knives of prehistory.

LOOKING AHEAD

Although bows were far and away the most complex and important component of the prehistoric hunting tool kit, to become operational they required arrows, whose design specifications were considerably more flexible. In the next chapter we will discuss techniques of arrow making and the procurement of the raw materials that were used to make the slender projectiles that absorbed the energy in a bow's draw pull, becoming in the process the high-speed bearers of destructive force.

Plate 1. A Sheep Eater man and his dog, with Electric Peak in the background. The 10,992-foot peak is located north of Mammoth Hot Springs in Yellowstone National Park and is named for the lightning storms that center around it. Illustration (detail) by Davíd Joaquín.

Plate 2. Autumn in Yellowstone, and Sheep Eaters and their dogs are packed for travel. Dog travois was feasible in more open, level places, but rougher terrain required that dogs carry packs. Illustration (detail) by Davíd Joaquín.

Plate 3. A Sheep Eater hunter and his dog crossing one of the many waterfalls in the Yellowstone area. Most of the mountain streams are permanent, but the volume of water flow throughout the year differs, depending on the amount of melting snow. Illustration by Davíd Joaquín.

Plate 4. A Sheep Eater family group at their campfire. Illustration by Davíd Joaquín.

Plate 5. A Sheep Eater man on a vision quest at a rock art site. A male or female supplicant would bathe in a nearby stream or lake, then take a purifying sweat bath. A person would pray for several days while awaiting the arrival of a guardian spirit. Illustration by Davíd Joaquín.

Plate 6. A Sheep Eater man wearing a typical tippet collar. This decorative garment was made famous by Meriwether Lewis, who was given one by the Mountain Shoshone. After returning from his expedition, Lewis would model the tippet for groups of admirers. Illustration by Davíd Joaquín.

Plate 7. A Sheep Eater young woman in her best buckskin dress. It is ornamented with a bighorn sheep tail and elk teeth across the chest. Illustration by Davíd Joaquín.

The Thing Belonging to the Bow: Sheep Eater
Arrows and the Raw Material They Transport

In the *Oxford English Dictionary*'s discussion of the derivation of the word *arrow*, one of two ancestral forms of the word is given as the "Goth[ic] *arhwazna* from *arhw* ... prob[ably] 'the thing belonging to the bow.'"[1] Now, if arrows could somehow speak for themselves, one of their first statements would protest the fact that for many years they have been viewed as merely an appendage of a bow or as the faceless vehicle for the delivery of a projectile point. Although it is not possible in one brief chapter to atone for the injustices of linguistic custom, we can offer some small redress by presenting what is known about the types of arrows used by the Sheep Eaters and their Shoshone brethren.

For instance, Nathaniel Wyeth has written that a favorite Shoshone raw material for arrow making was greasewood, and Lowie notes that arrows were made from serviceberry stems that had been dried and cured for a year.[2] Two other kinds of wood, chokecherry and red willow, were also apparently used for arrows, depending on their availability. A typical Sheep Eater arrow was between 25 and 32 inches long, which means that arrows were nearly the same length as the typical 34-inch bows. The similarity in length is testament to just how much strength and elasticity was provided by horn bow design. Describing the steps involved in making an arrow, Wyeth has written that a stem or branch was "made straight by wetting and immersing in hot sand and ashes, and brought into shape by the hand and eye. To reduce the short crooks and knobs, it was drawn between two rough grit stones, each [of] which had a slight groove in it, and coarse sand ... used to increase the friction."[3]

According to Shimkin, arrow makers sometimes straightened their shafts by relying on the ancient human strategy (now considered

dentally incorrect) of using their teeth as tools. At other times, hunters straightened their arrows using shaft wrenches made by drilling
holes through a flat piece of bighorn sheep horn. Such an implement
allowed an arrow to be fitted through a hole of the proper diameter,
after which the tool was used for leverage to straighten the shaft.

Shimkin learned from Shoshone consultants that a notch was cut
into the end of an arrow to accommodate the bowstring; Wyeth, on
the other hand, has stated that this feature was not present. It now
seems probable that both notched and unnotched arrows were common. A long fletching technique was characteristic of Shoshone
arrows, meaning that split feathers were attached with sinew to the
base of the shaft and along it for four to five inches.[4] Dominick learned
from informants that Sheep Eaters had a preference for owl or eagle
feathers because they would not absorb blood, but there appears to be
considerable variety in the species whose plumage was put to this
use.[5] For example, arrows collected from the Northern Shoshone
before 1869 are fletched with feathers from a red-tailed hawk, whereas
the fletching on arrows recovered from archaeological contexts came
from grouse and other unidentified large birds.[6]

Prehistoric technology and its maintenance often required considerable energetic investment, so it is not surprising that once Sheep
Eater arrows were broken, they were routinely recycled and reworked.
Arrows and arrow parts found with Sheep Eater remains in Mummy
Cave in Wyoming and in Wickiup Cave in Montana have been identified as compound arrows, whose shafts were made of several segments. One end of each segment was whittled into a tenon (or projec-
tion), and the other end into a mortise (or cavity), so that segments
could be joined by fitting complementary ends together. Most recycled arrows consisted of only two segments, but some compound
arrows found in Mummy Cave were made of three.

Often the replacement segments were made from *phragmites*, a hollow reed that grows in Wyoming's Bighorn Basin, or from *equisetum*, a
segmented hollow grass found in wetlands throughout the region.
The reeds appear to have been selected for their straightness and
appropriate diameter and most often replaced a broken arrow's fore
shaft, in which case the replacement section was fitted with a projectile point before being connected to the rear shaft. At other times
reeds were designed to replace the rear shaft and were fletched with

feathers and incised with a nock. Sinew was used to strengthen the shaft just below the nock and to hold the joint together. Evidence of constriction of the reeds by the surrounding sinew has suggested to archaeologists that hunters used fresh, green reeds to make replacement sections. According to Lewis and Clark, Shoshone arrows were sometimes tipped with rattlesnake venom or a compound made of the spleen of an animal mixed with crushed red ants, which produced a deadly poison, but it is not certain whether toxic substances were used in hunting, or war, or both.

Regardless of the Sheep Eaters' purpose in transporting sharp, lethal objects—and for convenience and accessibility—they made quivers for their arrows from the skins of long animals such as otters. Sometimes the pelts of young mountain lions were large enough to make a case capable of accommodating both a hunter's bow and his arrows. In his book entitled *Hunting with the Bow and Arrow*, originally published in 1923, Saxton Pope provides detailed instructions about how to make a deerskin quiver using twentieth-century implements such as scissors and leather hole punches.[7] The process would be more labor intensive if—as in the case of the Sheep Eaters—it were undertaken using only obsidian tools and bone needles.

THE BUSINESS END OF THE ARROW

Despite our concern for fairness and equal time for all components of Sheep Eater hunting paraphernalia, the truth is that from the standpoint of the creature at which a hunter is aiming, an arrow is merely the delivery system for a potentially lethal projectile point. A variety of lithic raw material, including high-quality cherts and chalcedonies, occurred in major outcrops throughout the Yellowstone region and were used by Indians as both arrowheads and tools of various kinds. But obsidian, the Rolls Royce of cutting materials, was abundantly present in Sheep Eater territory, and, not surprisingly, it was exploited extensively in hunting technology.

Obsidian, an igneous rock found in about a dozen known deposits in the greater Yellowstone region, is formed when episodes of vulcanism propel molten lava from deep within the lithosphere to the Earth's surface, where it cools and solidifies. The fact that each time a volcano produces obsidian-rich lava the ingredients differ slightly has meant that geologists and archaeologists can identify specific obsidian sources using a series of relatively inexpensive and readily available tests. The obsidian in the vicinity of Yellowstone Park comes in several different colors, each with its own characteristics. Research by Kenneth Cannon and Richard Hughes on obsidian in the greater Yellowstone region has demonstrated, however, that obsidian artifact colors alone do not identify the source from which a sample has come.[8]

The most highly valued obsidian is translucent black, although it changes to smoky black or silvery gray when a light is shone through it. This more vitrified form was used for fine projectile points or blades with extremely sharp edges. Another form of obsidian is black and opaque and tends to be less glassy. Obsidian from yet other sources has an opaque, brownish or rusty red color and was used less for the manufacture of utilitarian tools and more for ceremonial purposes.[9]

Figure 11.1. Obsidian Cliff, Yellowstone National Park. The designation of this feature of the landscape as a "cliff" is a misnomer because the obsidian deposits referred to actually encompass hundreds of square kilometers. The outcrop in the photograph is near an ancient trail—now a highway—and is therefore only the most apparent source of obsidian in the extensive formation. Photograph by F. J. Haynes, 1899; from the Haynes Foundation Collection, courtesy of the Montana Historical Society.

Contemporary as well as prehistoric flint knappers have preferred to use obsidian for stone tools because, with skillful reduction techniques, blades freshly struck from a core represent the sharpest cutting edge known, several times sharper than a surgical steel scalpel. Because obsidian blades cut cleaner, which results in more rapid healing and the formation of less scar tissue, at least one physician at the University of Michigan Medical Center uses obsidian scalpels to remove skin lesions and repair wounds.[10]

One of the most imposing and historically significant areas within the Yellowstone landscape has been given the name Obsidian Cliff (Figure 11.1). Although the term *cliff* summons the mental image of the 200-foot-high escarpment so frequently pictured on postcards of Yellowstone National Park, what photos do not show is that the site is simply the most prominent feature of a tree-covered plateau extending for hundreds of square kilometers in the northwest sector of the park. Within this large, obsidian-laden area, evidence of extensive prehistoric mining remains in the form of trenches that can be scores of meters long.

The debris from extraction is everywhere, despite the fact that in the years since the park's incorporation, so many souvenir hunters have pocketed pieces of obsidian that the area has now been declared off-limits to tourists and hikers. As a result of protective legislation making it a felony to remove arrowheads and other artifacts from public lands, unauthorized collecting of obsidian pieces occurs less frequently today than it did at the end of the nineteenth century. Collectors in the Yellowstone region have learned the hard way that the penalty for recreational pilfering of obsidian can include loss of a vehicle in addition to a court date and possible permanent identification as a convicted felon.

PROVOCATIVE RESEARCH QUESTIONS

The area surrounding Obsidian Cliff presents archaeologists with the same dilemma faced by persons who have just acknowledged that there is indeed an elephant in the living room. How does one cope? The task of trying to find out more about the specifics of the mining process through excavation is so daunting that it overwhelms attempts at rigorous archaeological inquiry. Archaeologists find themselves asking, Where should test pits be placed? How can they study the thousands of artifacts that would be assembled in such an effort?

Despite the tactical and physical problems excavation would entail, we think that someday it should be attempted in order to answer many questions about prehistoric resource procurement and use. For instance, how were chunks of obsidian dislodged from the parent rock? Were fires set on the surface, as some people theorize, and when the rock was hot enough would cold water then douse the flames and cause the rock to fracture? Or, if blocks were simply hammered free, what kinds of tools were used? Are there areas where miners actually followed an obsidian seam underground by excavating a mineshaft, or did all mining effort take place on the surface?

Fortunately, some questions can be answered by examining the debris remaining in many of the quarry areas. We know that once obsidian nodules had been extracted from a deposit, the raw material was reshaped by knapping it into tabular, leaf-shaped pieces called *preforms* that were the size of a man's hand. Units of this size could be packed and transported to locations, some quite distant, where they could be further reduced into smaller tools. Broken preforms are common on surfaces in the Obsidian Cliff area, which suggests that miners discarded pieces that were flawed or had fractured during the reduction process. Very few functional tools are found in the quarry sites, indicating that individuals were not coming to a quarry just to extract and rework obsidian into finished tools to be added to their personal tool kits. Rather, the presence of preforms is evidence that obsidian was being obtained for manufacture into tools, for personal use or for trade, at another location.

The distribution of obsidian outcrops is not uniform, however, so the fact that the material is fairly common in Yellowstone's Absaroka Mountains but is not present in the nearby Wind River Mountains (which were formed largely through block-faulted plate tectonics rather than vulcanism) means that, in the past, obsidian represented a tradable commodity as well as a material for personal use. Chemical analysis of obsidian from Yellowstone has shown that it moved hundreds of miles through prehistoric networks, turning up in archaeological sites from Ohio to Texas. It would have been a particularly desirable commodity in the eastern half of North America, which is volcanically much less active than the western parts of the continent.

Interestingly, geochemical evidence shows that obsidian from a number of different, nonlocal sources was used to make artifacts later recovered at Yellowstone National Park. The presence of such arti-facts demonstrates that people brought obsidian objects with them from places like southern Idaho, either discarded or lost them, and then made new tools from obsidian found in the park.[11]

There has been speculation that perhaps obsidian quarries were considered dangerous places in the past—places where people would not have wanted to linger because the resources would have been tar-geted for exploitation by many different, unknown groups from out-side the Yellowstone area. A variant of this supposition questions whe-ther resident Sheep Eater groups controlled access to the quarries, making outsiders feel as though they were trespassing. The notion of quarries as designated neutral zones or places whose resources were so extensive that no single group controlled access has also been advanced.

In fact, none of these suggestions is supported by the ethnographic record. The idea that Sheep Eaters considered the quarries to be assets that they defended against encroachment is offset by historical accounts describing the Sheep Eaters as living in small, mobile groups that avoided confrontation with others. When encountering unknown persons at a quarry, it is likely that Sheep Eaters would have either retreated to a safe place and returned when the coast was clear or gone to another location where obsidian was available. Because obsid-ian is found in many different places in the Yellowstone region, trying to control access to all sources would have been totally impractical, even if a group of Sheep Eaters had chosen to attempt it. The concept of a consensually neutral zone is equally irrelevant because obsidian sources were numerous and available to anyone who wanted to make the trek into the mountains to obtain the raw material.

It is important to remember that the Sheep Eaters' annual round, crisscrossing through high mountainous terrain and lower valley land-scapes, provided them with multiple opportunities to access obsidian sources, so they did not have to plan specific procurement expedi-tions like groups living elsewhere did. The documentary evidence that Sheep Eaters transported high-quality obsidian down from the mountains to trade with lowland groups is testimony to their unim-peded access to sufficient raw material to meet their own needs and provide a surplus that could be exchanged for other necessities.

LOOKING AHEAD

Archaeologists who work with the archaeological record of hunter–gatherers are invariably impressed by the intelligence, ingenuity, and craftsmanship of the men and women who depended for their livelihood on a skillful exploitation of natural resources. In this and the preceding chapter we have explored how Sheep Eater hunters outfitted themselves with the essential tools they would need to provide their families with animal protein and the sheepskin fleeces they needed to make their clothing. In the next chapter, the reader will learn how hunters armed with powerful bows and deeply penetrating arrows devised successful strategies for hunting bighorn sheep.

12

||||||

Hunting Bighorn Sheep for Food and "Hornware"

Despite the implications of their name, Sheep Eater Indians hunted dozens of the more than sixty different mammalian species that inhabited their range. They fished for half a dozen aquatic species, and they filled their larders with hundreds of plant foods. But it is true that one animal—the wily bighorn sheep (*Ovis canadensis*)—sustained them in many ways, none more than dietary. Archaeological excavations at stratified sites like Mummy Cave, where every layer is dominated by thousands of split and burned bighorn bones, reveal the important role these animals played in the Sheep Eater diet (Figure 12.1).

THE MIGHTY BIGHORN SHEEP

Wild bighorn sheep were once so abundant in the greater Yellowstone region that Osborne Russell, traveling in 1836 high in the Absaroka Mountains just south of Yellowstone Park, wrote in his diary nearly every day for more than a week that his party encountered "thousands of mountain Sheep . . . all very fat so that this could be called no other than high living both as regarded altitude of positions and rich provisions."[1] Through much of the Sheep Eater tenure in the mountains of the Yellowstone region, bighorns were as prolific as Russell described. It is astonishing, then, that by the end of the nineteenth century, twenty years after the Sheep Eaters were excluded from the park and domiciled at the Wind River Reservation and other federally defined Indian enclaves, the number of bighorn sheep had declined to the point that in an 1897 tour of the region, wildlife artist and naturalist Ernest Thompson Seton reported no—as in zero—sightings.

Sheep Eaters were not responsible for the near-extermination of the species, nor was the problem localized in the Yellowstone area. Diseases spread by the domesticated sheep brought by settlers into the region accounted for a significant drop in bighorn populations.

Figure 12.1. A group of bighorn sheep in Yellowstone National Park. The massive horns of the rams can weigh as much as 30 pounds. Ewes have much smaller horns. Photograph by William S. Keller, 1966; courtesy of the Yellowstone Slide Archive.

According to Seton, however, an "epoch of relentless destruction by the skin hunters" had decimated bighorn populations throughout their range, leaving fewer than 300 animals in the western United States.[2] Populations of bighorns began to rebound in the early 1920s, in Yellowstone and elsewhere, and their numbers have been recorded annually since then. The Park Service estimates that current herd size has stabilized in Yellowstone's northern mountains at somewhere between 150 and 225 animals.

Left to their own devices—which is sometimes difficult to ensure in areas such as a national park, where visitors regard wildlife with intense, sometimes intrusive interest—bighorn sheep adjust the size and composition of their social groups according to the seasonal expression of their biological imperatives. For much of the year, females (or ewes), their lambs, and their older but still immature offspring live in bands of between five and fifteen animals led by a dominant ewe. In winter, female bands aggregate and can form herds approaching

100 animals. For males (or rams), the group size averages five or fewer animals, except in the summer when groups coalesce and move to higher mountain pastures to feed. For many high-latitude herbivores, summer represents a time when their favorite foods are most abundant. During the warmer months, bighorns are able to indulge their taste for a variety of tender grasses and sedges that become dormant and inedible in the winter. When cold, snowy conditions prevail, the branches of woody species such as willow and sage become the target of grazing animals.

Bighorn sheep are large, impressive creatures and represent substantial protein packages for hungry hunters and their families. A mature ram may weigh between 260 and 280 pounds, with its horns accounting for as much as 30 of those pounds. Ewes weigh between 115 and 200 pounds and have much smaller, comparatively insignificant horns. Rams are typically 65 to 72 inches from head to foot, and ewes, about ten inches shorter. Bighorn skins are highly prized for clothing; the hair is double layered, with short gray fur underlying tougher, hollow, outer guard hairs—a combination producing superb insulation. Like many animals that are adapted to the seasonally changing palette of their environment, bighorns have coats that change from dark brown in the summer to a lighter brown in winter. In all seasons there are patches of white on the bellies, the backs of the legs, and the muzzle.

There is no mystery about how these sheep got their name. The massive horns on an eight- to ten-year-old ram may curl completely around in a full arc, with the tip beginning to form a second curve. These formidable horns are used to intimidate other males, sometimes with legendary ferocity. An aggressive display may be sufficient to frighten away a competitor, but, more often, a male will use its horns to deliver a karate chop that destabilizes or knocks over its opponent. On occasion, an aggressor will charge his opponent, running at more than 30 miles per hour and crashing skull-to-skull with a force equaling 2,400 pounds. The reason that bighorns are able to withstand an impact of such intensity is they have double-thick skulls—the original football lineman's helmet—coupled with the fact that their horns take the brunt of the blow. Males are driven by a powerful reproductive imperative, and the winner of such a contest earns the right to breed with any number of estrus ewes during the November–December mating season. Sometimes large-horned males breed with so many females, or so many times with the same female, that they become exhausted to the point of collapse.

Not only are bighorns especially horny beasts, at least in terms of their cranial armament, but they have developed a hoof structure that is particularly well adapted to the landscapes they traverse. The hard surface of their hooves surrounds the soft inner tissue of a flexible pad, which provides a good grip and surefooted tread on uneven rock surfaces and allows them to escape predators by running onto rocky slopes and outcrops. World-renowned authority on bighorn sheep behavior Valerius Geist has written that bighorns seldom graze more than 300 paces from the safety of the rocky outcrops to which they can retreat when menaced by a wolf, in the past their primary predator.[3] Although it is true that female bighorns ignore better grazing and foraging resources located outside the terrain in which they are safe but their predators are disadvantaged, recent studies have shown that rams forage further from their safety zones. For males, the risk associated with increased foraging distance appears to be offset by access to more diverse and plentiful vegetation, which results in better nutrition.[4]

Sheep Eater Hunting Strategies

As is the case for all hunter–gatherers, the Sheep Eaters' knowledge of the behavior of their prey was as comprehensive as the understanding that today's wildlife biologists have of the species they monitor with ear tags, radio transmitters, and global positioning systems. Their hunting tactics reflected an awareness that when bighorn sheep are surprised, they will run upslope onto rock outcrops, where their well-adapted feet provide a secure grip and make escape possible. In early spring, capitalizing on their knowledge and working as a team (Figure 12.2), a group of hunters would locate talus piles of basalt or other dark-colored rock from which the snow had melted but where, at the bottom of the slope, there were patches of the fresh new grass that represented prime forage to hungry bighorns. On such a rocky slope, about two or three hundred feet above the fresh grass, hunters would construct hiding places by stacking boulders in a circle to make pits or blinds. After putting branches and dead wood over the top of such a pit, which was typically four to five feet in diameter and three feet

Figure 12.2. Sheep Eater hunters and their dogs set out to hunt bighorn sheep. The important role played by dogs in hunting is one reason they were held in such high esteem by their masters. Illustration by Davíd Joaquín.

Figure 12.3. A Sheep Eater hunter, hidden in a hunting blind, aiming at fleeing bighorns. Hunting was a cooperative effort, and success depended on hunters who would direct their dogs to flush or scare the bighorns into running up the mountainside toward the hunter camouflaged in the blind. Illustration by Davíd Joaquín.

deep, several of the hunters would conceal themselves and await the arrival of their prey.

Meanwhile, the remaining hunters and their dogs would locate a group of sheep farther down the slope and begin to approach them from below. They would walk slowly into the open, in a quartering direction, until the sheep noticed them.[5] Once the sheep were alert to possible danger and were becoming skittish, the hunters would howl like wolves and urge their dogs to charge.[6] Afraid of the dogs and confused by the howling, the frightened sheep would move rapidly upward onto the rocky talus where the hidden hunters waited, revealing themselves only when the sheep were within range of their bows and arrows (Figure 12.3). This ancient hunting tactic was simplicity itself, and its effectiveness is confirmed by the dozens of hunting blind sites in the region.

In winter, the Sheep Eaters used a variant of the entrapment hunting strategy. Hunters wearing snowshoes and accompanied by their dogs would drive sheep into deep snowdrifts and then move across the top of the snow to shoot the floundering animals with their bows and arrows. In this case, the sheep's primary defensive weapons—their heavy horns—were their undoing. Not only did horns make the sheep immobile, but they were the source of the sturdy raw material for the snowshoes and bows that were essential for the hunters' success.[7]

Large, elaborate, V-shaped trapping structures were used for communal bighorn sheep drives in other seasons. Hunters coaxed sheep into the area between long wooden fence wings—the legs of the "V"—that met at the V's point and formed a corral or "catch-pen." It is possible to reconstruct the way sheep were manipulated into such a trap because fifteen to twenty traps remain in varying stages of disrepair in the mountains of Montana and Wyoming. The sites with largely intact traps are in the Absaroka and Wind River mountains near Dubois, Wyoming, the same area where the largest remaining herds of North America's bighorn sheep are found. Much of our understanding about how the catch-pen hunting strategy worked comes from John Mionczynski, a wildlife biologist who has lived with bighorn sheep for several summers while researching the causes of the low survival rate of a herd on Whiskey Mountain.

Before describing the catch-pen hunting strategy in detail, it is important to point out that the majority of the traps were built near sheep bedding grounds in the areas where bighorns congregated during the mating season in late November and throughout the following winter months. Bighorns tend to select bedding locations on open, bare ridges where they can see for considerable distances. If frightened, they may run downslope for a short distance, but invariably they will turn and run up the mountain to escape. The long, funnel-shaped "drivelines" were built of deadfall timber that was stacked to make fences, any gaps being filled by rock cairns. The drivelines were built across the most logical escape route for the sheep, so that once the bighorns were within the drivelines, they could be driven into the catch-pens and killed with clubs or spears. Some driveline structures were so elaborate that they had circular holding areas where the animals were apparently forced to march around and around until they were exhausted and could then be directed toward the catch-pen.[8]

Maneuvering the sheep into the area within the drivelines was the tricky step in the process, and Mionczynski has replicated the technique that he thinks Sheep Eaters used. He *sings* to the sheep in low, steady tones—as though he were humming a lullaby—and like children following the Pied Piper, they come toward him. As New Age and improbable as this luring tactic may seem, it is supported by the presence of nestlike areas built into the driveline walls that Mionczynski thinks may have sheltered a shaman or the hunt master. From such a vantage point, either participant could have coordinated the hunt and crooned softly to coax the animals into cooperating.

The catch-pen component of the entire structure was often hidden among the trees, the kind of place that bighorns avoided (Figure 12.4). The layout of the structure was designed so that all other escape routes led to steep precipices, leaving the bighorns with no alternative except to cooperate. The catch-pens, which were on average 15 to 24 feet long and 8 to 14 feet wide, were a number of feet deeper than the surrounding ground surface. They were accessed by a sloping entry ramp made of logs and covered with soil and vegetation that, to some extent, withheld from the cajoled and bewildered sheep the nature of their ultimate destination. Any bighorn unfortunate enough to have arrived at the catch-pen's outer precincts would then have been unceremoniously hustled down the ramp and forced to leap into the pen below.

All the remaining nineteenth-century catch-pens are somewhat eroded, but the tallest ones still stand a good five feet high. The walls were constructed of tiers of deadfall wood and built crib-style, like a

Figure 12.4. Sheep Eater hunters driving game into a "catch-pen." The remains of at least a dozen catch-pens have been found in the mountains surrounding Yellowstone Park. Many others have been destroyed by forest fires. Illustration by Davíd Joaquín, after a work by Grant Hagen on display at the Wind River Historical Center, Dubois, Wyoming.

crude log cabin. Because the diameter of the upper tiers was smaller than that of the lower ones, the walls would have appeared to converge over the heads of the animals. Once the sheep were in the pen, they were killed by a blow to the head with a short club. One club has been recovered, and it looks, as much as anything, like a street patrolman's billy club.[9] Such a simple implement sufficed because, in spite of their cranial armor, bighorn sheep are surprisingly vulnerable at the point behind their horns where the spine connects to the head.

We wish we could report more fully on the construction and contents of bighorn catch-pens, but, unfortunately, none has yet been excavated. There may not be much remaining in them, however, because once the sheep were killed, the entire carcass was apparently removed and butchered elsewhere.[10] Archaeological research at sites with large numbers of bighorn sheep bones has been completed in the area of sheep traps, but no one-to-one correlation between an actual trap and a butchering or processing area has yet been made.[11] In addition to Mummy Cave, the Bugas-Holding site in the Sunlight Basin, north of Cody, Wyoming, is a possible sheep-processing site to which animals were brought from a nearby trap.[12]

Additional evidence that some of the butchering took place near the catch-pens at a number of the sites comes from the presence of massive, trophy-size sheep's heads that were set in the crotch of a nearby tree. These large skulls are now bleached white and appear to watch over the sites like ancestral sentinels. It is likely that they are examples of the worldwide practice in hunting societies of leaving an offering for the dead animal's spirit as a sign of respect and a gesture of the hope that, by being honored in this way, the spirit will be contented and not motivated to interfere with the group's next hunt. Sheep Eater traditions maintained that the spirits of dead bighorns animate the narrow canyons, passageways, and rock shelters in the landscape that humans and sheep together called home, and, in a twist of fate that the hunters could not have foreseen, it is the bighorn sheep alone who continue an ancient way of life in the mountain fastness.

LOOKING AHEAD

In chapter 13, we will describe the wide range of resources in addition to bighorn sheep that Sheep Eater families hunted, gathered, prepared, and cooked as the seasons and environment changed in their mountain homeland.

13
||||||

Cutthroats, Bitterroots, and Whistle Pigs: Seasonal Variety in the Sheep Eater Diet

Living in an industrialized world in which food is often grown thousands of miles from where it is consumed, it is easy to forget that long before refrigeration and global transport systems made it possible for New Englanders to enjoy oranges from Florida and Israel, food consumers were also food producers. Prior to the adoption of agriculture, which tended to tether families to plots of land that were used repetitively to provide nutritional necessities, hunter–gatherer families transported themselves to where the food was concentrated. What people ate and when they ate it were governed by a complicated equation whose components included—but were not limited to—the mix of resources in the territory to which they had access and the timing of resource availability.

Seasonal transhumance is the term for a way of life based on "following the food," and it describes accurately the Sheep Eater adaptation to the changing suite of edible plants and prey animals available to them throughout an annual cycle. In chapter 12, we discussed some of the tactics that Sheep Eaters used in their pursuit of the biggest and most abundant protein package in their territory—bighorn sheep. Sheep Eaters hunted bighorns and other large-body-size animals year-round, and the general outlines of their lives were defined by the seasonal movement of sheep to high mountain meadows in the warmer months and to lower foothills and valleys in the colder months.

Rocky mountain mule deer (*Odocoileus hemionus*) were prevalent in Sheep Eater territory but were hunted individually, rather than captured in groups by means of trapping or driving strategies. Although bison were the largest animal in the Yellowstone area and could weigh as much as 1,800 pounds, they were wary and difficult to hunt, so little effort was invested in tracking and killing them. Of course Sheep Eaters did not ignore bison, but based on the hundreds of sheep bones and the relative absence of bison bones in sites like Mummy Cave, hunting them was more opportunistic and not part of a planned hunting strategy.

Sheep Eater hunters pursued elk—members of the deer family whose biological name is *Cervus canadensis*—when they could, but elk populations in their territory were low until the historic period. The ecological balance tipped in favor of elk and their numbers increased following the systematic extermination of wolves and beavers by Euro-Americans involved in the fur trade. It comes as no surprise that elk were the favorite prey of wolves, whose predation kept elk population levels depressed, but the connection between the number of beavers and the number of elk is not as obvious. It turns out that these two species were competing with one another for food, specifically the willows and other brushy, woody plants that grow along the edges of streams. The furry rodents devoured large quantities of the forage that elk needed to make their antlers grow—that is, until beaver pelts became a valuable commodity in nineteenth-century fur markets.

That elk and beaver occupied opposite ends of a survival teeter-totter is supported by the faunal records at archaeological sites on the Great Plains. At places next to large, fast-moving streams in which beavers would not have been able to build dams and dens, there are significant numbers of elk bones throughout the entire prehistoric record. This pattern indicates that from a beaver's perspective, in spite of the presence of good forage, the high-energy water flow created poor beaver habitat, and they had to look elsewhere. An elk would have seen things differently, of course: lots of food was available, and there was no creature with big front teeth at the front of the line.[1]

While sheep, deer, and elk contributed significantly to the Sheep Eater diet, many smaller critters were also important sources of nourishment. Beavers, porcupines, squirrels, birds—both aquatic and terrestrial—and fish often ended up baking in earth ovens or broiling on wood fires. Some of these species were encountered singly and opportunistically, whereas others—such as fish—were often harvested in great numbers, which required planning and teamwork.

Fishing: Cheaper by the Dozen

To understand just how abundant fish were and still are in the greater Yellowstone region, we need look no further than the memoirs of Philetus Norris, the second superintendent of Yellowstone Park. Norris was a legendary character in park history and a celebrated teller of tales, some of them a bit taller than others. He once described trekking in 1881 with two companions to Trout Lake, which is located in the Lamar River valley, very near the spot where Osborne Russell had encountered a group of Sheep Eaters some fifty years earlier (see chapter 1). By blocking off an inlet to the lake, Norris was able to trap spawning cutthroat trout, and, he claims, in a matter of *minutes* he and his companions had caught and tossed eighty-two fish onto the bank. In a sporting gesture, they returned about half of their catch to the water, keeping forty-two fish that had a combined weight of more than 100 pounds.[2]

In support of Norris's credibility, at least in this instance, let us assure readers that the inlets to Trout Lake and other high-latitude bodies of water are sometimes so choked with spawning trout that—Scout's honor—it is possible for a person to walk across the shallower areas supported entirely on the backs of fish. Resources of this magnitude not only sustained Sheep Eater populations but, then as now, are an extremely important component of the diets of grizzly bears, bald eagles, osprey, pelicans, and other species that exploit aquatic resources. In fact, the recent illegal introduction of lake trout to Yellowstone Lake, and the potential of this species to outcompete indigenous cutthroat trout, has biologists concerned that long-term changes to the ecosystem will result if the spawning cutthroats are no longer available to their customary predators in the food chain.

If we were to draw a pie chart diagram illustrating the various components of the Sheep Eater diet, fish would occupy a slice representing as much as 15 to 20 percent of the whole pie. Access to such a significant dietary resource required a specialized technology that was nearly as extensive as the gear of today's anglers and included weirs, basket traps, seines, dip nets, spears, leisters, harpoons, and bone hooks of different shapes and sizes.

Weirs and leisters—two words that break the "i before e" rule—represent sequentially used implements in a strategy to harvest fish in large numbers (Figure 13.1). Weirs are devices requiring preliminary

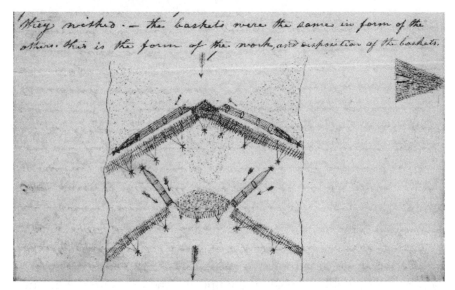

Figure 13.1. A drawing of a fish weir and the accompanying text from the journal of Meriwether Lewis. Note the baskets that are incorporated into the weir. Various rock dams and willows woven into fences were also set up in shallow water to serve as fish weirs. Image courtesy of the American Philosophical Society.

construction and setup, but once they are in place, the angler can temporarily relax and let the weir do the work. To make a weir, experienced persons would set a series of previously sharpened poles into a riverbed or lake bottom and then weave flexible strips of wood through them to form a lattice. The effort involved in construction rewarded those who designed their weir so that it could be rolled up, stored on shore, and reused in another season. The goal was to create a porous, maze-like device that spawning fish could easily penetrate but that prevented their attempts to escape and continue swimming upstream. Once a sufficient number of fish had been trapped in the weir, a leister—a handheld fishing spear with flexible outer barbs that grip the fish—was used to retrieve the larger fish from the weir. Anglers used a dip net to catch any smaller fish trapped by the weir.

Another strategy, more suitable for use in smaller streams, involved building water-channeling structures or rock dams. These funneled water into a large, conical basket trap made of woven willows that was usually five feet long and had an opening of about two feet in diameter (Figure 13.2). Persons positioned in the stream above the dam would wade downstream, beating the water to chase fish into the basket.

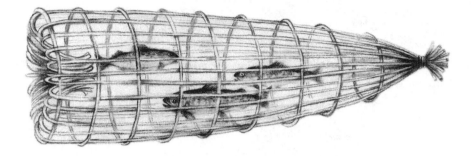

Figure 13.2. Fish trapped in a fish weir basket. Large fish weir baskets were commonly stored near a fishing area and were repaired before each season of use. Illustration by Davíd Joaquín.

Helpers on shore near the basket would monitor the catch, periodically pulling out a full basket and emptying the fish onto the ground. Sometimes the opening in a basket trap was on top, in which case the person watching would use either a spear or a dip net to remove the accumulating fish. Rock dams for use with basket traps can still be found in Dinwoody Creek on the Wind River Reservation, and though these are remnants of more-modern Shoshone fishing operations, they are very similar to the ancient ones.

Sheep Eaters also routinely used a special bone or antler toggle-head harpoon, whose pointed end was detachable and connected to the shaft by a thong or cord. A fisherman would impale a fish on the harpoon, and, once he had retrieved his catch, he would separate the point from the spear shaft and slide the fish onto the thong. If a fish were still vigorously struggling, the angler could release the harpoon and allow point, thong, and shaft (still attached to one another) to float until the effort of resisting the harpoon's weight was too much for the wounded fish.[3]

The freshness of the cutthroat trout, whitefish, grayling, and suckers that Sheep Eaters caught and consumed is a luxury by today's standards, but during the midsummer spawning season, when large quantities of fish were available, considerable effort was put into preserving the catch for later. Instead of smoking fish, which is how tribes along the Columbia River customarily processed salmon, Sheep Eaters would split fish down the back, remove their innards, and place them on the ground or on racks to dry in the sun.[4] If the volume of caught fish was substantial, this became a labor-intensive operation. In addition to the effort of preparation, sentry duty became necessary to fight off flies and to prevent the birds, coyotes, wolves, bears, and smaller mammals like raccoons attracted to the drying fish from claiming a share of the largesse. The normally well-behaved Sheep Eater dogs would also have tried to sneak a fish or two and would have had to be restrained.

Like vendors in open-air markets who spend hours setting up their wares in the morning only to pack up everything again in the evening, Sheep Eaters had to collect their drying fish every evening—fish will not sun dry in one day—and place them in storage vessels as protection from nocturnal predators. Then at first light, out the fish would come for another day of sun baking. Rainy days, too, were problematic, and, depending on conditions, the drying fish might require multiple episodes of storage and retrieval.

The archaeological record does not preserve the blood, sweat, and tears produced by the exertions of large-scale fish processing, but more tangible evidence of Sheep Eater fishing is found in several sites. The excavators' notes from Mummy Cave report that fish bones were found in Layer 36, along with a bone harpoon head and several net weights, but the bones themselves were initially thought to have been misplaced. Kenneth Cannon, an archaeologist at the National Park Service's Midwest Archeological Center, has recently reported to us that the fish bones were found in the comparative collection of the center and have been returned to the Buffalo Bill Historical Center.[5]

In any case, it would have been quite understandable had the bones been lost, because at the time Mummy Cave was dug, it was customary to screen the dirt from excavations using one-quarter-inch mesh, through which very small items like fish bones could easily pass, ending up in a back dirt pile and lost to prehistory. Today's archaeologists often use a water-screening technique that dissolves artifact-bearing sediments and catches any tiny objects in a mesh screen fine enough to use on windows to keep out mosquitoes.

The net weights in Layer 36 are somewhat problematic because it is possible that they might have been attached to nets used for catching small terrestrial mammals instead of for fishing. Arguing in favor of an aquatic-use context, however, is their association with fish bones and a harpoon head. The latter item is made from an elk antler tine and has a sharp point and barbs along one side.[6] The butt is broken, and it is not clear how it fitted into a haft, but presumably it was part of a spear that was used to remove fish from a weir or trap, either of which would have worked well in the Shoshone River, which flows only a few feet from the entrance to Mummy Cave.

DIGGING FOR DINNER

The food pyramid—that multilevel symbol of nutritional wisdom—has been redesigned several times in the last decade. For a while, the pyramid rested on an "indulge heartily" base of carbohydrates, and Americans became adept at preparing all sorts of pastas with names ending in -ini, -etti, and -oni. In a recent reshuffling, refined flour "fun foods" were booted up to the designated "eat sparingly" top of the pyramid, and seeds, nuts, fruits, and vegetables replaced them in the "recommended eating" precincts at the base. Although on a day-to-day basis the protein and carbohydrate components of the Sheep Eater food pyramid shifted in response to the availability of various food resources, it is interesting that, on an annual basis, their diet was quite congruent with newly approved, twenty-first-century nutritional guidelines.

In the day or so after a bighorn sheep carcass was brought into camp, for instance, the protein segment of the dietary pie chart would enlarge as tummies stayed full of delicious roasted meat. Following a family expedition to catch spawning lake trout, taste buds might become tired of a daily diet of fish stew. Overall, though, the most consistently available and most important sources of food came from the earth. Sheep Eaters ate a variety of root vegetables, many of which are unknown to generations brought up to think that "root" means fried or mashed potatoes and the occasional marshmallow-draped yam served on winter holidays. But nature's underground bounty offers balsam root, biscuit root, bitterroot, bistort, camas, sego lilies, spring beauty, tobacco root, wild onion, and yampa, all of which still grow abundantly in the mountain meadows of Sheep Eater territory and were essential for their survival (Figure 13.3). Berries, pine nuts, a variety of herbs, seeds, and insects were also gathered in season. As a rule of thumb, the growing season of plants is shorter in high-altitude, high-latitude settings, and the exploitation of the many varieties of plants available in the Sheep Eater areas of Wyoming, Montana, and

Figure 13.3. Important plants in the Sheep Eater diet: biscuit root (*top*), onion (*lower left*), and bitterroot (*lower right*). These examples represent a sample of the twenty-five to thirty important root vegetables that were included in the Sheep Eater diet. Illustration by Hannah Hinchman.

Idaho had to be scheduled to coincide with times of peak availability—but without interfering with other food-procurement activities.

George Drouillard, the skillful hunter who accompanied Lewis and Clark on their epic journey, has told a story underscoring the importance of root vegetables to the Mountain Shoshone.[7] On August 22, 1805, he was hunting near the forks of the Beaverhead River, close to present-day Dillon, Montana, when he encountered a small group of Mountain Shoshone that included several women who had been digging root vegetables. Drouillard was riding one of the expedition's newly acquired horses, from which he dismounted and joined the Indian group for a visit in sign language. When it was time to leave, Drouillard went to fetch his horse, leaving his rifle leaning against a tree. Seeing that the white man's attention was elsewhere, a young Shoshone man in the group grabbed the gun, leaped on his horse, and galloped away. Drouillard chased after him for about ten miles, and just as the young man was about to be overtaken, he emptied the powder from the pan, tossed the gun to the ground, and took off.

Retrieving his weapon, Drouillard returned to the Shoshone camp, from which by this time everyone had scattered, leaving behind their sacks of dried plants. Drouillard took two of the bags to Captain Lewis; one bag contained three different kinds of roots separated by rawhide folds, and the other was full of dried berries. In his journal (whose spelling and punctuation are presented as written), Lewis described the contents with great interest:

> One species of the roots were fusiform about six inches long and about the size of a man's finger at the larger end tapering to a small point. the radicles larger than in most fusiform roots. the rind was white and thin. the body or consistence of the root was white mealy and easily reduced by pounding to a substance resembleing flour which thickens with boiling water something like flour and is agreeably flavored. this rout is frequently eaten by the Indians either green or in it's dried state without the preparation of boiling.[8]

Several lines of evidence suggest that Lewis is describing biscuit root or one of the several species of *Lomatium* that are common to the region. Lewis's statement that the root can be eaten raw rules out camas and tobacco root, both of which contain a complex carbohydrate called inulin that the human digestive tract cannot process.

Because cooking transforms inulin into a digestible sugar, both camas and tobacco root were roasted before being consumed in great quantities by Sheep Eaters and other Indian groups. The mystery root was not yampa, which Lewis would have been able to identify, as it was introduced to him by Sacajawea. That leaves *Lomatium*, whose white, mealy texture resembles that frontier favorite, biscuits, and accounts for the name conferred on the plant by early white settlers. Just as in some parts of the United States a meal is not considered complete without biscuits, for Sheep Eaters, biscuit root was a dietary mainstay and almost always present in their portable larder.

Lewis described another root in the bags Drouillard retrieved as a small, round tuber with a nutty flavor. This is almost certainly the walnut-sized bulb of the sego lily (*Calochortus nuttallii*), which later became the state flower of Utah. In the middle 1800s, partly because of crop-devouring cricket infestations, food was scarce for Mormon settlers, and people resorted to digging and eating the roots of sego lilies until they were able to plant their usual crops once again. It is very likely that they learned about this lifesaving food from Shoshone Indians.

The third root that Lewis inspected and recorded was a member of the purslane family whose name—bitterroot—would have seemed appropriate, at least to Lewis. He described the root as "fibrous; the parts were brittle, hard of the size of a small quill, cilindric and as white as snow throughout, except some small parts of the hard black rind which they had not seperated in the preperation." The Shoshone explained that these roots became quite soft after they were boiled, a fact that Lewis verified, although he observed that they had a "very bitter taste, which was naucious to my pallate, and I transfered them to the Indians who had ate them heartily."[9]

Bitterroot (*Lewisia rediviva*) was identified and given its Latin name by the distinguished German-trained botanist Frederick Pursh and was later designated the Montana state flower. In the years following the expedition, Pursh was studying botany in Philadelphia when Lewis gave him a large part of the expedition's herbarium to examine. Not long afterward, Pursh transported the collection to England, where he analyzed it at the Royal Botanical Gardens, and he included the results in his well-known treatise, *Flora Americae Septentrionalis*.[10] By the time the treatise was published, Lewis had been dead for four years, and the United States was at war with Great Britain. Had Americans not been so preoccupied with martial pursuits, they might have been amazed by the multinational character of Pursh's work. It featured bitterroot, a plant that was indigenous to the cookery of western American Indians, collected by and named for Lewis, and studied by a German-trained botanist, who described it in a British publication.

The origin of bitterroot's species identification (*Lewisia rediviva*) was also uncommon. More than two years after the specimen was collected, pressed between papers, and dried, it was placed in water in Philadelphia, where it bloomed for a short time. Perhaps contemporary botanists would not be surprised by the recuperative powers of a plant acclimated to dry environments, but it amazed Pursh, who recognized its resiliency by adding *rediviva*, which means "restored to life," to its official botanical name.

In mid-August 1805, when Lewis and Clark were trying to find the Mountain Shoshone, they observed fields in which many holes had been dug in the ground. They later learned that these were the remnants of the large-scale extraction of root vegetables. In the division of labor typical of hunting and gathering societies, Sheep Eater women were the specialists who harvested a variety of highly nutritious roots. It has been said that a well-made digging stick, crafted from a fire-hardened piece of wood and topped with a padded T-shaped handle, was a woman's prized possession, with a value comparable to that placed by men on their horn bows. The handle was made of either bone or an elk antler tine to which part of the main antler beam was still attached, and the tool was so sturdy that it was often willed by a woman at her death to a close relative.

Once Sheep Eater women had filled their large baskets with roots and carried them back to camp, the roots had to be cleaned, and a deep pit had to be dug. Baking occurred in these underground ovens, which had first been lined with heated rocks and then filled with alternating layers of damp grass or tree moss followed by bulbs, more grass, and then another layer of heated rocks. The oven was then covered with dirt, and a fire was built on top to ensure that the temperature within stayed hot enough for several days to fully cook the contents.

In the course of archaeological research in Grand Teton and Yellowstone National parks, Stuart Reeve observed and measured the remnants of many earth ovens.[11] Two sizes predominated, those with diameters of seven feet or less, which were probably for family use, and bigger ones, sometimes approaching 15 feet in diameter, that were more likely used by community groups. Areas close to large meadows of prime root vegetable habitat contained the remains of thousands of pits, most of them probably associated with camas (*Quemasia*) baking.

In a discussion of the Henn site near Jackson Hole, Wyoming, archaeologist David Rapson and his colleagues have pointed out that many of these areas contain more than one kind of root vegetable, making them ideal locations for "mixed-bag" root vegetable processing. Apparently these sites are common in the Jackson Hole region: Melissa Connor and her colleagues have discovered and reported on several large sites with fired-rock features.[12]

Archaeologists have also observed that root baking was hard, dirty work, each episode lasting at least three days—an estimate that does not include digging the roots, an activity taking long days of backbreaking work. Once the digging, gathering, and cooking were done, however, the nutritional payoff was phenomenal. Archaeologist Julie Francis excavated a baking pit that could have accommodated nine bushels of roots. Francis has calculated the number of "digging days" needed to fill the pit with various root vegetables and concludes that one woman, digging a bushel of roots a day, would have had to work for nine days to fill the pit with camas and thirteen days to fill it with biscuit root. But when Francis determined that nine bushels of camas yield 226,000 calories, it became apparent that the laborious effort was justified. If one assumes that 2,000 calories will meet the nutritional requirements of one person for one day, a single pit of camas could meet the energetic needs of one person for 113 days or feed a family of four for a month. Another benefit of digging and processing camas is that once it has been baked and stored properly, it will remain edible for years.[13]

Even though camas has a higher caloric value than other root vegetables, the ones in Drouillard's bags were also very good food and were used by Sheep Eaters throughout the winter. Unlike camas, prior to storage such roots required only cleaning and sun drying because they contain no inulin and therefore did not need extensive baking to make them digestible. In fact, the suite of non-inulin root vegetables was more commonly used by the Mountain Shoshone than camas, which does not grow well above 8,000 feet.

THE PICK OF THE CROP

Regionally abundant berry crops, such as chokecherries, buffalo berries, or serviceberries, are also uncommon at the higher elevations where Sheep Eaters primarily lived, but we know from the bushel of dried serviceberries found in one of the bags recovered by Drouillard that berries were sometimes accessible and harvested. Although, in general, they were not sufficiently plentiful to be a major source of food, families would certainly have eaten their fill when they encountered the ripe, sweet little huckleberries that in some years can be found in dense patches in high forested areas. Especially abundant crops of berries would have been dried and added to winter soups. In fact, it is likely that had they not been left behind, the berries that became Drouillard's property would have been put to this use. In Meriwether Lewis's diary entry for July 17, 1805, his description of service berries is quite appetizing:

> The survice berry differs somewhat from that of the U'States. the bushes are small sometimes not more than 2 feet high and scarcely ever exceed 8 and are proportionably small in their stems, growing very thickly ascosiated in clumps. the fruit is the same form but for the most part larger more luscious and of so deep a perple that on first sight you would think them black.[14]

The Sheep Eaters' seasonal rounds sometimes took them in late fall to lower elevations where various berries would have been abundant earlier in the season. If they arrived too late for the harvest, they would have been unable to make pemmican, a nutritious combination of pulverized dried meat, mashed berries, and tallow that was the winter mainstay of Plains Indians.

IF YOU FEEL LIKE A NUT

On the same day that Drouillard met with the Mountain Shoshone and had to chase after one of their party to retrieve his purloined gun, Clark was searching for a passage over the mountains. He later wrote in his journal about encountering a fascinating gray, crow-like bird with a very sharp bill. The bird, later given the name Clark's nutcracker by ornithologists, uses its bill to extract seeds from pinecones. In Sheep Eater country, the bird's food of choice comes from the whitebark pine, a shrubby tree growing near the timberline. Whitebarks have small, egg-shaped, woody cones that range from one and one-half to three inches long. Although the cones mature in August, instead of opening to release its seeds, the entire cone falls from the tree and eventually decomposes enough for the seeds to become accessible. The dispersal of whitebark seeds is largely facilitated by Clark's nutcrackers, who cache them for winter food.

Whitebark pines and Clark's nutcrackers have such an important codependence that a threat to one species is an equal threat to the other. University of Denver biologist Diana Tomback has studied this interrelationship for more than thirty years and fears that a fungus now attacking and killing the pine trees will eventually lead to the extinction of the bird as well. Because the nuts are an important source of food for grizzly bears, mammalian biologists are concerned about the effect that the diminishing number of whitebark pine trees will also have on the species they study.[15]

Sheep Eaters, for whom pine nuts (*woŋgoduba*) were a favorite delicacy, also played a role in their dissemination. Hunters would usually climb trees to pick the cones, although occasionally they would fell a tree to get access. The cones were immediately spread on hot ashes to make them pop open, and, after extraction, the nuts were stored in buckskin bags and frequently cached under piles of rock and earth that were sometimes many miles from the trees.[16] By opening the cones and spreading them around, the Sheep Eaters had the same positive effect on the long-term survival of the whitebark pine as the Clark's nutcracker.

Not only are pine nuts delicious, they contributed important nutrients—about a quarter-cup contains nearly 200 calories, three-fourths of which are from fat—to the diet of a hardworking, hungry hunter–gatherer family. In contrast to contemporary "sitter-watchers," who indulge in many high-fat foods and are constantly encouraged to become less sedentary, to be more physically active, and to reduce their fat intake, prehistoric peoples regularly engaged in strenuous activities, ate much leaner meat, and needed the nutrients in a couple handfuls of high-fat pine nuts. Sheep Eaters added many different kinds of seeds to their handful, often mixing seeds from sunflowers and lamb's-quarter with those from a dozen other chenopodium and amaranth plants to make a high-protein trail mix. Lewis and Clark also reported that the Mountain Shoshone would pound together a mixture of seeds and service berries and let the resulting breadlike cake dry in the sun.[17]

Figure 13.4. Marmots, or whistle pigs, were an excellent source of protein for Sheep Eaters. These fatty animals were highly valued as a food source by fur trappers as well. Contemporary hunters who have tasted them, however, often describe a strong, offensive odor that is released during cooking. Illustration by Davíd Joaquín.

Whistle Pigs and Rock Chucks

Yellow-bellied marmots (*Marmota flaviventris*) are social, house cat–sized rodents living in colonies in Sheep Eater territory (Figure 13.4). Also called whistle pigs and rock chucks—names that mimic the noises and alarm calls they make when startled by a predator—they are about two feet long and weigh six to ten pounds. Another member of the marmot family, the woodchuck, has inspired a rhetorical question that might have been refashioned by Sheep Eaters as "How many rocks could a rock chuck chuck, if a rock chuck could chuck rocks?" In this case, however, young Sheep Eater boys would have been doing the rock chucking in the direction of the marmots—or shooting at them with their bows and arrows as part of their training as neophyte hunters. When they successfully bagged a rock chuck, it would have been welcomed at home because it was considered high-quality food.

Of the fourteen marmot species, those with yellow bellies live at high elevations in the rocky outcrops where mountain peaks give way to small meadows and open ridge crests. Even though marmots hibernate in deep dens beneath the winter snow, in order to keep from freezing during their long sleep, they eat large quantities of grass and other greenery during the warmer months to build the layers of fat that will protect them from the cold. Other marmot predators, including coyotes, bears, and eagles, find the chubby ground squirrels as delectable as Sheep Eaters did.

NOT-SO-WILY COYOTE

Coyotes were another species upon which Sheep Eater hunters cast a predatory eye. Coyote meat was on their menu of preferred foods, and they used the pelts to make warm winter clothing.[18] Not only was killing coyotes for clothing atypical of other Shoshone groups in the Great Basin and elsewhere, but an appreciation of the coyote as entrée material was simply unthinkable. It is said that because of their reverence for the animal's supernatural associations, Nevada Shoshone would starve to death rather than eat a coyote.

Just how Sheep Eater cookery prepared and served coyote has not been recorded, but it is likely to have been grilled in the coals of a wood fire. Today coyote meat is unlikely to turn up on the dinner table, but it is possible for the contemporary cook to replicate other favorites from the Sheep Eater hearth. We include here an approximation of a Sheep Eater one-pot stew based on an analysis of the residue from a cooking vessel at a Sheep Eater site called Medicine Lodge Creek. This typical winter ragoût is easy to prepare and will give the reader a whiff of the aromas of frontier food:

Basic Stone Pot Stew (Day 1)

1 to 2 pounds bighorn sheep, cut into bite-size cubes

12 to 15 nodding onions, peeled and cut in half

15 to 20 sego lily bulbs, washed and scraped

4 to 5 yampa roots, washed, cleaned of all dirt, and cut in half lengthwise

10 to 15 spring beauty bulbs, washed and scraped, if available

2 to 4 dried bitterroots for flavor

Place a two-quart stone pot in the fire and heat until a chunk of fat dropped on the cooking surface sizzles. Add bighorn meat and sauté, stirring until brown on all sides. When nearly done, add the nodding onions and stir until they are translucent—about three minutes. Fill the pot with fresh springwater and bring to a boil. Add the remaining ingredients and simmer until the root vegetables are soft, about thirty minutes.

Pepper Pot Stew (Day 2)

This simple recipe begins with leftover Basic Stone Pot Stew. Just toss fresh ingredients and water into the pot until it is full again. Simmer until newly added ingredients are soft. The process may be followed for up to five days, after which it is usually necessary to discard any remaining pot contents and begin again.[19]

"Mah-duh-k!"[20]

LOOKING AHEAD

In the preceding chapters we have presented what is known about the material, spiritual, and social aspects of Sheep Eater life: their history, the environment in which they lived, their worldview, the way life within families was organized, their relations with the world beyond their territory, their clothing, and the tools they used to exploit the resources available to them. In the final chapter of this book, we will trace what we know about the historical events that caused the removal of Sheep Eater families from their homeland and their relocation to federally defined reservations, where many of their descendants remain to this day. As for other descendants of First Americans, the process of being absorbed into large, mixed-tribe aggregations meant that the Sheep Eaters lost not only their territory and way of life but to some extent their knowledge of their own history and culture. The good news is that efforts have been made to retrieve from memory and record the information that ancestral Sheep Eaters hoped would continue to be at the heart of Sheep Eater life for all future generations.

14
||||||

The Sheep Eater Path to the Contemporary World

The full history of the troubled relationship between Euro-American immigrants and Native American nations is too extensive and complicated to recount here. But fast-forwarding through the documentary record makes clear that the path to independence for the thirteen American colonies, and their postwar pursuit of expanding national boundaries were realized at the expense of the continent's original inhabitants. Although the legality of claims to ownership of territory and resources made by the colonists and militias from three European nations can be robustly disputed—as can their right to dispossess the indigenous groups they encountered—nevertheless, prior to the American Revolution, an initial sequence of agreements had guaranteed Indian possession of vast regions. In the 1768 Treaty of Stanwix, for example, the British sweepingly ceded to various tribal groups "everything west of the Appalachians." Such grandiose gestures amounted to naught, however, because the terms of most treaties defined prior to 1780 were abrogated and replaced by the Founding Fathers with new ones, most of which were ignored as "the Europeans shoved west largely at will."[1]

Particularly egregious shoving occurred during the presidency of Andrew Jackson, as tens of thousands of eastern tribal peoples were forcefully resettled in the newly defined Indian Territory made up of parts of eastern Oklahoma and Kansas. Many who attempted to comply with governmental edicts died en route from hunger, disease, exhaustion, and attacks by marauding whites, and most of those who attempted to resist were exterminated. What was the result of a policy of dumping eastern tribal peoples into lands already occupied by Indian groups in the Plains and far West? In a word, conflict. The Sioux, Crow, Cheyenne, Arapaho, Kiowa, Flathead, Nez Perce, Coeur d'Alene, and various groups of Shoshones fought among themselves for access to rapidly shrinking land and resources—and sometimes fought together against American troops whose mission was their "pacification."

In 1837, Indian populations began to be severely reduced by a smallpox epidemic that in a decade brought death to half the tribal peoples on the Plains.[2] We all know the denouement of this tragic struggle for those whom disease and warfare did not kill. By 1880, almost all the remaining western Indians had been relocated to reservations, many of the groups forced to live side by side with ancient and more recent enemies.

For the indigenous peoples of Sheep Eater territory, whose residence on the continent was so enduring as to justify the phrase "from time immemorial," the preceding scenario transformed their lives in a mere three-quarters of a century.[3] The years between 1805—when Lewis and Clark's Corps of Discovery traded worn-out clothes and utensils for twenty-nine of Cameahwait's literally lifesaving horses— and 1880 saw the traditional Sheep Eater way of life go from stable, peaceful, and independent to threatened, under assault, and finally terminated. The many tribal groups in Sheep Eater territory were inundated by successive waves of trappers, traders, missionaries, land speculators, travelers, tourists, gold miners, and, ultimately, settlers who were fearful of Indians and wanted them "controlled." Between 1810 and 1840 American and British entrepreneurs were heavily involved in the fur trade. The Hudson's Bay Company operated an important trading post at Fort Hall, Idaho, until the 1840s, by which time—in roughly thirty-five years—commercial predation had decimated beaver populations. Fortunately for the species, the beaver hat had by then declined in popularity, otherwise that furbearer might have faced extinction.

In 1841, roughly coincident with the decline of the fur trade, an extensive overland migration of settlers to California and Oregon trekked through the mountains and valleys of Wyoming, Montana, and Idaho. As the immigrants moved west with their herds of cattle, they fed themselves and their livestock on local resources, leaving Shoshone lands overgrazed and overhunted. In the mid-1850s, Mormon missionaries intending to "civilize" the Indians established Fort Lehmi on a tributary of the Salmon River.[4] They led the way for increasing numbers of Mormon settlers, who further restricted Indian access to the land and resources on which they depended.

In 1860, the discovery of gold in central Idaho brought an onslaught of miners and commercial enterprises into the mountains of Northern Shoshone–Sheep Eater territory. All these incursions catalyzed Indian resentment, which was increasingly expressed in attacks on wagon trains, settlements, and mining camps. Violence by Indians led to the establishment of federal military garrisons in the region, some of whose troops, in 1863, radically escalated the level of attacks against persons in the Bear River valley by slaughtering all 200 members of a Shoshone band, most of them women and children.

There was no room in the dream of a manifest destiny—which entitled the descendants of American colonists and newer immigrants from European countries to populate the entire North American continent—for the notion that persons like Sheep Eaters might have a prior claim to the mountains, valleys, plains, and waterfronts that were now envisioned as "western real estate." Like so many other Indian polities, Sheep Eater society—with its kin cliques, healers, apprentice bow makers, skilled tailors, and petroglyph artists, its rhythms of life, seasonal migrations, and vision quests—was reduced in the public mind to just another expression of "savagery" that had to be neutralized and contained.

With their lands occupied, their lifeways disrupted, their access to resources cut off, and their lives seriously at risk, in 1868 the demoralized Shoshone of Idaho accepted the terms of the Fort Bridger Treaty with the federal government to reside, along with the remnants of Paiute-speaking Bannock Indian groups in the area, at the newly created 1.8-million-acre Fort Hall Reservation in southern Idaho, between present-day Idaho Falls and Pocatello. Subsequent surveying errors subtracted more than half a million acres from the reservation, and encroachments upon the resulting 1.2 million acres eventually left the Shoshone-Bannock as sovereign titleholders to their current one-half-million-acre site.

The enforcement of a zero-tolerance policy with regard to any Indian presence on nonreservation land resulted, in 1871, in a mandate given to J. A. Viall, the newly appointed superintendent of Indian Affairs in Montana. Viall was assigned responsibility for the relocation of all those Sheep Eater, Lemhi Shoshone, and Bannock groups not already settled on the Fort Hall Reservation. According to Viall, he dispatched A. J. Simmons to "Stinking Water Valley, Virginia City,

Beaverhead, and other places, to gather together the scattered remnants of these tribes, who were prowling around the country half starved, and in deplorable condition for the purpose of taking them to the Crow Reservation."[5] One of the places that Simmons was charged with depopulating of its resident Indians included that part of the historical homeland of the Sheep Eaters within which, the following year, the U.S. government would create Yellowstone National Park.

It is not surprising that Viall proposed placing the Mountain Shoshone on the Crow Reservation southeast of Billings, Montana, because it was known that on several previous occasions the Sheep Eaters had been allies of the Crows. Historical records of a longtime association between the two tribes include the account by François Larocque, a fur trader from Canada's Northwest Company, of his visit with the Crow in 1805.[6] He reports that the Shoshone were "very numerous and each tribe has different names." Although Larocque does not identify specific groups, he is referring to various bands of Sheep Eaters, Salmon Eaters, and Buffalo Eaters. He also notes that one of their bands had nearly been destroyed and that the remaining twelve tents "live with the Rocky Mountain Indians"—a reference to the Mountain Crow. It is likely that sixty to seventy Shoshone maintained a relatively permanent living arrangement with the Mountain Crow Indians and, based on Larocque's observation (quoted in chapter 7) that they had with them a "pot hewn out of solid stone," they were probably Sheep Eaters.

In 1836, African American explorer and trapper James Beckwourth reported that the Shoshone were so impressed with the trading relationships between the Crow and the American Fur Company that 200 Shoshone lodges permanently joined the Crow. Beckwourth claimed that the Shoshone men married Crow women and in only a few years became so assimilated that they "forgot" their Shoshone origins.[7] The logic of Viall's suggested placement of the Sheep Eaters on the Crow Reservation and the likelihood of its success notwithstanding, the Crows rejected the terms because some Bannock Indians—who were notorious for stealing horses and had, in fact, recently been in conflict with the Crows—were to have been included in the group.

From Simmons's perspective, his successful roundup of Sheep Eater and Bannock groups definitely had its downside. He had 600 Indians assembled but no reservation to escort them to, and winter was approaching. Fortunately for Simmons, Montana rancher Nelson

Story—the man who in 1866 drove 1,000 head of cattle from Texas to Montana and now ran the first large cattle ranch in the Yellowstone River valley just north of the park—received a government contract to feed Simmons's band of wayfaring Indians for the winter. A subsequent exodus and migration saw the group initially settled in Idaho on what came to be known as the Lemhi Farm or the Ross Fork Agency, located on the eponymous Ross Fork of the Salmon River. It was there that anthropologist Robert Lowie visited and interviewed many Sheep Eaters in 1906 and from there that, one year later, Sheep Eater and Bannock Indians were moved to their permanent home on the Fort Hall Reservation.

THE SHEEPEATER WAR OF 1878–79

The conflict identified by the misnomer the *Sheepeater War* was not a war, and the Sheep Eaters were not to blame for the instigating circumstances.[8] Rather, they were scapegoats for the violence that erupted in February 1878 at a mining camp on Loon Creek, near Oro Grande, Idaho, during which five Chinese gold prospectors were killed. According to a contemporary account in the *Yankee Fork Herald* of Bonanza City, Idaho,

> the Chinese were snugly in their warm cabins, with plenty of provisions on hand. Mr. Sheepeater made a call, and not meeting with that hospitality he thought due him on his own land, and his stomach calling loudly for that which he had not to give it, he resolved to do something desperate. After dark the Indians got together, and while most of the Chinese were sitting around a table in one of the largest cabins, engaged in the primitive and fascinating game of "one-cent ante," the Sheepeaters came down like a wolf on the fold, and the heathen, Oro Grande and all, were swept away as by a cyclone, while the victors returned to the bosom of their families on the Middle Fork to make glad the hearts of the little Sheepeaters with the spoils of the heathen.[9]

To twenty-first-century readers, this blatantly racist account, which refers to the Chinese miners by the colloquial term *the heathen* and depicts the Sheep Eaters as bloodthirsty and vengeful, reads more like a work of fiction with an omniscient narrator providing color commentary than it does supposedly fact-based journalism.

Although many years later the Sheep Eaters were absolved of responsibility for the Loon Creek massacre, and blame was placed where it belonged—with white residents of the area who had been hoping to steal the horde of gold they erroneously believed the Chinese miners were accumulating—the event set in motion a military campaign to track down the few remaining Sheep Eaters in the area. On May 31, several detachments of soldiers and supplies were sent out from Boise and Camp Howard to capture the perpetrators but became bogged down in the still-prevalent mountain snowdrifts. When they eventually reached Oro Grande, all structures had been burned to the ground, and the trail of the perpetrators—still thought to have been Sheep Eaters—was cold.

The soldiers retreated, regrouped, and set out again, this time accompanied by a party of Umatilla Indian scouts. In July, there was a skirmish in the Big Creek area with a small group of Sheep Eaters, who wounded but did not kill several soldiers. Near the end of August, still evading capture, the Indians managed to circle around and launch a surprise attack on the army's rear guard, killing one soldier. By September 16, just as winter was approaching and the troops had almost exhausted their supplies of both food and patience, a group of Sheep Eaters was tracked just before nightfall to a campsite near Impassable Canyon on the Middle Fork. Confirmation that the pursuers had cornered their quarry occurred when they heard a dog bark. In the morning, when the soldiers surrounded the camp and prepared to attack, they discovered that the Sheep Eaters had slipped away during the night and eluded them once again. The soldiers' frustration was short-lived, however, for a few days later, a Sheep Eater representative appeared and announced that the group was exhausted and prepared to surrender. In all, fifty-one men, women, and children became captives of the U.S. Army and were taken to the Fort Hall Reservation.

Much less is known about the circumstances leading to the relocation of a number of Sheep Eater families onto the Wind River Reservation in Wyoming, southeast of Yellowstone National Park. A fire in 1906 destroyed government records chronicling the reservation's formative events, but it is known that Shoshone–Sheep Eater groups must have been in residence before 1883, when Togwotee became the Sheep Eater guide for President Chester A. Arthur's expedition into the newly formed park (see chapters 4 and 8).

CAVEAT EMPTOR

Despite the nearly genocidal effects of the Euro-American treat-ment of native populations, those Indian groups that were not entirely decimated have managed to endure—and some have thrived—even though the loss of access to their lands and their inability to follow traditional customs have changed forever the character of their lives. Robert Lowie, Åke Hultkrantz, and Sven Liljeblad interviewed Sheep Eater descendants throughout the twentieth century, and an oral his-tory project at the Wind River Historical Center has recorded the recollections of some Eastern Shoshone residents about their experi-ences with reservation life. In contrast to the preceding body of infor-mation, we want to warn about two sources of *misinformation*, one main-taining that there are no living Sheep Eaters and the other arguing that Sheep Eaters were as much fictional creations as Harry Potter.

The claim of tribal extinction is made in a book by William Alonzo Allen entitled *The Sheep Eaters*, which was published by Shakespeare Press in 1913. Allen purports to have interviewed a 115-year-old Sheep Eater named "the Woman under the Ground" who, according to Allen, communicated with him in sign language. Allen's informant claimed to have been the only survivor of a smallpox outbreak that left her the last remaining Sheep Eater. We now know that much of the material in the book is false, including the tribal affiliation of its elderly central figure, who was actually a Crow Indian.[10] The follow-ing eloquent quotation from Allen's monograph contains at least one error that readers ought to be able to spot immediately: "We chanted our songs to the sun, and the Great Spirit was pleased. He gave us much sheep and meat and berries and pure water, and snow to keep the flies away. The water was never muddy. We had no dogs nor horses. We did not go far from our homes, but were happy in our mountain abode."[11] As even the most cursory historical accounts men-tion the centrality of dogs in Sheep Eater life, such a significant error (as well as others in the monograph that we have not cited) casts doubt on the veracity of the old woman's entire account and raises the suspi-cion that Allen completely fabricated the story.

As is true of many fabulists, William Alonzo Allen's own life was at least as interesting as the inventions he purveyed as true. Born in Ohio in 1848, Allen moved west in 1877, after hearing reports of the discov-ery of gold in the Black Hills. He left behind his wife, Josephine, and a son, William Orwin Allen, who later joined his father in Coulson, Montana, the town from which the city of Billings later developed. W. A. and W. O. Allen are often confused in the historical literature because, aside from the similarity of their names, both father and son were dentists. The elder Allen began his career as a blacksmith and turned to dentistry—legend has it—only after he arrived at the scene of a Nez Perce attack on a stagecoach and discovered the dental tools of a passenger who was missing in action. Allen apparently practiced amateur dentistry for two years and then went to Chicago for professional training. He is said to have learned enough in a month to hang out his DDS shingle and begin pulling teeth.

Teeth were not the only things that Doc Allen pulled, however. He may have been motivated to try to pull the wool over the public's eyes as a way of capitalizing on the interest in a recurrent theme in American popular literature. Beginning in 1826 with the appearance of *The Last of the Mohicans* by James Fenimore Cooper, the reading public was entranced with tales recounting the "last of the red man's race." Allen's contribution to this genre was successful in its time, although it has now been discredited by scholars. Amazingly, recent popular writers and video producers have ignored the scholarly caveats and continue to perpetuate the myth that all Sheep Eaters died of the dreaded pox. This belief is so prevalent that, as recently as 1997, after a meeting at Yellowstone National Park that was attended by persons identifying themselves as Sheep Eaters, a well-known scientist asked: "Did I hear correctly, that some of those Indians claimed they were Sheep Eaters? I thought all of the Sheep Eaters died of smallpox."

A more recent but equally problematic contribution to the Sheep Eater literature has been made by archaeologist Susan Hughes, who—in spite of the robust historical and archaeological records testifying to the existence and lifeways of the Sheep Eaters—would have us believe that such a group never existed in the first place.[12] Hughes sees similarities between historical accounts of Sheep Eaters and the medieval European folk fantasies about wild men who inhabited unexplored forests and wild recesses. She also writes that the "Sheepeater myth is a non-Indian invention, the application of a borrowed Northern Shoshone word [*Tukadika*] to an existing image replayed throughout colonial history. This myth developed during the 1870s, when Philetus Norris, second superintendent of Yellowstone National Park, popularized it to explain the abandoned Indian structures in Yellowstone Park."[13]

If Hughes's explanatory construct is correct, then the documentary record is full of incidents of mass hallucination. For instance, as early as 1855, Mormon Church records indicate that missionized Sheep Eater Indians were baptized at Fort Lemhi, located approximately 120 miles west of Yellowstone National Park.[14] Mormon use of the Sheep Eater name, nearly twenty years before Norris is supposed to have "invented" it for his own ends, suggests that the term predated not only Norris's tenure as park superintendent but the establishment of the park itself.

Hughes goes to considerable lengths to explain the logic of her assertion that the wickiups found in Yellowstone National Park should be construed as shelters built and used exclusively by non–Sheep Eater Indian groups. As part of her argument she cites Aubrey Haines, a respected Yellowstone Park historian, who claimed that wickiups at Lava Creek were constructed and occupied by Crow Indians. Haines's source of information about what group was responsible for the wickiups was a letter written in 1927 by George Bird Grinnell to Park Ranger Philip Martindale.

A closer reading of Grinnell's letter reveals that he never actually specifies that Crow Indians were responsible for the wickiup structures. Rather, he suggests that because the structures' poles were so close together, they must have been made by war parties who were trying to conceal their fires.[15] It is now known—and we presented this information in chapter 6 as part of our discussion of Sheep Eater housing—that the use of a large number of closely spaced poles was characteristic of Sheep Eater construction techniques. Does this mean that all the wickiups in the Yellowstone Park area were built and used by Sheep Eaters? Of course not. As we noted earlier, all western Indian groups constructed wickiups, and almost certainly they are responsible for some of the wickiups in western Wyoming and the surrounding region.

Had Hughes not been so committed to a denial of Sheep Eater existence, she might have consulted a significant number of sources of verification. Her research completely ignores Wickiup Cave and its rich inventory of Sheep Eater artifacts. She fails to mention the well-established link between the content of Dinwoody petroglyphs and Sheep Eater design principles and material culture. She does not discuss the excavations at Mummy Cave or its artifact assemblages and their dates. She ignores steatite pots, their sources, and their presence in Sheep Eater archaeological sites. Nor does she discuss the one artifact synonymous with Sheep Eater hunters: the sheep horn bows used in mountain settings.

In a baffling reference to the sheep traps that we discussed in chapter 12, Hughes grudgingly admits that "if the Shoshone did build these high altitude traps, then they were built by the Tukudeka or Sheepeaters in keeping with the traditional Shoshone use of the term."[16] Consistency would seem to demand that, once an author has denied the existence of an ethnic group, its members should not then be cited as the makers of a very real phenomenon such as a sheep trap. It can be hoped that other scholars, especially historians, who read the Hughes article and notice its logical flaws will overlook the fact that it purports to reflect recent archaeological scholarship and will reject its arguments.

Living Sheep Eaters

David Dominick has noted that "in Wyoming, the last official reports of a Sheepeater group concern their removal to the reservations in the 1870s. They soon lost their identity, at least from a group point of view, as there is no record that they were distinguished for long from the Shoshoni whom they joined on the reservation."[17] The important phrase in the preceding statement is "at least from a group point of view," and its accuracy can be confirmed by going to Web sites maintained by the tribal leadership of the Fort Hall and Wind River reservations. There, tribal history and contemporary affairs are discussed in terms of the Eastern Shoshone at Wind River and simply "the Shoshone" at Fort Hall.[18] On the other hand, in Dominick's archival research and personal interviews with consultants on the Wind River Reservation, he has established that the Sheep Eater ethos persisted well into the twentieth century. For instance, consultant J. T.

> spoke of the Tukudeka as being distinct from the other Indians of the reservation. He mentioned one of the few Tukudeka who after three generations kept his distinctiveness from the rest of the Shoshoni. This man, J. Q., lived on a part of the reservation away from all others...and was known by the other Shoshoni not to participate in the regular Shoshoni dances.[19]

Figure 14.1. A Sheep Eater woman in the 1950s. Contemporary Idaho and Wyoming Sheep Eaters continue to recognize the importance of the heritage left by their mountain-dwelling kinfolk. Illustration by Davíd Joaquín.

Interviews conducted thirty years later by Dr. Sharon Kahin as part of an oral history project sponsored by the Yellowstone National Park Ethnological Resources Survey reveal that a senior generation of residents at the Wind River Reservation has kept alive much traditional Sheep Eater knowledge (Figure 14.1). During an interview conducted on February 4, 1996, Fay (who said, "I used to belong to the Sheep-Eaters") and two others, Mary Jane and Zedora, had a wide-ranging conversation covering such topics as the use of the white clay available at hot springs (or *bow-we-ran* in Shoshone) as a treatment for indigestion and as a way to clean buckskins.[20] Discussion of the use of

obsidian as a tool for bloodletting led to the statement that Obsidian
Cliff in Yellowstone Park is probably a sacred site because, in the past,
"prayers were left there with what ever they left there. They would
offer, like we say now, we give them tobacco, or we leave something
there for the spirits to give a blessing for taking it."[21]

Several times during the interview, Fay and her companions
expressed concern that Indian access to Yellowstone Park to obtain
white clay or obsidian is restricted and that it can take a month or longer for a request for admission to be processed. Similarly, as Fay noted,
"when you go into Yellowstone for the Bear Root [a plant ground into
dosa and added to the fire during sweat lodges], you cannot even stop
along the road and pick the flowers.... Like Bear Root, even if you see
it along the road, you can't even touch it. You can go along there and
reach for it, but you can't stop and dig them up."[22]

This statement, and others like it in the transcript, leave one with
a sense of the impediments facing tribal peoples who want to maintain
continuity with past cultural practices. The bureaucratic regulations
that try to protect the park's resources from the thousands of visitors
each year who would like to take home a memento of their trip to one
of nature's grandest creations also make it very difficult for descen-
dant Sheep Eaters and others to maintain a connection with the lifeways of their ancestors.

The women interviewed at Fort Washakie nearly a decade ago
were well aware that the connection between the past and present is
tenuous and growing more so. As Fay said, "It's a pity that they didn't
do this project 20 or 30 years ago. Zedora has helped me on other
projects like this in the past, but the first one we did was in the [19]80s
and a lot of those people that we talked to are gone now."[23] Dennis,
who entered the discussion when it was nearly over, set the time line
even further back: "Stuff like this should have been done eighty years
ago. Like Fay said, when you are a kid you don't think of something
like this.... Kids now do not listen to grandparents." But he went on to
say, "Our daughter, Lua, she has been born and raised traditionally.
She will probably die traditional. She goes to sweats, she goes to
fasts.... She is always sweating and pow-wowing."[24]

Although it is true that younger Sheep Eater men and women may
be losing contact at a precipitous rate with their immediate forebears,
whose knowledge of ancient customs was passed down to them by
their forebears in the course of daily living, other forms of transmission

are available and beginning to provide links to the past. We hope that more books like this one will become available, enriching the lives of persons interested in researching their Sheep Eater ancestry and informing others about times, people, and events that history has temporarily overlooked or, worse, maligned. The electronic media, particularly video and DVD, are increasingly present at museums and cultural centers, augmenting more static exhibits and bringing the past to life. Fay's description of these presentations as "the screens that run with history" is particularly apt, for what makes history "run" are accounts of vital, resourceful people like the Sheep Eaters and their interaction with the forces at work in their lives.[25]

Epilogue

||||||||||||||||||||||||||||||

"By Diligent Discovery":
Learning More about the Sheep Eaters

The very good news is that although in this book we have presented what is currently known about the Sheep Eater Indians and their life-ways, we can say with confidence that the body of knowledge about these remarkable people will continue to grow. First of all, it is likely that unpublished documents and other source materials will continue to surface, essentially corroborating the Sheep Eater story as presently outlined. Just recently, Yellowstone National Park historian Lee Whittlesey discovered an account by Yellowstone traveler and newspaper editor Spencer Ellsworth, who described his 1882 encounter with a *Mr. Topham*.[1] As the two men sat around Ellsworth's evening campfire, Topham told of his trip some years earlier to the Madison mountain range in Montana, northwest of Yellowstone Park, to trade with a group of Sheep Eaters. In his narrative, Topham referred to his trading partners in the uncomplimentary terms that, as we have seen, were often used by Euro-American visitors to the frontier. But despite his cultural prism, which made the Sheep Eaters appear impoverished and timid, Topham was still able to walk away from the trading session with two horse-loads of furs.

The new, significant information in Topham's eyewitness account establishes a Sheep Eater presence in the Madison mountain region and thus anchors the results of archaeological fieldwork undertaken in the area over the past twenty-five years. Numerous sites in the area have been attributed to the Sheep Eaters by archaeologist Carl Davis and his colleagues, who identify their research problem in the following terms:

Archaeologists working in the Northwestern Plains and adjacent Rocky Mountains find it difficult to identify historic native peoples in the homogenous hunter–gatherer material culture of the recent past. Extant identifications tenuously rely on one or two items of material culture—certain pottery types and projectile point styles (i.e., Frison 1976). The singular exception may be the Northern Shoshone, and potentially, the Sheepeater. As derived from the ethnographic literature, a constellation of material culture traits—pottery, chipped stone tool forms, and habitation and game capture features—appear to be the archaeological residues of Northern Shoshone occupations.[2]

As the result of this group's deliberate research strategy, the most productive source of future new information about the Sheep Eaters is likely to come through archaeological inquiry.

Davis and associates have recognized the potential benefit of an approach that first identifies a Mountain Shoshone site through the presence of culturally distinctive artifacts and then carefully excavates the site to learn about the activities that took place there. To some extent, we have relied on the results of archaeological research in our presentation of material in this book. The study of a sheep horn bow recovered from archaeological deposits and the excavation of root-vegetable roasting features have added immensely to our knowledge of Sheep Eater lifeways. Davis and his colleagues are, however, proposing a departure from the previous, somewhat haphazard discovery of one Sheep Eater site here and another there. They advocate a research program that would seek out Sheep Eater sites and excavate them before they are lost to erosion and vandalism.

Thinking in a similar vein, Chris Finley led an expedition in summer 2003 to record suspected Sheep Eater sites on Boulder Ridge in the Washakie Wilderness, south of Cody, Wyoming. Finley is not part of the Davis team, but he has also recognized the importance of recording Sheep Eater sites—especially those with wooden features that might be destroyed by wildfires—before they disappear. With some funds provided by administrators at the Shoshone National Forest, Finley enlisted help from his son Judson Finley, a doctoral student in geoarchaeology at Washington State University, and archaeologist Dan Eakin, from the Office of the Wyoming State Archaeologist. This trio of archaeologists represents an excellent understanding of Wyoming cultural resources, they knew how to discover sites and describe their contents, and they were committed to learning more about sites through excavation.

Accompanied by a group of students from Northwest Wyoming College, they set out for Boulder Ridge, a roughly 13-kilometer-long landform east of Yellowstone Park. At an elevation of nearly 10,000 feet, the ridge is a difficult place to get to, but at the same time, it is prime bighorn sheep territory, and, as Finley's team discovered, it was once a major Sheep Eater hunting and camping area.

The list of features that the team found and mapped is extensive. Two of the long-abandoned sheep traps included rock cairns, low rock walls, and chunks of deadfall timber arranged into drivelines. There were places along the drivelines where hunters had constructed wooden fences or barricades, designed to keep sheep from escaping. The researchers found small circular or oblong rock-filled pits—that might have been used as hunting blinds—made by stacking rocks into low, U-shaped walls. Similar features were found within the drivelines, where they apparently served as places where persons could hide and then pop out, scaring the sheep and forcing them to stay within the lines. Several of these features are situated quite close to the edge of the mountain, where it drops off steeply into the South Fork of the Shoshone River, and they may have served as lookout posts for hunters watching for any game that might have been moving up or down the mountainside.

The Finley team also recorded a collapsed wickiup that had been built in a dense grove of spruce and fir trees. As they made a plan-view map of the feature, they noted that there were no associated surface artifacts. In fact, Finley's crew did not find many artifacts at all. There were a few isolated pieces of flaking debris—remnants of stone-tool production—and an artifact scatter consisting of fifty to sixty chipped-stone fragments, but the absence of arrowheads and other items led them to suspect that hikers and hunters had helped themselves to any portable objects originally left there. At the end of the project, the team's report indicated that clearly the most fascinating and significant finds were the sheep traps. These were somewhat confusing to sort out, but regardless of how they functioned, it was apparent that the rock blinds, cairns, rock walls, and deadfall timber walls had once been part of a sophisticated sheep-hunting system.

Then the unthinkable happened. In autumn 2003, ten days after Finley and his crew left the field, a wildfire swept over Boulder Ridge. The beetle-infested trees burned hot and fast as the fire consumed much of what was in its path, even as fire-fighting crews dropped

Figure E.1. The Boulder Ridge site after a fire in autumn 2003. Pin flags identify the locations of artifacts that were exposed by the fire. Photograph courtesy of Chris Finley.

retardant to slow its spread. Fortunately, the area ultimately devastated by the Boulder Ridge fire was not large compared to the extent of some forest fires, but the archaeologists were unable to assess the damage to the sheep traps and other features because heavy snow soon covered the burned ridge, preventing access to the area. Once the spring melt had made trails passable again, Chris Finley and Dan Eakin went back up on Boulder Ridge.

What they found is one of the most remarkable Sheep Eater discoveries since the excavation of Mummy Cave.[3] The fire had burned away between about ten and twenty centimeters of the forest floor— a humus layer composed of compacted pine needles and leaves—and in the process, it exposed thousands of burned bones and artifacts (Figure E.1). The fire had also incinerated the wickiup and some of the wood in the drivelines, but the number of newly exposed remains was extraordinary. In contrast to their previous visit less than a year before, this time the team found a flat-bottom Intermountain ware ceramic pot, rim fragments from a steatite vessel, stone awls or drills, dozens of projectile points, and the typically leaf-shaped Shoshone knives. There were large numbers of scrapers, including several split-cobble *teshoas*, which are diagnostic of the Shoshone. Perhaps the most surprising finds were a bone flesher with a serrated end that was used for cleaning hides, three bone discs, and a bone wedge.

Finley had thought that activities at segments of the site complex had taken place in the protohistoric and historic periods, and this expectation was confirmed by the presence of Euro-American trade goods such as iron awls, projectile points, and more than 1,000 glass beads scattered across the site. There was also extensive debris from attempts to manufacture tools from metal; several metal tools resulting from these episodes included one scraper and what looked like handles from broken knives.

Using global positioning equipment, the team carefully plotted the location of each artifact and took photographs. Patterns in the spatial distribution of artifacts immediately began to emerge. They found areas in which it was clear that the main activity had been butchering animals, and other areas where hides had been processed (Figure E.2). Not all the consequences of the fire were positive, however. The faunal remains at the site were so badly damaged that, although recognizable, the butchered bones, mostly from sheep, quickly disintegrated when touched. There were several sheep skulls with missing horns, but whether the horns had burned off in the fire or had been removed centuries before by hunters intending to make bows or other objects is not known. The fragility of the bone assemblage meant that it could not be collected, so questions about the age of the animals or the season of their deaths remain unanswered.

As we write this chapter in late summer 2005, the analysis of the collected artifacts is just beginning, so questions about the sources of the raw material used to make the stone tools are unanswered. Much of the lithic material is obsidian—very likely from the Yellowstone area—but whether it is from Obsidian Cliff or another source is not yet known. Many artifacts remain on Boulder Ridge awaiting collection, but until the process is complete, detailed summary statements about the artifact assemblage and what it tells us about the past are on hold.

Nevertheless, several conclusions seem justified. First of all, it is clear that a profitable approach to learning more about Sheep Eater lifeways consists of a targeted program of archaeological research. Archaeologists can use the Boulder Ridge site complex as a model for

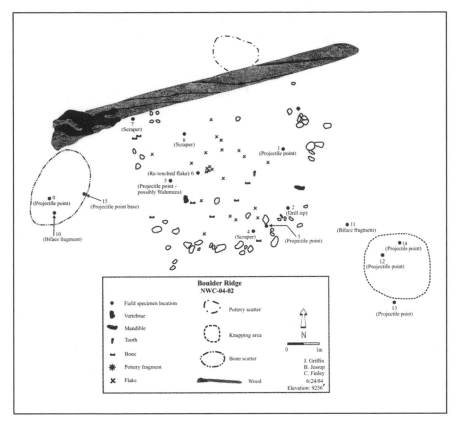

Figure E.2. A sketch map of one feature of the Boulder Ridge site showing the artifact distribution. The circular rock alignment may represent the base of a conical-shaped wickiup or lodge. Even though the fire destroyed some artifacts, the remaining ones represent an unparalleled opportunity to study the relationships between the tools. Original map courtesy of Chris Finley. Redrawn by Bonita Newman.

learning the appropriate techniques and methods for exploring *un-burned* sheep trap complexes and increasing the likelihood of finding intact deposits.

In the recent past, archaeologists excavated the interior floor areas of several dozen regional wickiups and were disappointed when the recovered artifact assemblage was so meager. After making maps and creating a good photographic record of the sites, they concluded that these features revealed very little about the past. A different lesson is learned from the investigation of the collapsed wickiup on Boulder Ridge that was consumed by fire. There, the artifacts exposed in the burning were found *outside* the structure, surrounding the wickiup, and not inside on the floor. In the future, investigators need to include excavation units in the area adjacent to a wickiup and not just inside the structure.

Through a combination of artifact analysis and site structural studies, it should also be possible to explore questions about the composition of the social units engaged in the hunt and related activities. This question has been addressed, if not completely answered, at the Boulder Ridge site complex, where it is clear from the presence of *tesboas*, typically women's tools, that women played an important role. All too often, assumptions about the division of labor in foraging groups have resulted in a static picture in which men were hunters and women were plant gatherers, housekeepers, or child minders. The evidence from Boulder Ridge suggests that women played an integral role in hunting activities, possibly sitting in the hunting blinds and jumping up when necessary to direct sheep into the trap. We can say with more certainty that the distribution of hide-processing and garment-making tools in areas near the bone beds suggests that women were there, right in the middle of the action, either during or immediately after a hunt. This kind of important information does not appear in the ethnographic record of Sheep Eater lifeways.

Many other questions about the Sheep Eaters might be answered through careful archaeological examination of the sites they once occupied. The eminent North American archaeologist Patty Jo Watson has written: "The archaeological record can reveal ancient culture—the mental activities of long dead people—if skillfully interrogated."[4] To learn more about the Sheep Eaters, from their day-to-day activities to their values and viewpoints, archaeologists need to become skillful interrogators. They need to devise research programs that bring appropriate questions to bear on the material remains of dynamic human systems left behind and buried by time. To recover more complete information about the highly capable mountaineering Sheep Eaters, we must, without question, be more diligent in our attempts at discovery.

Notes

Prologue—What's in a Name?

1. *Shoshone* is also spelled *Shoshoni*, most often by anthropologists and linguists wishing to emphasize that the pronunciation of the final syllable is "ee."

2. Various spellings include *Tukudeka*, *Tukaduka*, and *Tukurika* (Murphy and Murphy 1986:306). The English name *Sheep Eaters* was used as early as 1865.

3. Liljeblad 1957:56, emphasis added.

4. Prior to Lowie's research—initially published in 1909—the only information about the Shoshone had come from trappers and explorers, the best known being Meriwether Lewis. Lewis wrote about his encounters with the Kukundika (Lemhi), particularly noting their clothing and personal adornment, in his journals describing his experiences during the epic journey of the Corps of Discovery in the early historic period. In the twentieth century, the work of Robert and Yolanda Murphy presented an overview of historical references relating to the Idaho Shoshone. The most informative material on Shoshone social organization and religion was collected by two Swedish anthropologists, Sven Liljeblad and Åke Hultkrantz, whose research focused on the Idaho and Wyoming Shoshone, respectively. Readers interested in a comprehensive listing of the work of these researchers and many other sources should consult the excellent series of chapters on the Shoshone in the *Great Basin* volume of the *Handbook of North American Indians*, edited by Warren L. D'Azevedo and published in 1986 by the Smithsonian Institution.

5. Lowie 1909; Steward 1970 [1938]: preface.

6. Shimkin 1947.

7. For a comprehensive discussion of the Indian nations that lived in and around Yellowstone National Park, see Janetski 2002; and Nabokov and Loendorf 2004.

Chapter 1—Objects of Pity

1. *The Compact Edition of the Oxford English Dictionary* 1971: s.v. "history."

2. The most accurate description of the Sheep Eaters available until now was published in 1964 by David Dominick. His paper is called "The Sheepeaters" and appears in the *Annals of Wyoming* 36, no. 2, as well as on the Web site of the Wind River Historical Center at www.windriverhistory.org/exhibits/sheepeaters/Resources/Dominick.pdf. This Web site also lists a series of video programs about the Sheep Eaters containing up-to-date, factual information (see ch. 6, n. 13).

3. Chittenden 1964 [1895]:11.

4. Coutant 1899:705.

5. Harris 1952:109.

6. See Nabokov and Loendorf 2004:274–85; Weixelmann 1992, 2004.

7. Russell 1965 [1914]:26. Although it is clear in Russell's journal that he is describing the pedestrian Sheep Eater hunters who pursued bighorn sheep in the Absaroka Mountains, he refers to them as Shoshone. It was Aubrey Haines, editor of the 1965 edition of Russell's journal, who identified them as Sheep Eaters.

8. Irving 1843:4.

9. Irving 1843:157–58.

10. Irving 1843:176.

11. Ferris 1983:171.

12. Thompson 1854:490.

13. Olden 1923:13.

14. Humfreville 1899:271; Lander 1860:137.

15. Philetus Norris (1881:35) describes his trip to the Lemhi Agency in his Yellowstone National Park superintendent's report. Accounts of Indians hunting in the park appear in army records and have been published by Madsen (1980:131).

16. Sholly and Newman 1991:106–7.

Chapter 2—"We Are All the Same People, All the Way Back"

The quotation in the chapter title is from a Sheep Eater consultant who was interviewed by David Dominick in 1963.

1. Meriwether Lewis, journal entry, August 19, 1805, in Moulton 1988:119.

2. Sacajawea, a Mountain Shoshone woman, was captured by the Hidatsa near the headwaters of the Missouri River in Montana and taken 600 kilometers to the east. Through her subsequent association with the expedition of Lewis and Clark in 1805, she became well known in her own time and an icon to future generations.

3. Meriwether Lewis, journal entry, August 18, 1805, in Moulton 1988:117.

4. A discussion of the Shoshone use of horses and places with good pasturage in Idaho and Wyoming is found in Liljeblad 1957:41–56.

5. Liljeblad 1957:93.

6. Harris 1952:88–89; Skarsten 1964.

7. Hanson 1981.

8. Goss 1999:78; Liljeblad 1957:23.

9. Liljeblad 1957:23.

10. Steward 1970 [1938]:137.

11. John 1975:307; Moorhead 1968:146.

12. Hanson (1981:45–53) presents redrafted copies of Drouillard's maps and notations.

13. François Larocque, a Northwest Fur Company agent, encountered the Flathead near present-day Billings, Montana, in 1805 (Wood and Thiessen 1985). William Price Hunt, leading the overland Astor expedition, noted Flathead groups in the Bighorn basin in 1811 (Irving 1836). These separate accounts suggest that the Flathead may have been expanding their hunting territory into safer areas.

14. Lamb 1958.

15. We recognize that the distribution and age of Numic-speaking groups in the Wyoming region are controversial issues and that there are significant differences among the researchers who study these problems (for various views, see Madsen and Rhode 1994). At the same time, it is important to recognize that recent archaeological discoveries in Idaho and Wyoming point toward ancient cultural connections between these regions and the Great Basin.

16. Husted and Edgar 2002:145–46; Wright 1978.

17. Holmer 1990, 1994.

18. Francis and Loendorf 2002; but for another point of view, see Quinlan and Woody 2003.

19. Francis and Loendorf 2002:94–107.

20. Danny Walker (2004) reports on the house pits near Riverton. McKern and Harrel (2004) provide an up-to-date compilation of the house pit sites in Wyoming.

21. Southern Idaho examples are discussed by Butler (1986:131).

22. Susan Hughes (2003) offers the most comprehensive analysis of the faunal remains from Mummy Cave.

23. Thomas 1981.

24. Husted 1995:68.

25. For additional discussion, see Nabokov and Loendorf 2004.

26. Wright and Dirks 1983.

Chapter 3—Purple Mountain Majesties

The epigraph, quoted from Hayden (1872), is from a discussion titled *National Parks: The American Experience* and can be found on the National Park Service Web site at www.cr.nps.gov/history/online_books/runte1/chap2.htm.

1. Information about many aspects of the natural history of the Yellowstone National Park area is available online at www.nps.gov/yell. See also Despain 1990; Good and Pierce 1996; and Smith and Siegel 2000.

2. For a discussion of the slave raid as a precursor to the horse raid, see Ewers 1980 [1955]:310. An extensive discussion of slavery on the southern Plains is found in Brooks 2002 and includes information on the Comanche and Apache, groups formerly resident on the northern Plains.

3. Trenholm and Carley (1964:25) identify the Bighorn Medicine Wheel as Sheep Eater in origin, but Hultkrantz (1970) questions this assignment. A recent study of the Medicine Wheel by Campbell and Foor (2004) suggests it was constructed in a number of stages.

4. Facts about the size of Yellowstone National Park are available online at www.yellowstone-natl-park.com/facts.htm.

Chapter 4—Living among the Powerful Spirits

1. *The Compact Edition of the Oxford English Dictionary* 1971: s.v. "primitive."

2. Tylor 1871. Despite the fact that Tylor shared some of the biases of his time, he was an original thinker who played a formative role in the history of anthropology. Many of his ideas are still relevant to anthropological research today.

3. See Geraldine Hultkrantz's *Shoshone Tales* (n.d.b), an unpublished manuscript developed from the field notes of Åke Hultkrantz.

4. Hultkrantz offers an excellent overview of Shoshone religion in *Native Religions of North America*, first printed in 1987.

5. Hultkrantz 1981:34.

6. Francis and Loendorf 2002:113; Nabokov and Loendorf 2002:158.

7. An initial discussion regarding water ghost petroglyphs is presented in a paper by Loendorf (1993). Subsequent discussion of these figures is found in Francis and Loendorf 2002:116–18. A more lengthy presentation of the Sheep Eater worldview as depicted in rock art appears in Loendorf 2004.

8. Discussion of the vision quest at rock art sites is found throughout Shoshone literature. Hultkrantz (1981:35) offers a good description of the practice.

9. Keyser (1992) offers a series of references for Salish rock art sites.

10. Frison and Van Norman 1993.

11. For an illustration of this figure, see Francis and Loendorf 2002:93.

12. Hultkrantz 1951:36–37.

13. Unpublished interview notes in Hultkrantz n.d.b.

14. The plant's power is mentioned by several Shoshone ethnographers including Lowie (1924:297), Shimkin (1937–38, 1953, 1986:325), Steward (1943:389), and Hultkrantz (n.d.a).

15. Unpublished field notes in Hultkrantz n.d.b., "Love Puha-Medicine."

16. Hultkrantz n.d.b., "Love Puha-Medicine."

17. Whitley 1994:362–64, 2000:109–11.

18. Lowie 1909:217.

19. Lowie 1909:218; Vander 1997:486.

20. Vander 1997:486–87.

21. Vander 1997:67–71.

22. Hultkrantz 1957:135–36.

Chapter 5—Weaving the Social Fabric

1. Mead 1973.

2. Murdock 1981.

3. Binford 2001:430.

4. Murdock 1949:1.

5. Malouf 1966:4–5, 1967.

6. Malouf 1966:4.

7. Steward 1970 [1938]:114–16.

8. Information on Sheep Eater birth, childhood, and marriage conventions comes primarily from Lowie (1909) and Steward (1943). Neither of these authors differentiates between the Sheep Eaters and the Salmon Eaters, and, as noted earlier, these two

groups were very similar and had overlapping membership. As the members of one group could and did periodically become affiliated with the other, the customs of families of one group mirrored the practices of the other. During the time that Lowie conducted his research, the Shoshone and significant numbers of Sheep Eaters were still on the Ross Fork Agency Reservation in northern Idaho, prior to their relocation in 1907 to the Fort Hall Reservation.

9. Lowie 1924:272.

10. Liljeblad (1957:95) notes that the Sheep Eaters were known to observe cross-cousin marriage rules more than other Shoshone groups.

11. From James Russell Lowell's 1843 poem, "A Glance behind the Curtain," line 202 (Lowell 1924:52).

12. Haines 1965:26.

13. Shimkin 1947.

14. Henderson 1866:20.

15. Wood and Thiessen 1985.

16. Early trade is discussed by Hughes and Bennyhoff (1986).

17. For information about Sheep Eater tailoring of wolf pelts, see Liljeblad 1957:98.

18. Both Osborne Russell and Bart Henderson describe this Sheep Eater custom.

19. Malouf 1966:4.

Chapter 6—Sheltering Sheep Eaters

1. Bird 1960:176.

2. Earl of Dunraven 1917:221–22, 246. The Earl of Dunraven's record of his trip, *The Great Divide*, was originally published in 1876. In 1917 it was included in a book titled *Hunting in the Yellowstone*, edited by Horace Kephart.

3. Baillie-Grohman 1882:177. The Baillie-Grohman and Dunraven identification of Sheep Eater wickiups is based on their historical observations. Some of the wickiups they saw, however, may have represented shelters built by other tribes.

4. Lowie 1909:183; see also Clark 1885:337.

5. Dominick 1964:163–64. This information was provided by a living Sheep Eater.

6. Hoffman 1961:36.

7. Jack E. Haynes, letter to Åke Hultkrantz, October 23, 1955, in Hultkrantz's possession.

8. Stuart Conner and Ken Feyhl wrote unpublished accounts of their findings at the Parker Peak site. These can be obtained by contacting the Cultural Records Office in Yellowstone National Park or by access to Stuart Conner's personal files.

9. Davis and Scott 1987.

10. Davis and Scott 1987:89.

11. In 1975 Carl Davis published an informative article about Wickiup Cave in *Plains Anthropologist*.

12. Loendorf 1967.

13. Love describes his discovery on the video entitled *The Sheep Eaters: Masters of the Mountains* (2001), which is available at the Wind River Historical Center.

14. Frison 1991:265 contains a discussion of this cache of snares.

Chapter 7—Chip and Chisel versus Make and Bake

1. Wood and Thiessen 1985:185.

2. Thwaites (1904–06, 5:10) and Osborne Russell (1965 [1914]:23, 26) also mention these pots, and Nathaniel Wyeth (1851:211) described them in a letter published by Henry Schoolcraft.

3. Bridger's "green pipestone" is on a map drawn by Pierre-Jean DeSmet (see Gowans 1989). Adams 1992 is an excellent source for the distribution of steatite sources in Wyoming, and other source information is found in Schoen and Vlchek 1991; Frison 1982; and Feyhl 1997.

4. Richard Adams, Office of the Wyoming State Archaeologist, and Tory Taylor, mountain outfitter and guide, Dubois, Wyoming, have devoted significant research to steatite pots. They are currently working in tandem with Shoshone National Forest, and their knowledge of steatite vessels in Wyoming is extensive. Adams continues to measure steatite pots and remains the best source for the sizes and volumes of the large number of pots in his ever-growing inventory.

5. Wedel 1954:403.

6. Hoffman 1961:40–52.

7. More recently, archaeologists from the Midwest Archaeological Center found more ceramics at the site, possibly from the same vessel. The radiocarbon ages of the "old surface," described by Hoffman as yielding the ceramics, indicate that the weakly formed A-horizon soils date to between 1350 ± 80 and 1570 ± 90 BP (Cannon et al. 1996).

8. The Marceau manuscript (1980) is on file with the Wyoming Cultural Records Office in Laramie. The dissertation was not finalized.

9. Marceau 1980:23.

10. Information on the Lawrence Site can be found in Reeve et al. 1979.

11. On the basis of his comparative study, Marceau has also suggested that steatite pots were significantly smaller than ceramic ones. Evaluating this generalization is complicated by the fact that the two classes of artifacts are not comparable for several reasons. One problem is that the fragmentary nature of the ceramic vessels makes it hard to estimate their original size, whereas the more complete steatite pots are readily measured. Another difference is that the manufacture of a steatite vessel is a subtractive process during which the stone is cut away to form the pot, whereas making a ceramic vessel is an additive process. Also, within structural limits, more clay can be added to a ceramic pot during manufacture to increase its size, but one cannot cut away more steatite than was originally present in the outcrop. Last, it must also be kept in mind that steatite is a heavy material, and the potential weight of a pot placed practical limitations on how big a vessel could be and still be manageable.

12. Adams 1992:116.

13. Marceau 1980:51.

Chapter 8—Fleeced and Greased

1. Accounts of the Little People (called *Nynymbi*) are common among the Shoshone (see Liljeblad 1986:654). Culin (1901:21) describes their occasional capture by eagles.

2. The independent discovery of the mummified bodies of two infants found in the Pedro Mountains of central Wyoming may have contributed to public belief in the existence of a group of tiny prehistoric people. X-rays of the first mummy, discovered in the 1930s, established definitively that the body was an anencephalic infant, whose cranial deformity gave it the appearance of a miniature adult. In the 1990s, the second mummy was brought to the attention of Dr. George Gill, a professor of anthropology at the University of Wyoming, who arranged for physicians at Children's Hospital in Denver to examine the remains. These were also identified as belonging to an anencephalic infant, and subsequent DNA analysis determined that the infant was an American Indian. Radiocarbon dating placed the mummy's age at approximately 300 years.

3. This account appears in a *Billings Gazette* interview with Medicine Crow (see Peterson 1966). Hultkrantz (1970:253) makes this same observation.

4. It was the second Yellowstone Park superintendent, Philetus Norris (1881:35), who labeled the Sheep Eaters pygmies.

5. Susan Hughes transported the remains to Ohio for study; the results are published in Saul and Saul 1987. It should be clear that we identify the human remains from Mummy Cave as belonging to a Sheep Eater individual on the basis of the artifacts found in the associated level. No other scientific study makes this claim.

6. Hughes 1987:4.

7. Condon 1961 [1949]. Willey and Key (1992:36) report the measurements of the Yellowstone Park skeletal remains, but they worked with only a small comparative sample and do not suggest an ethnic affiliation for them.

8. The distinctive, leaf-shaped knife with sharpening that alternates from one face to the other is a documented Shoshone tool (Frison 1991:132; Larsen and Kornfield 1994; Reed 1994). Shimkin's 1937–38 field notes contain illustrations of these knives that were provided by Shoshone consultants. Rawhide wrapping around the bases of the handheld knives restricts the area for sharpening. With regard to accompanying animal companions, descendants of Sheep Eaters today claim that their ancestors interred dogs in human burials.

9. Lowie 1909:182.

10. Lowie 1909:182.

11. Husted and Edgar 2002:81, 210.

12. Susan Hughes (1987:4) presents a good description of ear ornaments.

13. Liljeblad 1957:97.

14. Shimkin 1937–38: May 20, 1937, notes.

15. Split-cobble hide-cleaning tools (*teshoas*) are mentioned in early accounts about the Sheep Eaters, in part because it was thought to be counterproductive for artisans to use such crude tools when there were iron alternatives available. We now know that the tools continued to be used because they were as effective as metal ones

and the raw material was freely available (see Jones 1875; Shimkin 1937–38: May 20, 1937, notes).

16. Liljeblad 1957:97.

17. Husted and Edgar 2002:81, 216.

18. On Great Basin Shoshone, see Steward 1943:274.

19. Meriwether Lewis, journal entry, August 20, 1805, in Moulton 1988:128.

20. Steward (1943:274) discusses the rejection of coyote skins for clothing, whereas Liljeblad (1957:98) describes the uses that Sheep Eaters made of these skins.

21. What we know about the use of wolf skins also comes from Liljeblad (1957:98). Not all Sheep Eater groups regarded the use of coyote and wolf skins as taboo. The difference in perspective may relate to how long various groups had lived in the northern mountains. Those Sheep Eaters arriving later from the Great Basin may still have maintained the Shoshone aversion to exploiting predators such as coyotes and wolves.

22. Egan 1917:238.

23. Rabbit fur was found in deposits from Layer 36 at Mummy Cave, but only four rabbit bones, representing one or at most two individuals, were recovered (Hughes 2003: table 5.1). In contrast, Layers III–IV at Pictograph Cave near Billings, Montana, contained eighty rabbits (Mulloy 1958:220). Although rabbits do occur at higher elevations at Yellowstone Park and elsewhere, they are found in the significant numbers required for communal drives only in Wyoming's lower basins.

24. Husted and Edgar 2002:90–91.

25. Liljeblad 1957:98.

26. Husted and Edgar 2002:90, 227.

27. Meriwether Lewis, journal entry, August 14, 1805, in Moulton 1988:94n8. Julian Steward (1970 [1938]:187) has expressed the belief that the term "Broken Moccasin Indians" is another name for the Sheep Eaters.

Chapter 9—Barkeology, or, What We Know about Sheep Eater Dogs

1. Savolainen et al. 2002.

2. Hare et al. 2002.

3. Powell 2002:2.

4. Young and Goldman 1944:181, quoted in Henderson 1994:146.

5. Kurz 1937:239.

6. Belden 1974 [1870]:162.

7. Scott and Fuller 1965:30.

8. Haag 1956.

9. Nabokov and Loendorf 2004:xxx.

10. Ferris 1983:181.

11. Russell 1965 [1914]:26.

12. Lowie 1993 [1918]:165–69.

13. Ewers 1980 [1955]:306.

14. Roe 1955:22–27.

15. Shimkin 1937–38.

16. Henderson 1994:150. For sources comparing the relative strength and endurance of dogs and horses, see Henderson 1994.

17. For a discussion of canine castration, see Henderson 1994:148. For claims that the Sheep Eaters did not castrate their dogs, see Shimkin 1937–38.

18. Shimkin 1986:320.

19. Scott and Fuller 1965:45–51.

20. The estimate of the number of dogs kept by Plains groups is from Ewers 1980 [1955]:307.

21. Jones 1875:274.

22. Vigne et al. 2004:259.

23. Ewers 1980 [1955]:286; Roe 1955:274.

24. Stewart 1994.

Chapter 10—The Call of the Bow

1. Kroeber 1967.

2. Pope 1920:178.

3. Pope 2005:26.

4. Alice Biel (2004:7) relates that Yellowstone Park Superintendent Albright apparently regretted issuing the permit for this hunting expedition.

5. Pope 1926.

6. Holm 1982:116.

7. Hamilton 1982:98.

8. Wyeth 1851:212.

9. Russell 1965 [1914]:26–27.

10. Belden 1974 [1870]:112.

11. Miller 1951:7.

12. The McKey sheep horn bow was among the items in the Bob Scriver collection that was transferred in 2002 to the Scriver Center at the Montana Historical Society. Despite the fact that the center had received a permit to house and display the bow, it was later confiscated by the U.S. Fish and Wildlife Service on the grounds that eagle feathers were associated with it. Although it is true that the arrows accompanying the bow were fletched with feathers from birds of prey, none of them was from eagles. Nevertheless, the State of Montana allowed the seizure to stand. The bow was eventually given to the Blackfoot tribe of Montana.

13. Tom Lucas describes the making of a sheep horn bow in a video program, *The Sheep Eaters: Archers of the Yellowstone* (2003). Copies are available from the Wind River Historical Center.

14. Holm 1982.

15. The single-piece horn bow is described by Laubin and Laubin (1980:84).

16. Frison 1980:173.

17. Laubin and Laubin 1980:83.

18. William Peck, letter to Gary Everhardt, June 4, 1973, on file at Grand Teton National Park, Moose, WY.

19. Laubin and Laubin 1980:83–84.

20. Wilson (1985 [1919]:107) and Beckwourth (1972:285–86) describe the use of hot springs to soften horn for making bows.

21. Wyeth 1851:212.

22. Frison 1991:364–65.

23. Shimkin 1937–38.

24. Frison 1991:132–34.

25. Shimkin 1937–38.

Chapter 11—The Thing Belonging to the Bow

1. *The Compact Edition of the Oxford English Dictionary* 1971: s.v. "arrow."

2. Wyeth 1851:212; Lowie 1924:246.

3. Wyeth 1851:212.

4. Lowie 1909:192; Wyeth 1851:213.

5. Dominick 1964:156.

6. Davis 1975:301; Husted and Edgar 2002:91; Murphy and Murphy 1986:301.

7. Pope 2005:57–58. *Hunting with the Bow and Arrow* by Saxton Pope was originally published in 1923 but is now available online in a free, downloadable format at Project Gutenberg (www.gutenberg.org) and in book form in various other editions.

8. Cannon et al. 1997; Cannon et al. 2001.

9. Shoshone consultants noted that red obsidian was particularly prized for making ceremonial artifacts.

10. More about Dr. Lee A. Green's use of obsidian blades to correct dermatological problems can be found online by going to www.umich.edu/~urecord/9798/Sep10_97/surgery.htm.

11. Cannon et al. 1997; Cannon et al. 2001.

Chapter 12—Hunting Bighorn Sheep

1. Russell (1965 [1914]:21–25) is describing bighorn sheep in the Absaroka Mountains to the north of the present town of Dubois, Wyoming. In this area and in the Wind River Mountains to the south, the remnants of more than a dozen sheep traps have been discovered that were probably in use in Russell's time.

2. Seton's discussion of bighorn sheep populations in Yellowstone Park is included on the park's Web site at www.yellowstonenationalpark.com/sheep.htm in a section titled "Bighorn Sheep."

3. Geist 1993:155.

4. Ruckstuhl and Festa-Bianchet 2001.

5. Barrette 1963:32.

6. Lowie 1909:185; Steward 1970 [1938]:37.

7. Shimkin 1937–38.

8. George Frison and Danny Walker have made maps of many of these traps (Frison et al. 1990).

9. Frison et al. 1990.

10. In 2004, a remarkable discovery of bighorn sheep–butchering areas was made in Wyoming. In the epilogue, we discuss this important extension of our knowledge of Sheep Eater subsistence tactics.

11. Frison 2004:160.

12. Rapson 1990.

Chapter 13—Cutthroats, Bitterroots, and Whistle Pigs

1. We recognize that researchers disagree about the causes of fluctuating elk populations in Yellowstone National Park and that there are no straightforward explanations for the current overpopulation of that species. Zooarchaeological research, however, is a promising approach to understanding elk population levels in the past, and we recommend that interested readers consult Lyman and Cannon 2004 for an excellent overview of this subject. Cannon and Cannon (2004:51–52) point out that elk remains have been relatively common at the Myers-Hindman site near Livingston, Montana, over the past 3,000 years. The site is in a narrow valley near the rocky banks of the fast-moving Yellowstone River. It is not exceptionally good habitat for beaver, and, as the archaeological remains suggest, apparently the location was better suited for elk. Excavated sites from locations like the Lamar River valley in Yellowstone National Park are needed to determine if elk are equally common along a slow-moving stream. See also Kay 2002:221–22.

2. Norris 1881:31–32.

3. Nathaniel Wyeth illustrates one of these harpoons in his letter to Henry Schoolcraft written at Fort Hall on April 18, 1848; see Wyeth 1851.

4. Demitri Shimkin's 1937–38 field notes contain excellent descriptions of Shoshone fishing and fish drying.

5. The bones were not included in Hughes's (2003) analysis of the site's faunal remains.

6. For a photograph of the harpoon, see Husted and Edgar 2002:217.

7. The following encounter between George Drouillard and a small group of Shoshone was recorded in Meriwether Lewis's journal entry of August 22, 1805 (in Moulton 1988:143).

8. Lewis, journal entry, August 22, 1805, in Moulton 1988:143.

9. Lewis, journal entry, August 22, 1805, in Moulton 1988:143.

10. The publication date of Pursh's monumental study of North American plants, *Flora Americae Septentrionalis*, is variously listed as 1813 or 1814. This confusion results from the fact that the date of publication appears as 1814 on the title page of the two-volume work, whereas it was actually available in December 1813.

11. Stuart Reeve's 1986 dissertation, titled "Root Crops and Prehistoric Social Process in the Snake River Headwaters, Northwestern Wyoming," is an excellent source of information about the long-term importance of root vegetables; see also Rapson et al. 1995.

12. Connor 1998; Connor et al. 1991.

13. Francis 2000; for a discussion of pit baking, see also Wandsnider 1997.

14. Meriwether Lewis, journal entry, July 17, 1805, in Moulton 1987:392.

15. More information about Diana Tomback's studies of the interrelationship between pine nuts and the Clark's nutcracker is available online at www.whitebark-found.org/tomback.htm.

16. For a discussion of felling whitebark pine trees, see Steward 1943:362. Information about storing pine nuts under rock cairns can be found in a number of sources (see Mallery 1886:156). A rock cairn near Obsidian Cliff in Yellowstone National Park may have once served this purpose (Loendorf 2003).

17. Meriwether Lewis, journal entry, August 13, 1805, in Moulton 1988:81.

18. Liljeblad (1957:97) identifies coyotes as included in the Sheep Eater food spectrum.

19. This recipe is only partly conjectural. Wyoming archaeologists have recovered the "pot dumps" from this kind of stew, some of which are discussed in a master's thesis by Danny Walker (1975).

20. *Mah-duh-k* means "eat it" or "please eat" and is the Shoshone equivalent of "bon appétit."

Chapter 14—The Sheep Eater Path to the Contemporary World

1. Page 2003:194.

2. Page 2003:280.

3. We want to remind readers that there were a dozen or more tribes in and around Yellowstone National Park that were affected by these changes. Our focus on the fate of Sheep Eaters during the last part of the nineteenth century is not meant to suggest that other groups did not suffer in similarly disruptive and tragic ways.

4. The original site was named "Fort Lihmi" after King Lihmi, a personage in the *Book of Mormon* "who had preserved a colony of his people in the wilderness" (Bigler 2003:35).

5. Viall 1871:831.

6. Wood and Thiessen 1985:220.

7. Beckwourth 1972:366.

8. What has been described as "a few" Sheep Eaters did participate in a raid on the Mormon settlement of Fort Lemhi led by 150 Bannock Indians in winter 1858. Community leader Thomas Smith had tried to negotiate a settlement of grievances between feuding Nez Perce and Bannock groups in the vicinity of the fort following a complicated sequence of thefts of cattle and horses, but he had been unsuccessful. In the melee two missionaries were killed, and five others were wounded, with the result that plans for an expanded Mormon presence in the area were abandoned (Bigler 2003:38–39).

9. Quoted in Idaho Historical Society 1965:2.

10. See Nabokov and Loendorf 2004:292–93. Hultkrantz 1970 contains the most complete discussion of the Allen book.

11. Allen 1989 [1913]:16.

12. Hughes 2000, 2004.

13. Hughes 2000:63.

14. Bigler 2003.

15. Nabokov and Loendorf 2002:145.

16. Hughes 2000:78.

17. Dominick 1964:137.

18. Information about the Wind River Reservation can be found at www.eastern-shoshone.net. Two Web sites maintained by the Shoshone-Bannock tribes at Fort Hall have comparable information: www.shoshonebannocktribes.com and www.sho-ban.com. A scholarly treatment of the history of the tribes relocated to the Fort Hall Reservation can be found at a Web site associated with Idaho State University: www.challenge.isu.edu/multicultural/NativeAm/ShoBan/forthall/htm.

19. Dominick 1964:138.

20. Yellowstone National Park 1996:3.

21. Yellowstone National Park 1996:6.

22. Yellowstone National Park 1996:13.

23. Yellowstone National Park 1996:9.

24. Yellowstone National Park 1996:20.

25. Yellowstone National Park 1996:17.

Epilogue—"By Diligent Discovery"

The quotation in the chapter title is a snippet from Shakespeare's *King Lear*, act V, scene 1, line 65.

1. Whittlesey n.d.

2. Davis et al. n.d.:2. See Davis 1975; Davis and Scott 1987; Keyser 1976.

3. We have already noted that the Sheep Eaters and the Crow had various close relationships, especially in the historic period, so there is no certainty at present that all the Boulder Ridge sites were produced by Sheep Eater activities. Some may represent the remains of Crow hunting parties.

4. Watson 1995:685.

Bibliography

Adams, Richard. 1992. Pipes and Bowls: Steatite Artifacts from Wyoming and the Region. M.A. thesis, Department of Anthropology, University of Wyoming, Laramie.

Allen, W. A. 1989 [1913]. *The Sheep Eaters.* Reprint. Fairfield, WA: Ye Galleon Press (original: New York: Shakespeare Press).

Baillie-Grohman, William. 1882. *Camps in the Rockies: Being a Narrative of Life on the Frontier and Sport in the Rocky Mountains, with an Account of the Cattle Ranches of the West.* London: Sampson Low.

Barrette, K. 1963. Ghost Tribe of the West. *Frontier Times* 37(6):32–33, 58.

Beckwourth, James. 1972. *The Life and Adventures of James P. Beckwourth.* Lincoln: University of Nebraska Press.

Belden, George P. 1974 [1870]. *Belden: The White Chief: Twelve Years among the Wild Indians of the Plains.* Reprint. Athens: Ohio University Press (original: Cincinnati: C. F. Vent Publishers).

Biel, Alice Wondrak. 2004. History of Research Permitting in Yellowstone National Park. *Yellowstone Science* 12(3):5–20.

Bigler, David. 2003. Mormon Missionaries, the Utah War, and the 1858 Bannock Raid on Ford Limhi. *Montana* 53(3):30–43.

Binford, Lewis R. 2001. *Constructing Frames of Reference: An Analytical Method for Archaeological Theory Building Using Ethnographic and Environmental Data Sets.* Berkeley: University of California Press.

Bird, Isabella L. 1960. *A Lady's Life in the Rocky Mountains.* Intro. by Daniel J. Boorstin. Norman: University of Oklahoma Press.

Brooks, James F. 2002. *Captives and Cousins: Slavery, Kinship, and Community in the Southwest Borderlands.* Chapel Hill: University of North Carolina Press.

Butler, B. Robert. 1986. Prehistory of the Snake and Salmon River Area. In *Handbook of North American Indians, vol. 11: Great Basin,* ed. Warren L. D'Azevedo, 127–34. Washington, DC: Smithsonian Institution Press.

Campbell, Gregory R., and Thomas A. Foor. 2004. Entering Sacred Landscapes: Cultural Expectations versus Legal Realities in the Northwestern Plains. *Great Plains Quarterly* 24(3):163–83.

Cannon, K. P., D. Bringelson, W. Eckerle, M. Sittler, M. S. Boeka, J. Androy, and H. Roeker. 2001. *The Results of Archeological Investigations at Three Sites along the Wilson-Fall Creek Road Corridor, Teton County, Wyoming.* Lincoln: Midwest Archeological Center.

Cannon, K. P., and M. B. Cannon. 2004. Zooarchaeology and Wildlife Management in the Greater Yellowstone Ecosystem. In *Zooarchaeology and Conservation Biology,* ed. R. L. Lyman and K. P. Cannon, 45–60. Salt Lake City: University of Utah Press.

Cannon, K. P., G. M. Crothers, and K. L. Pierce. 1996. *Archeological Investigations along the Arnica Creek to Little Thumb Creek Section of the Grand Loop Road, Yellowstone National Park, Wyoming.* Lincoln: Midwest Archeological Center.

Cannon, K. P., K. L. Pierce, P. Stormberg, and M. V. MacMillan. 1997. *Results of Archeological and Paleoenvironmental Investigations along the North Shore of Yellowstone Lake, Yellowstone National Park, Wyoming: 1991–1994.* Lincoln: Midwest Archeological Center.

Chittenden, H. M. 1964 [1895]. *The Yellowstone National Park.* Ed. Richard A. Bartlett. Reprint. Norman: University of Oklahoma Press.

Clark, William. 1885. *The Indian Sign Language, with Brief Explanatory Notes.* Philadelphia: L. R. Hamersly.

The Compact Edition of the Oxford English Dictionary. 1971. Oxford: Oxford University Press.

Condon, D. 1961 [1949]. American Indian Burial Giving Evidence of Antiquity Discovered in Yellowstone National Park. *Plains Anthropological Conference Newsletter* 1(5):87–91.

Connor, M. A. 1998. *Final Report on the Jackson Lake Archeological Project, Grand Teton National Park, Wyoming.* Technical Report No. 46. Lincoln: Midwest Archeological Center.

Connor, M. A., K. P. Cannon, S. E. Matz, D. C. Carlevato, and C. A. Winchell. 1991. *The Jackson Lake Archeological Project: The 1987–1988 Field Work.* 2 vols. Technical Report No. 7. Lincoln: Midwest Archeological Center.

Coutant, C. G. 1899. *The History of Wyoming,* vol. 2. Laramie: Chaplin, Stafford and Mathison.

Culin, Stewart. 1901. A Western Trip among Western Indians: The Wanamaker Expedition. *Bulletin of the Free Museum of Science and Art of the University of Pennsylvania* 3(1–3):1–22.

Davis, Carl M. 1975. Wickiup Cave. *Plains Anthropologist* 20(70):297–305.

Davis, Carl M., Leslie B. Davis, Ann M. Johnson, and Patricia A. Dean. N.d. The Late Prehistoric Intermountain (Ceramic) Tradition and the Historic Sheepeater Shoshone. Unpublished MS, in possession of the authors.

Davis, Carl M., and Sarah A. Scott. 1987. Pass Creek Wickiups: Northern Shoshone Hunting Lodges in Southwestern Montana. *Plains Anthropologist* 32(115):83–92.

D'Azevedo, Warren L., ed. 1986. *Handbook of North American Indians, vol. 11: Great Basin.* Washington, DC: Smithsonian Institution Press.

Despain, D. G. 1990. *Yellowstone Vegetation: Consequences of Environment and History in a Natural Setting.* Lanham, MD: Roberts Rinehart Publishers.

Dominick, David. 1964. The Sheepeaters. *Annals of Wyoming* 36(2):131–68.

Earl of Dunraven. 1917. *The Great Divide.* In *Hunting in the Yellowstone,* ed. Horace Kephart. New York: Outing Publishing Co.

Egan, Howard R. 1917. *Pioneering the West, 1846–1878: Major Howard Egan's Diary.* Richmond, UT: Howard Egan Estate.

Ewers, John C. 1980 [1955]. *The Horse in Blackfoot Indian Culture: With Comparative Material from Other Western Tribes.* Bureau of American Ethnology Bulletin 159.

Reprint. Washington, DC: Smithsonian Institution, Government Printing Office.

Ferris, Warren. 1983. *Life in the Rocky Mountains: A Diary of Wanderings on the Sources of the Rivers Missouri, Columbia, and Colorado, 1830–1835.* Ed. Leroy R. Hafen and Fred A. Rosenstock. Denver: Old West Publishing Co.

Feyhl, K. S. 1997. Steatite: Some Sources and Aboriginal Utilization in Montana. *Archaeology in Montana* 38(2):55–83.

Francis, Julie E. 2000. Root Procurement in the Upper Green River Basin: Archaeological Investigations at 48SU1002. In *Intermountain Archaeology*, ed. David B. Madsen and Michael D. Metcalf, 166–75. Anthropological Papers No. 122. Salt Lake City: University of Utah Press.

Francis, Julie E., and Lawrence L. Loendorf. 2002. *Ancient Visions: Petroglyphs and Pictographs of the Wind River and Bighorn Country, Wyoming and Montana.* Salt Lake City: University of Utah Press.

Frison, George. 1980. A Composite, Reflexed, Mountain Sheep Horn Bow from Western Wyoming. *Plains Anthropologist* 25(88):173–75.

———. 1982. Sources of Steatite and Methods of Prehistoric Procurement and Use in Wyoming. *Plains Anthropologist* 27(1):273–86.

———. 1991. *Prehistoric Hunters of the High Plains.* San Diego: Academic Press.

———. 2004. *Survival by Hunting: Prehistoric Human Predators and Animal Prey.* Berkeley: University of California Press.

Frison, George C., A. Reher, and D. N. Walker. 1990. Prehistoric Mountain Sheep Hunting in the Central Rocky Mountains of North America. In *Hunters of the Recent Past*, ed. L. B. Davis and B. Reeves, 208–40. One World Archaeology 15. London: Unwin Hyman.

Frison, George, and Z. Van Norman. 1993. Carved Steatite and Sandstone Tubes: Pipes for Smoking or Shaman's Paraphernalia? *Plains Anthropologist* 38(143):163–76.

Geist, Valerius. 1993. *Wild Sheep Country.* Minocqua, WI: NorthWord Press, Inc.

Good, J. M., and K. L. Pierce. 1996. *Interpreting the Landscape: Recent and Ongoing Geology of Grand Teton and Yellowstone National Parks.* Moose, WY: Grand Teton Natural History Association.

Goss, James. 1999. Rocky Mountain High Culture: Look the Utes Aren't Marginal Anymore! Plenary paper presented at the Fourth Rocky Mountain Anthropological Conference, Glenwood Springs, CO, September 30.

Gowans, Fred. 1989. *A Fur Trade History of Yellowstone Park, Notes, Documents, Maps.* Orem, UT: Mountain Grizzly Publications.

Haag, William G. 1956. Aboriginal Dog Remains from Yellowstone National Park. MS on file at Yellowstone Library, Mammoth, WY.

Haines, A. L. 1965. A Supplementary Report on High-Altitude Indian Occupation Sites near the North Boundary of Yellowstone National Park. MS on file in the Yellowstone National Park Archives, Mammoth, WY.

Hamilton, T. M. 1982. *Native American Bows.* Special Publication 5. Columbia: Missouri Archaeological Society.

Hanson, Jeffrey. 1981. The George Drouillard Maps of 1808. *Archaeology in Montana* 27(1):45–53.

Hare, Brian, Michelle Brown, Christina Williamson, and Michael Tomasello. 2002. The Domestication of Social Cognition in Dogs. *Science* 298:1634–36.

Harney, Corbin. 1995. *The Way It Is: One Air, One Water, One Mother Earth*. Nevada City, CA: Blue Dolphin Publishing Co.

Harris, Burton. 1952. *John Colter: His Years in the Rockies*. New York: Charles Scribner's Sons.

Hayden, F. V. 1872. *Preliminary Report of the U.S. Geological Survey of Montana and Portions of Adjacent Territory*. Washington, DC: Government Printing Office.

Henderson, A. B. 1866. Journal of the Yellowstone Expedition of 1866 under Captain Jeff Standifer. Original MS in the Beinecke Library, Yale University, New Haven; copy at Yellowstone National Park Research Library, Mammoth, WY.

Henderson, Norman. 1994. Replicating Dog Travois Travel on the Northern Plains. *Plains Anthropologist* 39(148):145–59.

Hoffman, Jake. 1961. A Preliminary Archaeological Survey of Yellowstone National Park. M.A. thesis, Montana State University, Bozeman.

Holm, Bill. 1982. On Making Horn Bows. In *Native American Bows*, by T. M. Hamilton, 116–30. Special Publication 5. Columbia: Missouri Archaeological Society.

Holmer, Richard. 1990. Prehistory of the Northern Shoshone. *Rendezvous, Idaho State University Journal of Arts and Letters* 26(1):41–59.

———. 1994. In Search of the Ancestral Northern Shoshone. In *Across the West: Human Population Movement and the Expansion of the Numa*, ed. D. Madsen and David Rhode, 179–87. Salt Lake City: University of Utah Press.

Hughes, Richard, and James A. Bennyhoff. 1986. Early Trade. In *Handbook of North American Indians, vol. 11: Great Basin*, ed. Warren L. D'Azevedo, 238–55. Washington, DC: Smithsonian Institution Press.

Hughes, Susan. 1987. Description of the Mummy Cave Burial. In The Mummy from Mummy Cave: Preliminary Report, by F. P. Saul and J. M. Saul, 4. *Paleoanthropology News* 60:4–10.

———. 2000. The Sheepeater Myth of Northwestern Wyoming. *Plains Anthropologist* 45(171):63–83.

———. 2003. Beyond the Altithermal: The Role of Climate Change in the Prehistoric Adaptations of Northwestern Wyoming. Ph.D. dissertation, University of Washington, Seattle.

———. 2004. The Sheepeater Myth of Northwestern Wyoming. In *People and Place: The Human Experience in Greater Yellowstone*, ed. Paul Schullery and Sarah Stevenson, 2–29. Proceedings of the 4th Biennial Scientific Conference on the Greater Yellowstone Ecosystem, October 12–15, 1997, Yellowstone National Park. Mammoth, WY: Yellowstone Center for Resources.

Hultkrantz, Åke. 1951. The Concept of Soul Held by the Wind River Shoshone. *Ethnos* 16(1–2):18–44.

———. 1957. Indians in Yellowstone Park. *Annals of Wyoming* 29(2):125–49.

————. 1970. The Source Literature on the "Tukadika" Indians in Wyoming: Facts and Fancies. In *Languages and Cultures of Western North America: Essays in Honor of Sven S. Liljeblad*, ed. E. H. Swanson Jr., 246–64. Pocatello: Idaho State University.

————. 1981. *Belief and Worship in Native America*. Ed. Christopher Vecsey. Syracuse, NY: Syracuse University.

————. 1987. *Native Religions of North America: The Power of Visions and Fertility*. San Francisco: Harper Collins Publishers.

————. N.d.a. The Sheepeaters of Wyoming: Culture History and Religion among Some Shoshoni Mountain Indians. Handwritten MS, 2 vols., in possession of the author.

Hultkrantz, Geraldine. N.d.b. *Shoshone Tales*. MS developed for eventual publication from the field notes of Åke Hultkrantz, in possession of the author.

Humfreville, J. Lee. 1899. *Twenty Years among Our Hostile Indians*. New York: Hunter and Co.

Husted, Wilfred M. 1995. The Western Macrotradition Twenty-Seven Years Later. *Archaeology in Montana* 36(1):37–92.

Husted, Wilfred M., and Robert Edgar. 2002. *The Archaeology of Mummy Cave, Wyoming: An Introduction to Shoshonean Prehistory*. Midwest Archeological Center and Southeast Archeological Center Special Report No. 4. National Park Service Technical Reports Series No. 9. Lincoln.

Idaho Historical Society. 1965. *The Loon Creek Mines*. Reference Series No. 366, August. Boise: Idaho Historical Society.

Irving, Washington. 1836. *Astoria or Anecdotes of an Enterprise beyond the Rocky Mountains*. Philadelphia: Carey, Lea, and Blanchard.

————. 1843. *The Adventures of Captain Bonneville*. New York: Frank F. Lovell and Co.

Janetski, Joel C. 2002. *Indians in Yellowstone National Park*. Salt Lake City: University of Utah Press.

John, Elizabeth. 1975. *Storms Brewed in Other Men's Worlds: The Confrontation of Indians, Spanish, and French in the Southwest, 1540–1795*. Lincoln: University of Nebraska Press.

Jones, William A. 1875. *Report on the Reconnaissance of Northwestern Wyoming, Including Yellowstone National Park, Made in the Summer of 1873*. 43rd Congress, 1st Session, House Executive Document 285. Washington, DC: Government Printing Office.

Kay, Charles E. 2002. Are Ecosystems Structured from the Top-Down or Bottom-Up? In *Wilderness and Political Ecology: Aboriginal Influences and the Original State of Nature*, ed. Charles E. Kay and Randy T. Simmons, 215–37. Salt Lake City: University of Utah Press.

Keyser, James D. 1976. The LaMarche Game Trap: An Early Historic Game Trap in Southwestern Montana. *Plains Anthropologist* 19(65):173–79.

————. 1992. *Indian Rock Art of the Columbia Plateau*. Seattle: University of Washington Press.

Kroeber, Theodora. 1967. *Ishi in Two Worlds: A Biography of the Last Wild Indian in North America*. Berkeley: University of California Press.

Kurz, Frederick. 1937. *Journal of Rudolph Frederick Kurz*. Bureau of American Ethnology Bulletin No. 115. Washington, DC: Smithsonian Institution.

Lamb, Sydney. 1958. Linguistic Prehistory in the Great Basin. *International Journal of American Linguistics* 24(2):95–100.

Lander, F. W. 1860. *Report of F. W. Lander, Superintendent, Wind River Agency, Wyoming, to the Commissioner of Indian Affairs*. 36th Congress, 1st Session, Senate Executive Document No. 1033:121–39. Washington, DC: Government Printing Office.

Larsen, M. L., and M. Kornfeld. 1994. Betwixt and between the Basin and Plains: The Limits of Numic Expansion. In *Across the West: Human Population Movement and the Expansion of the Numa*, ed. D. Madsen and D. Rhode, 200–10. Salt Lake City: University of Utah Press.

Laubin, Reginald, and Gladys Laubin. 1980. *American Indian Archery*. Norman: University of Oklahoma Press.

Liljeblad, Sven. 1957. *Indian Peoples in Idaho*. Pocatello: Idaho State College.

———. 1986. Oral Tradition: Content and Style of Verbal Arts. In *Handbook of North American Indians, vol. 11: Great Basin*, ed. Warren L. D'Azevedo, 641–59. Washington, DC: Smithsonian Institution Press.

Loendorf, Lawrence L. 1967. A Preliminary Archaeological Survey of the Clark Fork River, Carbon County, Montana. M.A. thesis, Department of Anthropology, University of Montana, Missoula.

———. 1993. The Water Ghost Being along the Wind River, Wyoming. Paper presented at "Shamanism and Rock Art: Interpretations from around the World," Trinity University and the Witte Museum, San Antonio, February 27.

———. 2003. Ethnographic Resources on the Mammoth Hot Springs to Norris Junction Road. Report on file with Cultural Resources, Yellowstone National Park.

———. 2004. Places of Power: The Placement of Dinwoody Petroglyphs across the Wyoming Landscape. In *The Figured Landscapes of Rock-Art: Looking at Pictures in Place*, ed. Christopher Chippindale and George Nash, 201–16. Cambridge: Cambridge University Press.

Lowell, James Russell. 1924. A Glance behind the Curtain. In *The Complete Poetical Works of James Russell Lowell*, ed. Horace E. Scudder, 49–53. Boston: Houghton Mifflin and Co.

Lowie, Robert. 1909. The Northern Shoshone. *Anthropological Papers of the American Museum of Natural History* 2(2):165–306.

———. 1924. Notes on Shoshonean Ethnography. *Anthropological Papers of the American Museum of Natural History* 20(3):185–314.

———. 1993 [1918]. *Myths and Traditions of the Crow Indians*. 2nd ed. Lincoln: University of Nebraska Press (original: *Anthropological Papers of the American Museum of Natural History, New York* 25[11]:1–308).

Lyman, R. Lee, and Kenneth P. Cannon. 2004. *Zooarchaeology and Conservation Biology*. Salt Lake City: University of Utah Press.

Madsen, Brigham D. 1980. *The Northern Shoshone*. Caldwell, ID: Caxton Printers.

Madsen, D. B., and D. Rhode, eds. 1994. *Across the West: Human Population Movement and the Expansion of the Numa*. Salt Lake City: University of Utah Press.

Mallery, Garrick. 1886. Pictographs of the American Indians: A Preliminary Paper. In *Fourth Annual Report of the Bureau of [American] Ethnology [for] 1882–1883*, 4–256. Washington, DC: Smithsonian Institution, Government Printing Office.

Malouf, Carling. 1966. Ethnohistory in the Great Basin. In *Current Status of Anthropological Research on the Great Basin: 1964*, ed. Warren L. D'Azevedo, 1–38. Desert Research Institute Social Sciences and Humanities Publication 1. Reno: University of Nevada.

———. 1967. Historic Tribes and Archaeology. *Archaeology in Montana* 8(1):1–10.

Marceau, Thomas. 1980. Steatite, Intermountain Pottery and the Shoshone: Problems in Association. MS on file at the Wyoming Cultural Records Office, Laramie.

McKern, Scott T., and Lynn L. Harrel. 2004. Archaic Way Stations: A Prelude of Things to Come? In *Ancient and Historic Lifeways in North America's Rocky Mountains, Proceedings of the 2003 Rocky Mountain Anthropological Conference, Estes Park, CO*, ed. Robert H. Brunswig and William B. Butler, 315–30. Greeley: Department of Anthropology, University of Northern Colorado.

Mead, Margaret. 1973. *Coming of Age in Samoa: A Psychological Study of Primitive Youth for Western Civilization*. New York: American Museum of Natural History.

Miller, Alfred Jacob. 1951. *The West of Alfred Jacob Miller (1837)*. Norman: University of Oklahoma Press.

Moorhead, Max L. 1968. *The Apache Frontier: Jacobo Ugarte and Spanish–Indian Relations in Northern New Spain, 1769–1791*. Norman: University of Oklahoma Press.

Moulton, Gary E., ed. 1987. *The Journals of the Lewis and Clark Expedition, vol. 4: April 7–July 17, 1805*. Lincoln: University of Nebraska Press.

———. 1988. *The Journals of the Lewis and Clark Expedition, vol. 5: July 28–November 1, 1805*. Lincoln: University of Nebraska Press.

Mulloy, William. 1958. *A Preliminary Historical Outline for the Northwestern Plains*. University of Wyoming Publications 22(1–2):1–255. Laramie: University of Wyoming.

Murdock, George P. 1949. *Social Structure*. New York: Macmillan.

———. 1981. *Atlas of World Cultures*. Pittsburgh: University of Pittsburgh Press.

Murphy, Robert F., and Yolanda Murphy. 1986. Northern Shoshone and Bannock. In *Handbook of North American Indians, vol. 11: Great Basin*, ed. Warren L. D'Azevedo, 284–307. Washington, DC: Smithsonian Institution Press.

Nabokov, Peter, and Lawrence L. Loendorf. 2002. *American Indians and Yellowstone National Park: A Documentary Overview*. National Park Service, Yellowstone Center for Resources, YCR-CR-02-1. Mammoth, WY: National Park Service.

———. 2004. *Restoring a Presence: American Indians and Yellowstone National Park*. Norman: University of Oklahoma Press.

Norris, P. W. 1881. *Annual Report of the Superintendent of Yellowstone National Park, to the Secretary of the Interior*. Washington, DC: Government Printing Office.

Olden, Sarah. 1923. *Shoshone Folk Lore, as Discovered from the Rev. John Roberts, a Hidden Hero, on the Wind River Indian Reservation in Wyoming.* Milwaukee: Morehouse Publishing.

Page, Jake. 2003. *In the Hands of the Great Spirit: The 20,000-Year History of American Indians.* New York: Free Press.

Peterson, Helen. 1966. The Pryor Mountains, Land of Legend, History, Mystery. *Billings Gazette Magazine Section*, April 10: 9–11.

Pope, Saxton T. 1920. *The Medical History of Ishi.* University of California Publications in American Archaeology and Ethnology 13(5):175–213. Berkeley: University of California Press.

————. 1926. *The Adventurous Bowmen: Field Notes on African Archery.* New York: G. P. Putnam's Sons.

————. 2005. *Hunting with the Bow and Arrow.* Project Gutenberg, EText-No. 8084. Available online at www.gutenberg.org/etext/8084.

Powell, Kendall. 2002. Stone Age Man Kept a Dog. *Nature Science Update*, November 22. Available online at www.nature.com/nsu.

Pursh, Frederick. 1814. *Flora Americae Septentrionalis.* London: White, Cochrane and Co.

Quinlan, Angus R., and Alanah Woody. 2003. Marks of Distinction: Rock Art and Ethnic Identification in the Great Basin. *American Antiquity* 68(2):372–90.

Rapson, D. J. 1990. Pattern and Process in Intrasite Spatial Analysis: Site Structural and Faunal Research at the Bugas-Holding Site. Ph.D. dissertation, Department of Anthropology, University of New Mexico, Albuquerque.

Rapson, D. J., M. Kornfeld, and M. L. Larson. 1995. The Henn Site Today and in Prehistory. In *The Henn Site, 48TE1291: Early Archaic to Protohistoric Occupation at the Jackson National Fish Hatchery, Wyoming*, ed. M. L. Larson, 234–39. Technical Report No. 7. Laramie: Department of Anthropology, University of Wyoming.

Reed, Alan D. 1994. The Numic Occupation of Western Colorado and Eastern Utah during the Prehistoric and Protohistoric Periods. In *Across the West: Human Population Movement and the Expansion of the Numa*, ed. D. Madsen and D. Rhode, 188–99. Salt Lake City: University of Utah Press.

Reeve, S. A. 1986. Root Crops and Prehistoric Social Process in the Snake River Headwaters, Northwestern Wyoming. Ph.D. dissertation, State University of New York, Albany.

Reeve, Stuart A., Thomas E. Marceau, Gary A. Wright, and Priscilla Meachum. 1979. Archeological Investigations of the Lawrence Site (48TE509), Grand Teton National Park, Wyoming. MS on file at the Midwest Archeological Center, National Park Service, Lincoln.

Roe, Frank Gilbert. 1955. *The Indian and the Horse.* Norman: University of Oklahoma Press.

Ruckstuhl, Kathreen E., and Marco Festa-Bianchet. 2001. Group Choice by Subadult Bighorn Rams: Trade-off between Foraging Efficiency and Predator Avoidance. *Ethology* 107:161–72.

Russell, Osborne. 1965 [1914]. *Journal of a Trapper*. Ed. Aubrey L. Haynes. 4th ed. Lincoln: University of Nebraska Press (original: *Journal of a Trapper, or, Nine Years in the Rocky Mountains: 1834–1843*, ed. L. A. York, Boise: Syms-York Co.).

Saul, F. P., and J. M. Saul. 1987. The Mummy from Mummy Cave: Preliminary Report. *Paleoanthropology News* 60:4–10.

Savolainen, Peter, Ya-ping Zhang, Jing Luo, Joakim Lundeberg, and Thomas Leitner. 2002. Genetic Evidence for an East Asian Origin of Domestic Dogs. *Science* 2998:1610–13.

Schoen, Jamie, and David Vlchek. 1991. Steatite Procurement and Source Areas in Western Wyoming. Paper presented at the Northwestern Plains Archaeological Symposium, Billings, MT, April 13.

Scott, John Paul, and John L. Fuller. 1965. *Genetics and the Social Behavior of the Dog*. Chicago: University of Chicago Press.

Shimkin, Demitri B. 1937–38. Unpublished Field Notes on the Eastern Shoshone. Demitri Boris Shimkin Papers, 1890–1993, Accession Number 9942, Box 1-3. American Heritage Center, University of Wyoming, Laramie.

———. 1947. Wind River Shoshone Ethnogeography. *University of California Anthropological Records* 5(4):245–90.

———. 1953. *The Wind River Shoshone Sun Dance*. Anthropological Paper 41, Bureau of American Ethnology Bulletin 151:195–484. Washington, DC: Government Printing Office.

———. 1986. Eastern Shoshone. In *Handbook of North American Indians, vol. 11: Great Basin*, ed. Warren L. D'Azevedo, 308–35. Washington, DC: Smithsonian Institution Press.

Sholly, D. R., and S. M. Newman. 1991. *Guardians of Yellowstone: An Intimate Look at the Challenges of Protecting America's Foremost Wilderness Park*. New York: William Morrow and Co.

Skarsten, M. O. 1964. George Drouillard. In *The Mountain Men and the Fur Trade of the Far West*, vol. 4, ed. L. R. Hafen, 260–70. Glendale, CA: Arthur H. Clark.

Smith, R. B., and L. J. Siegel. 2000. *Windows into the Earth: The Geologic Story of Yellowstone and Grand Teton National Parks*. Oxford: Oxford University Press.

Steward, Julian. 1943. Culture Element Distribution. XXIII: Northern and Gosiute Shoshoni. *University of California Anthropological Records* 8(3):263–392.

———. 1970 [1938]. *Basin–Plateau Aboriginal Sociopolitical Groups*. Reprint. Salt Lake City: University of Utah Press (original: Bureau of American Ethnology Bulletin 120, Washington, DC: Government Printing Office).

Stewart, James. 1994. A Short Analysis of the Legend Rock Petroglyph Sites, as to Other Wind River, Wyoming, Area Rock Art. Unpublished MS on file at the Wyoming Cultural Records Office, Laramie.

Thomas, David Hurst. 1981. How to Classify the Projectile Points from Monitor Valley, Nevada. *Journal of California and Great Basin Anthropology* 3(1):7–43.

Thompson, R. R. 1854. *First Annual Report—Oregon Territory—South Side of the Columbia River between the 46th and 44th Degrees Latitude between the Summits of the Rocky and Cascade Mountains*. Washington, DC: Government Printing Office.

Thwaites, R. G., ed. 1904–06. *Original Journals of the Lewis and Clark Expedition 1804–1806*. 8 vols. New York: Arno Press.

Trenholm, V. C., and M. Carley. 1964. *The Shoshonis: Sentinels of the Rockies*. Norman: University of Oklahoma Press.

Tylor, Edward B. 1871. *Primitive Culture: Researches into the Development of Mythology, Philosophy, Religion, Art, and Custom*. London: J. Murray.

Vander, J. 1997. *Shoshone Ghost Dance Religion: Poetry, Songs and Great Basin Context*. Urbana: University of Illinois Press.

Viall, J. A. 1871. *The Montana Superintendency. Office of the Superintendent of Indian Affairs. Annual Report of the Commissioner of Indian Affairs*. 42nd Congress, 2nd House Session, House exdoc (42-2), SN-1505. Washington, DC: Government Printing Office.

Vigne, J.-D., J. Guilaine, K. Debue, L. Haye, and P. Gérard. 2004. Early Taming of the Cat in Cyprus. *Science* 304(5668):259–61.

Walker, Danny N. 1975. A Cultural and Ecological Analysis of the Vertebrate Fauna from the Medicine Lodge Creek Site (48BH499). M.A. thesis, Department of Anthropology, University of Wyoming, Laramie.

Walker, Danny N., ed. 2004. Year 2000 Archaeological Investigations at the Sand Draw Dump Site, 48FR3123, Fremont County, Wyoming. Report on file at the Wyoming State Archaeologist's Office, Wyoming Department of Parks and Cultural Resources, Laramie.

Wandsnider, L. A. 1997. The Roasted and the Boiled: Food Composition and Heat Treatment with Special Emphasis on Pit-Hearth Cooking. *Journal of Anthropological Archaeology* 16:1–48.

Watson, Patty Jo. 1995. Archaeology, Anthropology, and the Culture Concept. *American Anthropologist* 97:683–94.

Wedel, Waldo. 1954. Earthenware and Steatite Vessels from Northern Wyoming. *American Antiquity* 29(4):403–09.

Weixelmann, Joseph O. 1992. The Power to Evoke Wonder: Native Americans and the Geysers of Yellowstone National Park. Project Director Tom Tankersley, Park Historian, National Park Service, Yellowstone National Park. MS submitted to the Wyoming Council for the Humanities, Laramie, Project #145-91.

———. 2004. Fear or Reverence? Native Americans and the Geysers of Yellowstone Park. In *People and Place: The Human Experience in Greater Yellowstone*, ed. Paul Schullery and Sarah Stevenson, 50–66. Proceedings of the 4th Biennial Scientific Conference on the Greater Yellowstone Ecosystem, October 12–15, 1997, Yellowstone National Park. Mammoth, WY: Yellowstone Center for Resources.

Whitley, David S. 1994. By the Hunter for the Gatherer: Art, Social Relations and Subsistence Change in the Prehistoric Great Basin. *World Archaeology* 25(3):356–73.

———. 2000. *The Art of the Shaman: Rock Art of California*. Salt Lake City: University of Utah Press.

Whittlesey, Lee. N.d. Storytelling in Yellowstone: Interpreting the Grand Old Park 1872–1920. MS awaiting publication, in possession of the author.

Willey, P., and P. Key. 1992. Analysis of Human Skeletons from Yellowstone National Park. University Foundation, California State University, Chico. MS prepared for the Midwest Archeological Center, National Park Service, Order No. PX-61159-0012.

Wilson, E. N. 1985 [1919]. *The White Indian Boy; or, The Story of Uncle Nick among the Shoshones.* Reprint. Yonkers-on-Hudson, NY: World Book Co. (original: Rapid City, SD: Fenske Printers).

Wood, W. Raymond, and Thomas D. Thiessen. 1985. *Early Fur Trade on the Northern Plains: Canadian Traders among the Mandan and Hidatsa Indians, 1738–1818.* Norman: University of Oklahoma Press.

Wright, G. A. 1978. The Shoshonean Migration Problem. *Plains Anthropologist* 23(80):113–37.

Wright, G. A., and Jane B. Dirks. 1983. Myth as Environmental Message. *Ethnos* 3–4:160–76.

Wyeth, Nathaniel J. 1851. Indian Tribes of the South Pass of the Rocky Mountains: The Salt Lake Basin; The Valley of the Great Säaptin or Lewis River, and the Pacific Coasts of Oregon. In *Historical and Statistical Information Respecting the History, Conditions and Prospects of the Indian Tribes of the United States*, vol. 1, by Henry R. Schoolcraft, 204–28. Philadelphia: Lippincott, Grambo.

Yellowstone National Park. 1996. Ethnological Resources Survey. Transcript of interview conducted by Dr. Sharon Kahin, February 4, Fort Washakie, WY.

Additional Reference Material

The Sheep Eaters: Archers of the Yellowstone. 2003. Videocassette. Produced by Sharon Kanin. Directed by Gary Wortman, Everyman Productions, Reston, VA. Available from the Wind River Historical Center, P. O. Box 896, Dubois, WY 82513.

The Sheep Eaters: Masters of the Mountain. 2001. Videocassette. Produced by Sharon Kanin. Available from the Wind River Historical Center, P. O. Box 896, Dubois, WY 82513.

Acknowledgments

In 1993, Loendorf and Associates, a cultural resource firm, initiated a project to research and identify the ways that Indians in the past used the landscapes and resources of Yellowstone National Park. From the beginning it was clear that the available information about how traditional Indians interacted with the park's "features and creatures," as well as with one another, was woefully out of date and inaccurate. Especially egregious was the misinformation that was prevalent in the available literature—and accepted by both park personnel and the public—about the Sheep Eater Indians, the Shoshone group most closely associated with Yellowstone.

At the conclusion of the project, the results of the research were published first as a report and then as a book with the title *Restoring a Presence: American Indians in Yellowstone National Park* by Peter Nabokov and Lawrence Loendorf (2004). Both publications include a major section on the Sheep Eaters; and, at the time, the information presented about this group appeared to represent the sum of current knowledge, and the goal of its presentation seemed to have been met.

As sometimes happens, however, as we continued to find new material and develop new ideas about those remarkable mountaineers, what had seemed to be the end of a journey became merely the midpoint in a longer excursion. We decided to reorganize the results of previous research and incorporate new material in a different format, this time in a more popularly written book, so that a wider audience might come to appreciate the remarkable lives and legacy of the Sheep Eater Indians of Yellowstone.

In a project that has consumed more than a decade, there are many people who contributed to our effort and whom we wish to thank. Foremost is David Joaquín, whose enthusiasm has never waned and whose wonderful illustrations have really brought the Sheep Eaters to life. We truly appreciate his talent, and we encourage readers interested in seeing more of his original artwork to seek him out.

We are also indebted to colleagues Peter Nabokov, Tim McCleary, and Patricia Albers, who continue to offer insights into the native cultures of the greater Yellowstone region. Sharon Kahin has been a steadfast supporter and helped us throughout the research and writing of the book. It was Sharon who asked Reba Jo Teran to translate a particular English expression into Shoshone for us, which Reba graciously did. We are deeply indebted to Swedish anthropologist Åke Hultkrantz, who gave us unpublished materials on the Sheep Eaters, and we also thank his wife, Geraldine Hultkrantz, for sharing materials destined for, but not yet in, book form. Another strong supporter has been David Dominick, who wrote an important essay on the Sheep Eaters. He generously shared with us his notes and interview information from living Sheep Eaters.

Many individuals provided us with field notes, photographs, unpublished reports, and lots of ideas. These include Rich Adams, Mike Bies, Jeani Borchert, Carl Davis and Sara Scott, Dan Eakin, B. J. Earle, Chris Finley, Julie Francis, George Frison, Hannah Hinchman, Ann Johnson, Chris Loendorf, Bonita Newman, Linda Olson, Lori Orser, and Danny Walker. We hope we can one day repay the debt we incurred as beneficiaries of their generosity. Many other archaeological advocates who are interested in the Sheep Eaters kindly offered us their assistance, and we profited greatly from it. These include Stuart Conner, Ken Feyhl, and John Rogers, Billings, Montana; Bob Baker, the mayor of Dubois, Wyoming, and his son, Monty Baker, who led us to sheep traps; Tom Lucas of Lander, Wyoming, who knows as much about sheep horn bows as any person in the American West; and Tory Taylor, Dubois guide and outfitter, who somehow finds another steatite pot every few years. We wish we could express our thanks to all these colleagues in a measure commensurate with the help they have given us.

We thank John Mionczynski, who spends his summers high in the Wind River Mountains with the Whiskey Mountain herd of bighorns. His knowledge of sheep behavior and his understanding of the edible plants and other natural resources of the region are unbeatable, and we drew heavily on it.

This book would not have been possible without the help of staff members at museums, archives, libraries, and site-information repositories. We are grateful for help from Nathan Bender and Ann Marie Donoghue, Buffalo Bill Historical Center; Janet Sperry, formerly with the Montana Historical Society; Mark Halvorson, North Dakota Heritage Center; Valerie-Anne Lutz, American Philosophical Society;

Felicia Pickering, Smithsonian Institution; Glen Hisey, Pope and Young Club; Jim Woods, Herrett Center for Arts and Science at the College of Southern Idaho; the Museum of the Mountain Man, Pinedale, Wyoming; the American Heritage Center, Laramie, Wyoming; and the Wind River Historical Center, Dubois, Wyoming. Mary Hopkins and Steve Sutter at the Wyoming Cultural Records Office have been strong supporters of this project, and we thank them, too.

We are indebted to Jeff Grathwohl, the director of the University of Utah Press, for his kindness and enthusiasm throughout the lifecycle of our manuscript and for his important contribution to its title. We are grateful to Glenda Cotter, managing editor at the press, for keeping the project on track in the most artful way. Elisabeth Graves's careful copyediting has greatly improved the text, and we thank her for her efforts.

We were very fortunate that Rosemary Sucec, a cultural anthropologist with Yellowstone National Park, and Kenneth Cannon, an archaeologist with the Midwest Archeological Center, were given our manuscript to review. They suggested a number of important changes, and we thank them for helping us clarify important issues and correct some errors. Any remaining imperfections, however, are solely our responsibility.

Persons near and dear to us also contributed considerably to our efforts. Larry thanks his wife Paula for her love and support, as well as Miss Brandy for guarding the home front. Nancy thanks Damon English, Ford Stone, Susanne and Jake Page, and Robert Hitchcock for encouragement all along the way.

About the Authors

LAWRENCE L. LOENDORF is an archaeologist at New Mexico State University. His recent books include *Ancient Visions: Petroglyphs and Pictographs of the Wind River and Bighorn Country, Wyoming and Montana*, written with Julie Francis and published by the University of Utah Press; and *Restoring a Presence: American Indians and Yellowstone National Park*, written with Peter Nabokov and published by the University of Oklahoma Press.

NANCY MEDARIS STONE is a writer and editor with a background in archaeology. She lives in Corrales, New Mexico.

DAVÍD JOAQUÍN is an artist who lives and paints in Tigard, Oregon. His paintings and limited-edition prints are represented by Waters Meet Gallery, Taos, New Mexico; American Trails Gallery, Ashland, Oregon; the Gallery Black Bear, Mt. Shasta, California; and Eagles Perch Fine Art, Garberville, California. More of his artwork and contact information are available at www.DavidJoaquin.com.

Index

archaeological context, 120; and
steps in making, 122–25, *123f6,
124f7;* Wyeth description of, 117,
125; x-rays of, 120, *121f5,* 122;
value placed on, 126. *See also* bows
bowyer, 114, 118
Bridger, Jim, 78
Bruce, Ed, 70
buckskin, 94, 96. *See also* hide, sheep
buffalo berries, 158. *See also* diet
Buffalo Bill Historical Center, 22,
91, 151
Bugas-Holding site, 144–45
burials: Condon burial, 92; evidence
for, 92, 189n2; in Mummy Cave,
91; radiocarbon dating of, 91; similarities among, 91–92; with dogs,
92, 110, 189n8

California Academy of Science, 113
Calochortus nuttallii. See sego lily
camas, 152, 154, 157. *See also* diet
Cameahwait: and encounter with
Lewis and Clark, 12–13; and
reunion with Sacajawea, 13;
and trade of horses and information, 13
Canis familiaris. See dogs
Cannon, Kenneth, 132, 151
caps and headbands, 100. *See also*
clothing
catch-pens: dimensions of, 143;
positioning of, 142; prehistoric
remains of, 143–45, *144f4*
cat's cradle, 56, *56f1*
ceramic vessels: estimates of age of,
88; Intermountain tradition of,
84f3, 85; Loendorf's study of distribution of, 86; Marceau's study
of distribution of, 85–87; and
presence in Wyoming and Montana, 83
Cervus Canadensis. See elk
Cheyenne Indians, 163
Chief Washakie, 14
children's play, 55–56
Chittenden, Hiram, 2, 8, 10

chokecherry, 126, 129, 158
Clark, William: maps prepared by,
14–17 (*see also* 1814 Clark map;
1810 Clark map); and meeting
with Cameahwait, 13
Clark's nutcracker, 158–59
clothing: embellishment of, 98–99;
and garments worn by men,
97–98; and garments worn by
women, 98–99; *99f2;* skins used
for, 99–100, 190n21; tailoring of,
97–99, 101; tools used to make,
96–97
Coeur d'Alene Indians, 163
Colter, John, 2, 15–16
Comanche Indians, 14, 62
Coming of Age in Samoa (Mead), 52
Condon, David. *See* burials
conflict avoidance, 64–65
Conner, Stuart W., 70, 187n8
Continental Divide, 11, 85. *See also*
Great Divide
Corps of Discovery, 12, 14, 164,
183n4. *See also* Lewis and Clark
expedition
Connor, Melissa, 157
cooking, nutritional payoff from, 157.
See also food preparation
Coutant, Charles, 2
coyotes, 161, 190n20
Craik, Bob, 66
Crocket pot, *84f3. See also* ceramic
vessels
cross-cousin marriage, 57. *See also*
social organization
cross-cultural comparison, 52–53.
See also George P. Murdock
Crow Indians, xiv, 3, 61, 107, 163.
See also Mountain Crow
cutthroat trout, 148, 150

dances. *See* rituals
Davis, Carl: and excavations at Wick-
iup Cave, 72–73; research strate-
gies of, 176–77
D'Azevedo, Warren L. See *Handbook of
North American Indians, Great Basin*

Wind River Historical Center, 83, 169
Wind River Mountains: lakes in, *xii*; as
    part of Sheep Eater territory, 33,
    34; trails through, 33; "warm val-
    ley" in, 60
Wind River Reservation, 6, 50, 168,
    172–73
wokaimunbitsch, 38. *See also* world view
"Woman under the Ground," 169. *See
    also* Sheep Eaters
wongoduba. See pine nuts
Woodring, Samuel T., 70
world view: animism in, 37; dancing
    in, 48; dream or trance states in,
    41–42; interweaving of religion
    and medicine in, 45; medicine and
    healing in, 42–48; spirits and spir-
    itual hierarchy in, 37–42; spiritual
    power in, 38; types of souls in, 41
Wright, Gary, 18, 27
Wyndham-Quin, Thomas. *See* Dun-
    raven, 4th Earl of
Wyeth, Nathaniel, 117, 129
Wyoming: Beartooth Mountains, 16,
    37; Cody, 15, 16, 17, 18, 33, 61,

145; Dubois, 60; earliest ceramics
in, 89; Lander, *xiii*, 4; Legend
Rock, 19; Lovell, 17; Thermopolis, 43, 60

yampa, 152, 161. *See also* diet
Yankee Fork Herald, 167
Yellowstone National Park: absence of
    rock art sites in, 47; archaeologi-
    cal sites in, 3; creation of, 7; ejec-
    tion of Indians from, 7; Ethnologi-
    cal Resources Survey of, 173;
    human burials in, 92, 104; Indian
    trails through, 33, 34*f*2; Lamar
    Valley, 60, 107; obsidian sources
    in, 132; Sheep Eater use of, 1;
    tribal groups in, *xiv*, 3; wickiups
    in, 69, 171
Yellowstone River, Clark's Fork of, 17
Yeppe Indians, 16, *16f1*
Young, Art, 113, *114f1*

Zedora (Sheep Eater consultant),
    173–74